Tea and T

TOURISM AND CULTURAL CHANGE

Series Editors: Professor Mike Robinson, *Centre for Tourism and Cultural Change, Leeds Metropolitan University Leeds, UK* and Dr Alison Phipps, *University of Glasgow, Scotland, UK*

Understanding tourism's relationships with culture(s) and vice versa, is of ever-increasing significance in a globalising world. This series will critically examine the dynamic inter-relationships between tourism and culture(s). Theoretical explorations, research-informed analyses, and detailed historical reviews from a variety of disciplinary perspectives are invited to consider such relationships.

Other Books in the Series
Irish Tourism: Image, Culture and Identity
  Michael Cronin and Barbara O'Connor (eds)
Tourism, Globalization and Cultural Change: An Island Community Perspective
  Donald V.L. Macleod
The Global Nomad: Backpacker Travel in Theory and Practice
  Greg Richards and Julie Wilson (eds)
Tourism and Intercultural Exchange: Why Tourism Matters
  Gavin Jack and Alison Phipps
Discourse, Communication and Tourism
  Adam Jaworski and Annette Pritchard (eds)
Histories of Tourism: Representation, Identity and Conflict
  John K. Walton (ed.)
Cultural Tourism in a Changing World: Politics, Participation and (Re)presentation
  Melanie K. Smith and Mike Robinson (eds)
Festivals, Tourism and Social Change: Remaking Worlds
  David Picard and Mike Robinson (eds)
Tourism in the Middle East: Continuity, Change and Transformation
  Rami Farouk Daher (ed)
Learning the Arts of Linguistic Survival: Languaging, Tourism, Life
  Alison Phipps

Other Books of Interest
Recreational Tourism: Demand and Impacts
  Chris Ryan
Shopping Tourism: Retailing and Leisure
  Dallen Timothy
Sport Tourism Development
  Thomas Hinch and James Higham
Sport Tourism: Interrelationships, Impact and Issues
  Brent Ritchie and Daryl Adair (eds)
Tourism Collaboration and Partnerships
  Bill Bramwell and Bernard Lane (eds)
Tourism and Development: Concepts and Issues
  Richard Sharpley and David Telfer (eds)

For more details of these or any other of our publications, please contact:
Channel View Publications, Frankfurt Lodge, Clevedon Hall,
Victoria Road, Clevedon, BS21 7HH, England
http://www.channelviewpublications.com

TOURISM AND CULTURAL CHANGE 11
Series Editors: Mike Robinson and Alison Phipps

Tea and Tourism
Tourists, Traditions and Transformations

Edited by
Lee Jolliffe

CHANNEL VIEW PUBLICATIONS
Clevedon • Buffalo • Toronto

Library of Congress Cataloging in Publication Data
Tea and Tourism: Tourists, Traditions and Transformations/edited by Lee Jolliffe, 1st ed.
Tourism and Cultural Change; 11
Includes bibliographical references and index.
1. Tea–Social aspects–Case studies. 2. Tea trade–Case studies. 3. Culture and
tourism–Case studies. 4. Heritage tourism–Case studies. I. Jolliffe, Lee. II. Title. III. Series.
GT2905.T413 2007
394.1'2–dc22

British Library Cataloguing in Publication Data
A catalogue entry for this book is available from the British Library.

ISBN-13: 978-1-84541-057-5 (hbk)
ISBN-13: 978-1-84541-056-8 (pbk)

Channel View Publications
An imprint of Multilingual Matters Ltd

UK: Frankfurt Lodge, Clevedon Hall, Victoria Road, Clevedon BS21 7HH.
USA: 2250 Military Road, Tonawanda, NY 14150, USA.
Canada: 5201 Dufferin Street, North York, Ontario, Canada M3H 5T8.

The policy of Multilingual Matters/Channel View Publications is to use papers that
are natural, renewable and recyclable products, made from wood grown in
sustainable forests. In the manufacturing process of our books, and to further support
our policy, preference is given to printers that have FSC and PEFC Chain of Custody
accreditation. The FSC and/or PEFC logos will appear on those books where full
accreditation has been granted to the printer concerned.

Typeset by Florence Production Ltd.
Printed and bound in Great Britain by the Cromwell Press.

Dedication

This book is dedicated to Rabindranath B. Gunasekara (1959–2003) who died in Sri Lanka while undertaking the field research for his chapter.

Contents

Acknowledgements ix
The Contributors xi

Part 1: Introduction
  1 Connecting Tea and Tourism
    Lee Jolliffe 3

Part 2: Tea Histories, Collections and Traditions
  2 Tracing the History of Tea Culture
    Paul Leung Kin Han 23
  3 Tea and Travel: Transforming the Material Culture of Tea
    Lee Jolliffe 38
  4 Tea Traditions in Taiwan and Yunnan
    Paul Leung Kin Han 53

Part 3: Tea and Tourism: Political, Social and Economic Developments
  5 Tea Production and Tourism Development in Assam:
    A Missed Opportunity?
    Kevin Hannam 71
  6 Amidst the Misty Mountains: The Role of Tea Tourism in
    Sri Lanka's Turbulent Tourist Industry
    Rabindranath B. Gunasekara and Janet Henshall Momsen 84
  7 The New Tea Appreciation Festival: Marketing and
    Socio-economic Development in Hunan Province, China
    Rong Huang and Derek Hall 98
  8 Tea Culture and Tourism in Fujian Province, China:
    Towards a Partnership for Sustainable Development
    Honggen Xiao 115

9   Tourism Development and the Tea Gardens of Fuding, China
    Lee Jolliffe and Peifen Zhuang 133
10 Tourism and Tea in Kenya: Opportunity for Development?
    Jacquelyne Muhati and Lee Jolliffe 145

**Part 4: Transforming Tea: From Tea Experiences to
Tea Destinations**
11 China's Tea and Horse Trade Route and its Potential for
    Tourism
    Hilary du Cros 167
12 Hangzhou: China's Green Tea City
    Keith Dewar and Wen Mei Li. 180
13 Teapot Trails in the UK: Just a Handle or Something Worth
    Spouting About?
    Derek Hall and Steven Boyne. 206
14 Tea Tourists and Tea Destinations in Canada: A New Blend?
    Lee Jolliffe 224

Part 5: Conclusion
15 Towards a Research Agenda for Tea Tourism
    Lee Jolliffe 247

Index 253

Acknowledgements

I am grateful to the individuals and organizations that made this book possible. First I thank my family, Darrell, Naomi and Aaron as well as Christian Tschirhart and Channarong Intah-chompoo, who put up with my tea obsession, visiting tea rooms and travelling to tea shops and gardens both with me and on my behalf – consuming many cups and pots of tea along the way. The active interest of colleagues Keith Dewar and Wen Mei Li and of my editor and friend Noni Regan encouraged the work. Faculty and staff at the Faculty of Business, University of New Brunswick Saint John are also to be thanked for their interest in the manuscript as it progressed. A visit to tea gardens in China was funded by a University of New Brunswick Canadian International Development Agency project. And in China colleague Peifen Zhuang took up the tea tourism cause and facilitated research there. Professional development funds from the University of New Brunswick made possible a visit to a tea village in Northern Thailand.

In addition Louise Roberge of the Tea Council of Canada, Des McCarthy (tea blender at Barbour's in Sussex, New Brunswick) and Judith Baxter of Kingston Heritage all provided practical insights into the tea business. Patrons at Mrs Profitt's Tea Room at the Orient Hotel in Victoria-by-the-Sea, Prince Edward Island, Canada are thanked for participating in my early efforts as a tea-tourism practitioner. The proprietors of a number of fine tea shops are also to be thanked for sharing their insights: Camellia Sinesis in Montreal, Quebec, Canada; the Red Tea Box in Toronto, Ontario, Canada; Infusions in Saint John, New Brunswick, Canada; Granville Island Tea Co., Vancouver, British Columbia, Canada; and Chiangmai Tea Shoppe in Chiang Mai, Thailand. The students at the University of New Brunswick Saint John worked with me on aspects of tea-tourism research and this includes Yan Cong, Pengbo Zoe, Anand Mohan, Lynn Lee, Karen Kwan and David Gao. The contributors to this volume have come through with work that is literally steeped in the various aspects of tea and tourism. The encouragement of the series editor, Mike Robinson, and comments on an early draft manuscript by contributor Derek Hall and other reviewers are acknowledged, as is the assistance provided by the staff of Channel View Publications. While all of the above have contributed to 'the brew', I take full responsibility for any errors or omissions and indeed for any oversights on behalf of the able cast of many who provided the materials for the blend of tea tourism cases that is presented in this book.

The Contributors

Steven Boyne, Scottish Agricultural College, Scotland

Hilary du Cros, Institute of Tourism Studies, Macau, PR China

Keith Dewar, University of New Brunswick, Canada

Rabindranath B. Gunasekara, University of California, Davis, United States (1959–2003)

Lee Jolliffe, University of New Brunswick, Canada

Derek Hall, Hame Polytechnic, Finland

Kevin Hannam, University of Sunderland, England

Rong Huang, University of Surrey, England

Wen Mei Li, University of New Brunswick, Canada

Paul Leung Kin Han, Hong Kong Polytechnic University, Hong Kong

Janet Henshall Momsen, University of California, Davis, United States

Jacquelyne Muhati, University of Greenwich, England

Honggen Xiao, University of Waterloo, Canada

Peifen Zhuang, Fujian Agriculture and Forestry University, China

Part 1: Introduction

Chapter 1

Connecting Tea and Tourism

LEE JOLLIFFE

Tea means many things to many people. It has an immensely rich and intriguing history and can be considered to be a plant, an agricultural product, a beverage, a meal service or a pastime. Tea has been both the focus of colonization and the subject of revolutions. Tea is closely connected with the ancient and modern history of world trade and travel. Tea as a commodity and a tradition can be transported from one culture to another and through cultural adaptation transformed from the traditions of one culture to the heritage of another.

Beginning in ancient times in China, tea derived from the *Camellia sinensis* plant was cultivated, processed and consumed. In China it was one of the tribute crops grown for the ancient Chinese rulers. In Japan the Japanese adopted their tea ceremony. A related variety of tea was also discovered and cultivated in India and the development of tea plantations were part of the intense colonization of the country under British rule. The cultivation of tea was subsequently introduced to many other countries, including Ceylon (now Sri Lanka), Kenya and Malawi. As a beverage, tea became the drink of choice for many nations around the world, including England, Russia and Canada.

Tea and its many aspects can clearly be a fascinating and most interesting subject of study. This is a book about one particular aspect of tea: tea and its myriad connections to tourism. It is also a book about the tourism of tea. Traders have long travelled in search of tea. Travel itself also has a rich connection with tea and has contributed to disseminating tea cultures and traditions. Tea is part of many tourist activities, whereby local tea traditions, cultures, services and attractions are experienced. This may vary from experiencing tea in the tea houses of Hangzhou, China or Taipei, Taiwan to visiting the tea museums of London, England and Ping Lin, Taiwan or purchasing tea as a souvenir in the airport shops of Hong Kong and Beijing, China.

Both tea-producing and tea-consuming countries have adopted tea as an inherent part of their national identities and this is important to the tourism process. For the Chinese it is the 'art of tea', for the Japanese 'the way of tea', for the British 'afternoon tea' and for the Russians tea served in a 'samovar'. Regional identities can be based on tea as well, as is evidenced by the 'cream teas' popular in the south of England, the tea festivals of the northern regions of India or the New Tea Appreciation Festival of Hunan, China.

There are many varieties, types and blends of tea. The leaf from the *Camellia sinensis* plant is processed, resulting in a number of types of tea which include white and green (unfermented), *oolong* (partly fermented) and black (fermented) teas. Different types of tea have been adopted by different cultures. In China green (unfermented) tea has been identified as a national drink, whereas in England black (fermented) tea has some associations as a national drink. Tea-producing areas in the Fujian Province of China, Taiwan and the north of Thailand have adopted *oolong* (partly fermented) tea as their drink of choice. In all of these cases, the consumption of tea forms an important aspect of social interaction and business dealings.

There is less caffeine in tea than in the popular beverage coffee and consuming tea has beneficial health effects (Manil & Zbinden, 2001). Today, there is thus an increased and renewed interest in the consumption of tea, particularly as a specialty beverage and for its health benefits. However the health benefits of tea are just one aspect of a beverage valued by most of the world's population.

Tea has many roles in relationship to tourism, society and its institutions. In this book, tea is being considered as a central analytical tool for tourism and the discourses, networks and impacts created by the relationship between tea and tourism. The following sections therefore discuss the role of tea and its consumption as: an instrument of hospitality; an influencer in terms of tourism and social change; a component of tourism experiences; and a dedicated focus for tourism attractions.

Tea and Hospitality

Tea is closely linked with hospitality and can be seen as its instrument. When tea is offered as a sign of hospitality in both domestic and commercial contexts the meanings and the significance behind it are complex. Tea in some situations may be a symbol of the commoditized guest–host relationship. For commercial hospitality operations tea may represent a potentially profitable product. The beverage of tea, with its ability to reflect local cultures and tastes may offer an opportunity for the hospitality industry to blend new specialty products and services, with positive results for investors.

Being the most consumed beverage in the world after water (Walker, 1996), tea is an integral part of food service. Hotels and restaurants (to a lesser extent) all over the world have seized upon the provision of 'afternoon tea' not only as an added meal service and luxury product, but as an added revenue stream. Vacant dining facilities can be utilized for the afternoon tea service in the time between lunch and dinner. Some hotels such as the Fairmont Empress in Victoria, Canada have built their reputation around their afternoon tea service.

In both Canada and the United Kingdom, tea councils are involved with certifying food service establishments that serve tea. The Tea Council of Canada has a certification programme and the Tea Council in the UK also certifies tea rooms (including those in hotels). In the latter case the certification process is administered through a tea guild. Practitioners in Canada interviewed for an investigation into tea provision in hotel and resort properties (Jolliffe, 2004) acknowledge that tea offered in such settings is an experience, and the current evolution of tea into a 'trendy' product does not surprise them.

That tea has a strong historical link with hospitality is reflected by the evolution of the tea room in the UK during the late 19th century, as a safe place where women could go to socialize with friends. Tea provision in the contemporary lodging sector is an extension of these historical roots. This provision also reflects the transference of the traditions of home, whereby a welcoming 'cuppa' (a colloquialism for a cup of tea), offered in a cosy setting, is transferred over to the commercial domain of today's food service and lodging industry.

Tea, Tourism and Social Change

It is evident that tea, as both a consumable product and an experience, is changed and adapted through both travel and tourism. The social changes within society with regard to tea are widespread and today are experienced as tourism. For example, the adoption and popularization of tea in 18th- and 19th-century Britain and the concurrent development of tea traditions represent the changes taking place in society. Tea is a barometer of social change, as seen in the case of many indigenous societies that have adapted tea as a beverage after contact with the outside world. For example, both the Inuit people of northern Canada and native tribes in Kenya have adopted the drinking of black tea as part of their cultures. In contemporary society the social and contextualized cultural performances of tea drinking in international travel and exchange are evident in the many different forms of tea provision and tea ceremony. This ranges, for example, from the Japanese tea ceremony to the British afternoon tea.

Present-day tea-related tourism has the potential to be an instrument of social change in terms of sustainable development projects in conjunction with tea gardens. Such projects have been established in Sri Lanka and proposed in China. In these cases tea tourism is seen as a means of generation of local revenue and poverty reduction. The irony of this situation is that very often the projects seek to address the very inequalities in local societies created by the initial development of the tea gardens (Moxham, 2004). It was common in the establishment of tea plantations in India and Ceylon for the large tea companies to keep the costs of production down in part through low wages for the workers. This situation allowed tea to be marketed to the masses in other countries at a low price.

Shapira (Shapira _et al._, 1975: 233) indicates that 'ceremonies, customs and rituals that have grown up around the practice of tea drinking are an integral part of the life and culture of many societies'. These tea customs and traditions are part of social change, arising as tea has been adapted from one society to another. While this has been a gradual process that has taken centuries, even today contemporary tea traditions experienced through tourism have the ability to influence the tea traditions of other societies. For instance, the Taiwanese tradition of 'bubble tea shops' is now being introduced in other countries, for example in the major cities of North America several of these shops are now open. In Taiwan the popularity of English-style tea houses is reported to be on the increase, especially among female customers who are attracted to the English-style tea service (Euromonitor, 2004). These trends demonstrate the transference of tea cultures and traditions across borders and continents.

In summary, tea traditions reflect social changes in society. Additionally, travel has had an important influence on nurturing these changes. Even today, the traditions and cultures related to tea are constantly being adapted and influenced by societies and their institutions. Tea tourism has the potential to address social inequalities at tea-producing locations and to be employed in the development of tourism, in both tea-producing and tea-consuming countries. Tourism also has the potential to impact local tea cultures as hosts develop the tea services they think tourists would like to experience.

Tea and Tourism Experiences

Tea plays a role in a large proportion of tourism trips. It may be a beverage served during a trip on a plane, a ship or a train; it may be a beverage served at the destination, at breakfast, lunch or dinner; it may form a meal service itself at the destination, for example as an afternoon tea; or it may be experienced at the destination as part of a tea attraction such as a museum or an exhibition. Tea can be experienced as part of traditions considered to reflect national identities, such as afternoon tea in England (Howard, 2003) or the Japanese tea ceremony in Japan (Pettigrew, 2001). In these circumstances the serving of tea can take on a ritualistic or religious approach. For example in the case of British afternoon tea, Pettigrew (1999: 71) indicates that 'traditionally served in the drawing room or garden at 4 p.m., a full afternoon tea in Britain always includes a spread of food as well as the beverage'. Another British institution, the tea room has taken on some of the characteristics of the afternoon tea (Boniface, 2003).

In the case of tea the Japanese way, Pettigrew (1999: 74) indicates 'the ritual of the Japanese ceremony is based on Zen Buddhism and involves much more than just drinking tea'. It is said that the Chanoyu tea ceremony can last up to four hours. Pratt (1982) reports that during its 700 or so years of history the Japanese tea ceremony has gone through at least three stages of development. During the second stage, in the 1400s, tea tournaments were popular. At these events a number of teas were sampled and guests who guessed correctly received a prize.

In both North America and the United Kingdom a whole genre of literature has encouraged the public to think of the mysterious and romantic appeal of tea and to become consumers of the tea experience. This includes a number of compendiums of tea facts, history and lore, for example: James Norwood Pratt's informative book *The Tea Lover's Treasury* (1982); Joel, David and Karl Shapira's (1975) guide *The Book of Coffee and Tea*; and the classic volume by Michael Smith, *Afternoon Tea* (1986). Also, some authors have documented their experiences running tea rooms, for example: Naughton and Perry (2002) *Tea and Sympathy*. Others, such as Jane Pettigrew, have used this experience as a jumping-off point for a career investigating tea, producing a number of works, including *A Social History of Tea* (2001). Those formerly involved in the tea trade have also written about their experiences and using this perspective as a starting point have delved into the various aspects of the background of tea. This group includes Roy Moxham (2004) *Tea: Addiction, Exploitation and Empire*. The author uses his experiences as a tea plantation manager in Africa as a starting point for tracing the history of tea and colonization.

With so much to experience in terms of tea it is no surprise that tea will appeal to tourists and that some tourists will be dedicated to searching out tea products and experiences during their travels. Some are extreme in terms of their dedication to the search; for example, Boniface (2003) refers to those who search out tearooms as 'tea room enthusiasts' and Jolliffe (2003a) refers to 'dedicated tea tourists' as those who will make or alter travel decisions according to their interest in tea. Others have searched out the meanings and stories behind tea; for example, Goodwin (2003) is one of the many who have travelled to countries such as China and India to uncover some of the facts and myths behind tea. The account of Goodwin's tea travels, first published in 1991 was reissued in 2003. Tea is also the subject of dedicated tea tours, taken to destinations that have a rich tea history, either in terms of consumption or production of tea, as described by Pratt's (2002) vivid account of a tea tour to China in his essay 'Pilgrimage to the Holy Land of Tea'.

Tea is a social custom and as such is part of many celebrations that tourists will experience. Tea as a daily event is one that serves as a marker of the tourism experience and a link between the other experiences of the day. Beyond the daily experiences of taking tea or experiencing tea as a meal service, tea events may include tea parties, tea tastings and tea interpretations. Tea parties offer a chance for tourists to socialize over a cup of tea. Tea is such an integral part of many societies that its service and customs may be stereotyped. Shapira (Shapira *et al.*, 1975: 235) observes 'the Briton, to be happy must have this tea, good tea, wherever he wants it; at the railway station, the tea trolley, on the trains, the tea basket, the cinema, the tea room'. Such stereotypes have an impact on what tourists expect and can cause tourism providers to offer what might fulfil the tourist image of a particular tea service. This in turn can threaten the authenticity of tea traditions. Boniface (2003: 116) notes that afternoon tea is an anachronism in that it 'represents an experience that is essentially now entirely heritage, but it is a heritage much pursued and regarded with enthusiasm and affection'. Much has been written about afternoon tea. There are books on afternoon tea, tea trails, tea walks and cream tea guidebooks. In this way tradition becomes attraction, and the tourist is part of the changing and adapting culture of tea.

The Attraction of Tea

There is evidence that tourists are interested in cuisine and are culinary purists (those who strive for correctness and authenticity in cuisine) (Wolf, 2003). There is a growing interest in culinary tourism which consists of travelling to experience culture through food and drink. Tea-related tourism has parallels with other food-related tourism pursuits such as wine tourism that have been investigated by tourism researchers (for example, Hjalager & Richards, 2002). There are obvious commonalities between wine and tea tourism with both beverages having rich histories and connections with travel. However, tea as a beverage is more commonly drunk and adapted to different cultures and societies. A service such as afternoon tea therefore acts as an attraction for the cultural tourist but also as a link between other activities in the day, and in many cases forms a symbolic element of cultural distinctiveness.

For tea drinkers worldwide, tea serves to attract them to experiences related to the consumption and appreciation of tea, and the appreciation of the tea cultures of other societies. Tea has a complex global history and a number of attractions have been developed that focus on tea. This includes both natural attractions such as tea gardens and estates and man-made attractions, such as interpretation centres and museums. Special events focusing on tea or with a tea component can also serve as attractions. Attractions can be classified by the length of stay and there is much potential for the development of what Gunn (1988) refers to as touring-circuit attractions. In the case of tea, this type of attraction might include designated tea trails and routes.

Defining Tea and Tea Tourism

The word tea is defined by the *Oxford English Reference Dictionary* (2001) as having four contextual meanings:

(1) an evergreen shrub or small tree, *Camellia sinesis*, of India, China, etc. and its dried leaves;
(2) a drink made by infusing the tea leaves in hot (at first preferably boiling) water;
(3) a similar drink made from the leaves from another plant or another substance;
(4) a light afternoon meal consisting of tea, bread, cakes, etc. or a cooked (especially early) evening meal.

This book is only concerned with the tea derived from the *Camellia sinesis* plant and the beverage served from the harvested and processed leaf of this plant, or that has this authentic tea as an ingredient. It thus does not deal with the third aspect of the definition, which deals with other herbs and substances that are brewed and served as a beverage called 'tea'. In the fourth aspect, the case of tea as a meal service, several chapters of this book shed light on issues related to the light afternoon meal that has developed into the afternoon teas, high teas and cream teas that have become popular tourism products.

What then is tea tourism? Jolliffe (2003b: 136) proposed a working definition of tea tourism as 'tourism that is motivated by an interest in the history, traditions and consumption of tea'. This is clearly tourism related to experiencing the many aspects of tea, including its history, growth, production, processing, blending and consumption. Experiencing the history of tea includes visiting the historic sites, locations and districts that reflect this story of tea, as well as attending exhibitions to learn from artefacts about the evolution of tea cultures and traditions. The tea experience will be influenced by many factors, such as host–guest relationships (Smith, 1977) in the case of community tea experiences, and the impact of curators and designers in the case of tea exhibition experiences. Tea tourism may be seen as part of the overall tourism phenomenon, as part of both cultural tourism and culinary tourism, and also as a small, specialist niche for dedicated tourists.

Who then are the tea tourists? As a working definition the tea tourist (Jolliffe, 2003a) can be described as a tourist experiencing history, culture and traditions related to the consumption of tea. Much work has been done on tourism typologies that can inform an assessment of the motivations and characteristics of tea tourists. Tourism researchers observe that a primary motive for pleasure tourism is the desire to escape from the routine situations of the home and the workplace and the familiarity of related social and physical environments (Williams, 1998). A number of theories can inform our understanding of the motives of tea tourists. For example, Iso-Ahola's (1982) model of the social psychology of tourism juxtaposes elements of escaping from normal routines with the quest for intrinsic rewards in the environments visited. In the case of tourists experiencing tea they may seek out commercial tea settings that offer this escape from normal routines (such as the consumption of afternoon tea) yet offer the familiar comfort of tea consumption found in their own homes. On the other hand, experiencing ancient tea traditions (as in the Japanese and Chinese tea ceremonies) refers to an inversion in tourism, experiencing, for example, an ancient ritual versus a modern ritual, or a foreign ritual versus a home ritual. Williams (1998) cites other researchers, for example Plog, who have postulated a psychographic view of tourist behaviour, classifying tourist types as psychocentrics, near-psychocentrics, mid-centrics, near-allocentrics, and allocentrics. The destinations these types of tourists will prefer will fall into a parallel continuum ranging from familiar to exotic. All of these theories are useful to the examination of tea tourists in terms of their underlying motivations and their choice of tea experiences and destinations.

Initial investigation into the motivations of tea tourists (Jolliffe, 2003a) classified both their motivation and the nature of the encounter with the tea experience as either accidental or intentional. The web sites of the tea companies and tour companies in the United States offering dedicated tea tours to a number of countries offer evidence that intentional tea tourists do indeed exist. Further work (Jolliffe 2003b) proposed a typology of types of tea tourists, including the accidental tea tourists previously identified and further subdividing the intentional tea tourists into the categories of dedicated and extreme. More study is needed to substantiate these suppositions about the varieties of behaviours exhibited by different types of tea tourists.

On what scale can we envisage tea tourism occurring? To imagine this, it is necessary to understand the commonality and universality of tea as a consumed beverage, as well as the extent of the tourist sites associated with it and the numbers of food outlets with tea services. As stated above, tea is, after water, the most commonly drunk beverage in the world. The basic resource for developing tea for tourism includes tea gardens where tea is grown, tea factories where it is processed, establishments where it is for sale and served, and institutions that preserve and interpret the objects that represent its traditions and culture. In a number of areas of the world there are also tea hotels located either adjacent to or within the tea gardens, or it is possible to obtain lodgings within the tea garden site.

Several examples give some idea of the extent of tea-related tourism. The first is the number of afternoon teas served by some of the major hotels around the world: this reflects the current state of tea tourism. The second is the numbers of tea farms, gardens, plantations and estates and related tea factories around the world: this gives an indication of the potential for developing tea tourism at these sites, keeping in mind that political situations will not always allow for this development. Select examples of hotels serving afternoon tea include:

- The Fairmont Empress in Victoria, Canada is reported as serving from 110,000 (2003 Tourism Victoria) to 115, 000 (2003, Gostello Report) afternoon teas annually.
- In London, England formal afternoon tea services are offered as featured meal services at a number of hotels, including the Ritz-Carlton, The Four Seasons and the Dorchester Hotel.

The extent of the resource available for tea tourism is also evident when we examine the number of tea gardens in the 57 tea-producing countries of the world. For example, it is reported:

- Outside of China there are close to 6000 tea estates (Pratt, 1982).
- In India, in Darjeeling alone, there are 86 operational tea gardens producing 'Darjeeling Tea'.
- There are an estimated 160 tea gardens in the North Bengal area of India (Hussain, 2004).

- In Kenya there are approximately 350,000 tea family smallholders (growing tea on their farms) licensed by the Kenya Tea Development Agency (KTDA).

Tea factories are less numerous than tea farms, tea gardens and tea plantations. This is because tea is often collected from a number of small-scale farmers and then processed in large factories. For example, the KTDA is mandated by the government of Kenya to collect tea from farmers and process it in centrally located factories. Tours of tea factories such as these are another attraction for tourists dedicated to experiencing tea although redundant tea factories also provide an architectural resource to be developed into facilities for tourists. An award-winning example of such a development is the conversion of a Victorian tea factory into a luxury hotel – The Tea Factory Hotel in Sri Lanka. On the other hand, in some tea villages such as Mae Salong, Thailand and Ping Lin, Taiwan, the processing of tea is all done on a small scale and these family-based tea enterprises can be visited just by strolling down the main street of the village.

Because of the large scale of both tea-production and tea-consumption facilities, it is clear that there is much potential for developing products for tea-related tourism. In addition there are augmented resources for tea tourism, those that use the basic resource components, and assemble and package them for tourism consumption (McKercher & du Cros, 2002). This includes tea events (such as tea parties, tea dances, special teas and tea festivals) and tea tours (incorporating visits to tea gardens, tea houses and tea hotels), as well as tea attractions (assembling tea artefacts and collections into interpreted exhibitions). In addition there is tea cuisine, as a number of restaurants around the world feature tea in their cooking. The distribution system for this product includes specialty tea companies, tour companies and travel agents.

In a number of regions there are also festivals and special events that focus on tea, for example:

- In Taiwan, a Tea Festival in Shimen Village, Taipei was held in December, 2003 with activities that included a celebration of winter tea complimented by tours of tea farms in the area.
- In Korea, annual green tea festivals are held each May at green tea plantations in Boseong-gun, Jellanam-do and at Hadong-gun, Gyeongsangnam-do.

In tea-producing situations in developing countries, there is opportunity for tea tourism projects to be a form of sustainable development, and for those in the developed countries to assist with these projects at arm's length.

This is reflected by the UK organization Tourism Concern and their involvement with developing 'pro-poor tourism' in conjunction with Sri Lankan tea gardens. Other development projects, such as the World Community Development Education Society project (based in Vancouver, Canada) with tea gardens in Assam, may have potential as sustainable tea tourism projects.

Research Framework

To study the connection between tea and tourism it is necessary to take an interdisciplinary approach. Much of the information available about tea comes from the study of history. However, the history of tea itself, extending across many centuries, is so lengthy that there is much that is legend, and historical records do not always exist. Some classic works on tea do exist, however, for example Lu Yu's treatise on tea (780 AD) and Sadler's work on the tea ceremony in Japan (1962 [1933]). Information on the growth, processing and distribution of tea comes from both the study of agriculture and from the tea industry itself. A classic example in this area is Harler's (1956) *Culture and Marketing of Tea*. The context for the development of tourism related to tea can be found in historical, political, sociological and anthropological studies of regions where tea has been produced, as well as at the locations where tea was exported to. An example of a seminal work in these aspects is Gardella's *Fujian and the China Tea Trade: 1757–1937* (1994). To develop a picture of the development of tea-related tourism at individual locations researchers must therefore draw on many different disciplinary sources.

For the study of tea and tourism it is useful to understand not only the history but also the marketing of tea. Harler (1956) describes the two sides to this process. Simply stated, on the one side is the broker who disposes in bulk of the tea, and, on the other, the distributor who blends, packages and distributes to the consumer. Sometimes the distributor also owns his own tea estates and so does not need the services of a broker. The major tea-producing areas all hold physical tea markets, and it is only recently that the Internet has been used for virtual tea auctions. In London, England, where tea auctions are no longer held, the Brahmn Tea and Coffee Museum occasionally holds mock 'tea auctions' as an attraction for visitors.

Tea researchers must also be adept at personal observation, experiencing and taking note of their own experiences with tea in different situations and cultures. These researchers must therefore travel, and in the context of preparing this book, researchers have travelled to the tea gardens of India, Sri Lanka, China and Thailand. They have surveyed visitors at tea festivals and tea rooms in both China and Canada. They have visited tea hotels in Kenya and Sri Lanka, as well as tea museums in China and England. Along the way they experienced afternoon tea at historic locations in England and Scotland and tea Chinese-style in the tea houses of Hangzhou and Fuzhou, China. They have had to visit the tea destinations of Victoria (British Columbia), Hangzhou (China), London (England) and Mae Salong (Thailand). These various investigations have given the researchers added insights that would not have been gained through a pure research-based academic investigation. As both observers and participants in the tea experience, they have taken part in action-based research (Kirby & McKenna, 1989) and become 'tea tourists' themselves. Contact has also been made with the tea industries in a number of countries, visiting tea blenders and talking to tea industry representatives, in order to gain insight into the industry perspective and attitudes towards the development of tourism related to tea.

This type of participatory research is not without bias. Each researcher carries with them the conceptual baggage related to their prior experience with tea. For example, the editor of this book, formerly a tea room proprietor, is seen by some as a 'tea lover' and has had to accommodate for this bias, searching out other viewpoints and perspectives regarding the romance of tea, balancing this perspective with examinations of the darker side of tea history. Each author also brings with him a unique appreciation of the quality of the leaf and its potential role in tourism, whether it is from working at a tea farm in China, having a tea farm in Kenya in one's own family, or coordinating a development project with organic tea growers in China. The contributors thus bring not only their own expertise as tourism researchers but also their own life experiences as tea consumers and tea tourists.

This book builds on previous work on tea, travel and tourism (Jolliffe, 2003a: Jolliffe, 2003b), which explored in a general sense the connections between tea history, tea traditions and the resulting tea attractions available for tourism. This initial work on tea tourism identified the connections between tea and travel as well as tea and cuisine, and provided examples of emergent tea attractions and tea destinations. The author asserted that tea tourism was developing 'in concert with the growing interest, and demand for authentic tourism experiences' and that the recent development of tea attractions and tea cuisine 'reflects a growing interest in culinary tourism' (Jolliffe, 2003a: 136). These observations were taken as evidence of the emergence of tea tourism as a special-interest or niche area of culinary tourism.

This book develops further the insights into the emergence of tea tourism, delving into the nature, characteristics and experiences of tea tourists, and examining the transformation of tea cultures and material for the purposes of tourism. In addition, through a mix of case studies of tea tourism destinations and empirical investigations of tea tourism experiences, the book further delineates the ability of tourism to transform tea into a tourism product, for the benefit of local communities around the world, as well as identifying the social and political situations that either nurture or hinder the development of tea-related tourism in particular geographic contexts.

Being the first substantive volume to focus on tea tourism, the book accommodates various geographical perspectives of tea-related tourism from the west, the east and the south. The preponderance of case material from China, considered by many as both the home and the birthplace of tea culture, is a particular strength. This inclusion has allowed for tea-related tourism in China to be viewed from the viewpoints of history, development, destinations and events, providing a snapshot of the state of tea tourism in China today, and providing insights and examples that may benefit the development of tea tourism in other countries.

Rationale for this Book

The many aspects of tea and its relationship to both travel and history demonstrate the need for a volume such as this, which explores the nature of these relationships. The central aim of the book is to trace and explain the relationship between tea and tourism. As a potentially seminal work on tea tourism the collaborative process for preparing this volume had some limitations as relatively few tourism researchers have worked exclusively in this area. However, the idea of tea tourism was taken up by an extremely able cast of authors, writing from their own perspectives as both academics and practitioners.

The contributors include specialists on cultural heritage tourism, tourism geography, tourism and development, and tourism and political ecology. This multidisciplinary approach brings much to the study of tea and tourism; however, it has limitations when case information on destination tea tourism is presented from different perspectives. Looking beyond these disciplinary differences in approach and method, it is possible through the chapters presented to see a glimpse of the global occurrence of a newly recognized niche type of tourism, which, in this book, is identified as tea tourism. This glimpse includes a palette of tea tourism products, experiences, services, destinations and tourists, as well as the identification of challenges and issues in developing this type of tourism.

In terms of developing knowledge on tea tourism, the book is a beginning and not an end. It answers some of the fundamental questions about such tourism but also poses others. For example, in the case of some well-known tea-producing areas, such as Assam, why has more tea tourism not developed? Within the answers to questions such as these are the germs of future research. If the political and socio-economic conditions for tourism should improve in these locations then the further development of tea tourism may be nurtured. Tea, its consumption and experience and its relation to travel is the filter through which tourism is viewed within this book.

Organization of this Book

The purpose of this book, through its various chapters, is therefore to explore the rich connections between tea, tourism and tourists, tracing the transformations of tea and tea cultures that have resulted from travel and tourism, and documenting the current state of tea-related tourism. In order to achieve this purpose, the book is divided into five parts.

The first part introduces the book. The second part traces tea history and culture and gives examples of its transformation into a tourism experience product. The third part examines the political and socio-economic context for tea tourism, highlighting issues that account for the apparent lag in the emergence of tea-related tourism. The fourth part examines the emergence and marketing of tea-related tourism at a number of destinations and in a number of regions of the world. Featuring case studies of tea tourism in a number of contexts, each chapter also provides analytical information on the development of this type of tourism. The fifth and final part of the book provides a conclusion and proposes directions for future research on tea tourism.

The introduction provides the background, purpose and organization of the volume. The second part of the book then traces both historical and contemporary tea cultures and gives an indication of their potential relevance to tourism. Chapter 2, 'Tracing the History of Tea Cultures' by Leung Kin Han, traces the history of the major tea cultures in the world and looks at contemporary tea-consumption patterns and behaviours that provide a context for the development of tea tourism. Using China as an example, he notes the potential for developing customized tea experiences in conjunction with tea, tea origins, tea products and tea customs. Chapter 3, 'Tea and Travel: Transforming the Material Culture of Tea' by Jolliffe, identifies the material culture associated with tea and examines how, through travel and the activity of collecting, this material has been transformed into providing other tea experiences for the tea tourist. Chapter 3 also identifies issues such as the influence of curatorial practices on the meanings associated with tea collections that may result in altered interpretations of tea cultures. Leung Kin Han in Chapter 4, 'Tea Traditions in Taiwan and Yunnan', compares two contemporary Chinese tea cultures, concluding that traditional tea cultures are being adapted to contemporary Chinese society, providing new experiences for tea tourists to discover. The make-up and variety in the tea tourism product is identified and a potential market segment for tea tourism is outlined as consisting of the three categories of tea hobbyists, novelty-seekers and cultural/eco-tourists.

These introductory chapters provide a foundation for understanding the ways in which tea histories, traditions and cultures are transformed from one culture to another, and the tea cultures of individual societies are transformed into tourism experiences.

The third part of the book examines both the political and socio-economic contexts for the development, or in some cases the lack of development, of tea-related tourism. In Chapter 5, 'Tea Production and Tourism Development in Assam: A Missed Opportunity?', Hannam, taking a politico-ecological approach, examines the history of tea production and subsequent tourism development in Assam Province, India. Here we can see the colonial history of tea has a direct relationship with the fact that 'tea tourism' has not yet developed to any significant extent in the province, with visits to tea gardens being conducted on an ad hoc basis. Hannam asserts that current opportunities for developing tea tourism in Assam have been mitigated by political conflicts in the area. Continuing with the theme of the development of tea tourism in a difficult political situation, in Chapter 6, 'Amidst the Misty Mountains: The Role of Tea Tourism in Sri Lanka's Turbulent Tourist Industry, Gunasekara and Momsen examine the role of tea tourism. Tea tourism here is identified as being linked to eco-tourism, heritage tourism, health tourism, and rural and farm tourism. It is denoted as having the ability to be either high-end and exclusive (as illustrated by the case of the Tea Factory Hotel), or community-based and 'pro-poor' (as illustrated by the Woodlands Network in Bandarawela, Sri Lanka – the group that coined the term tea tourism). Since the Tea Factory Hotel has no real links with the tea industry that can be experienced by guests, Gunasekara and Momsen note that small-scale developments may be more effective in linking tea and tourism for positive economic results for local communities. Huang and Hall in Chapter 7, 'The New Tea Appreciation Festival: Promotion and Socio-economic Development in Hunan Province, China", first outline the health benefits of green tea and then consider the related promotional and socio-economic aspects of the New Tea

Appreciation Festival. They note the potential of the festival for enhancing local and regional economy, promoting image and identity and generating a sense of the cultural continuity of the area's tea culture. In Chapter 8, 'Tea Culture and Tourism in Fujian Province, China: Towards a Partnership for Sustainable Development', Xiao reviews Fujian's tea culture and identifies the current state of tea tourism in this province of China in relation to tourism development, indicating ways in which the tea and tourism industries might work together towards sustainable development. In Chapter 9, 'Tourism Development and the Tea Gardens of Fuding, China', Jolliffe and Zhuang highlight tea-related tourism in Fuding, China and profile a development project proposed in conjunction with one of the organic tea gardens of rural Fujian. By profiling a local tea company, insights are gained into the potential role of small tea enterprises in facilitating tea tourism and implementing related pro-poor tourism projects. In Chapter 10, 'Tourism and Tea in Kenya: Opportunity for Development', Muhati and Jolliffe examine the relationship between Kenya's tea and tourism industries and discuss the political and economic context for tea-related tourism in what is now the world's largest tea-exporting country. The authors scrutinize the potential contribution of tea to the much-needed diversification of the country's tourism industry. While only limited evidence of existing products for tea tourism is uncovered, a number of potential developments are highlighted.

The fourth part of the book profiles the development and marketing of tea tourism destinations and products at different locations and in different countries. In Chapter 11, 'China's Tea Horse Trade Route and its Potential for Tourism', du Cros profiles China's Tea Horse Trade Route, less known and less developed than the Silk Road, and assesses it as a heritage asset. The market appeal of the route for tourism is discussed; and it is concluded that the trail does indeed have appeal and potential for development as a tea tourism route. This dual assessment of robustness and market appeal provides a blueprint for the future management and possible development of the route. In Chapter 12, 'Hangzhou: China's Green Tea City', Dewar and Li examine the development of Hangzhou, China as a tea destination. They profile the city's long history as the production source of Dragon Well Longjing tea, highlight its current efforts to promote itself as a tea destination, and also discuss issues regarding to branding and trade marking of this well know tea. In Chapter 13, "The UK's Teapot Trails: Just a Handle or Something Worth Spouting About?', Hall and Boyne examine the nature, concept and development of the UK's teapot trails, detailing the potential for tea-related tourism in local and regional development processes. This includes consideration of the tea room as a national symbol and the evaluation of the teapot trails as themed trails. In Chapter 14, 'Tea Tourists and Tea Destinations in Canada: A New Blend?', Jolliffe relates domestic tea consumption to a possible profile of domestic tea tourists in Canada. Several developing tea destinations are profiled, examining the role of the tea trade and the potential for further development of these destinations in the context of Canada's emerging culinary tourism industry.

While each chapter presents a particular view of the relationship between tea and tourism, overall this book is concerned with tea in relation to tourism, with the transformation of tea for tourism development, and with the related social changes that accompany these processes. The fifth part of the book thus contains a concluding chapter that draws upon the issues and themes introduced in the body of the text, creating a picture of the role of tea in tourism. Furthermore, a commentary is provided on the contemporary state of tea tourism, and issues critical to future development and study in this area are identified. As the background to tea tourism is uncovered, discussed and debated, the reader of this book is invited to get a cup of tea, to sit back, and to enjoy!

References

Boniface, P. (2003) *Tasting Tourism: Travelling for Food and Drink*. Aldershot: Ashgate.

Euromonitor (2004) *Hot Drinks in Taiwan*. Euromonitor International.

Gardella, R. (1994) *Fujian and the China Tea Trade: 1757–1937*. Berkeley, CA: University of California Press.

Goodwin, J. (2003) *The Gunpowder Gardens: Travels Through India and China in Search of Tea*. London: Penguin Books.

Gostello Report (2003) *The List: 10 Best Afternoon Teas*. Enroute. June 2003.

Gunn, C.A. (1988) *Tourism Planning*. New York: Taylor & Francis.

Hjalager, A.M. and Richards, G. (2002) (eds) *Tourism and Gastronomy*. London: Routledge.

Harler, C.R. (1956) *The Culture and Marketing of Tea*. Oxford: Oxford University Press.

Howard, P. (2003) *Heritage: Management, Interpretation, Identity*. London: Continuum.

Hussain, Syed Zaris (2004) Starvation kills hundreds of Indian tea garden laborers. *One World South Asia*. March 31, 2004.

Iso-Ahola, S.E. (1982) Towards a psychological theory of tourism motivation. *Annals of Tourism Research* (9) 2, 256–62.

Jolliffe, L. (2003a) *Something's Brewing: Tea and Tourism in Canada*. Presented at Travel and Tourism Research Association Canada Chapter Annual Conference. Saint John, New Brunswick, October 2003.

Jolliffe, L. (2003b). The lure of tea: History, traditions and attractions. In M, Hall, L. Sharples, R. Mitchell, N. Macionis and B. Cambourne (eds) *Food Tourism Around the World: Development, Management and Markets* (pp. 121–36). London: Butterworth-Heinemann.

Jolliffe, L. (2004) 'Not just a cuppa: Tea and commercial hospitality'. *Proceedings Bangkok International Conference on Applied Business Research 2004*. Bangkok, Thailand: Faculty of Business Administration, Kasetsart University.

Kenya Tea Development Authority (2004). Online document athttp://www.ktdateas.com/ (accessed 30 July 2004).

Kirby, S. and McKenna, K. (1989) *Experience Research Social Change*. Toronto: Garamond Press.

Manil, C. and Zbinden, M. (2001) *Tea Time*. London: Cassell & Company.

McKercher, B. and du Cros, H. (2002) *Cultural Tourism: The Partnership between Tourism and Cultural Heritage Management*. Binghamton, New York: The Haworth Press.

Moxham, R. (2004) *Tea: Addiction, Exploration and Empire*. New York: Carroll & Graf Publications.

Naughton, A. and Perry, N. (2002) *Tea and Sympathy*. New York: G.F. Putnam's Sons.

Oxford English Reference Dictionary (2001) Oxford: Oxford University Press.

Pettigrew, J. (1999) *Tea and Infusions*. London: Carleton.

Pettigrew, J. (2001) *A Social History of Tea*. London: The National Trust.

Pratt, J.N. (1982) *The Tea Lover's Treasury*. San Ramon, CA: 101 Productions.

Pratt, J.N. (2002) 'Pilgrimage to the Holy Land of tea', *Imperial Tea Court/China Tea Tour Essay*. Online document: http://www.imperialtea.com/tea/tours. (accessed 20 March).

Sadler, A.L. (1962 [1933]) *Cha-no-yu: The Japanese Tea Ceremony*. Rutland, VT: Charles E. Tuttle Company. Reprint of first edition.

Shapira, J., Shapira, D. and Shapira, K. (1975) *The Book of Coffee and Tea*. New York: St Martin's Press.

Smith, M. (1986) *Michael Smith's Afternoon Tea*. London: Macmillan.

Smith, V.L. (1977) *Hosts and Guests: The Antropology of Tourism*. Philadelphia, PA: University of Pennsylvania Press.

Tourism Victoria (2003) *Afternoon Tea in Victoria*. Online document: http://www.tourismvictoria.com (accessed 30 July 2003).

Walker, J. R. (2001) *Introduction to Hospitality*. Upper Saddle River, NJ: Prentice Hall.

Williams, S. (1998) *Tourism Geography*. London: Routledge.

Wolf, E. (2003) *Culinary Tourism: A Tasty Economic Proposition*. Portland, OR: International Culinary Tourism Association.

Part 2: Tea Histories, Collections and Traditions

Chapter 2
Tracing the History of Tea Culture

PAUL LEUNG KIN HAN

The background to tea is complex and the objective of this chapter is to provide a brief anthropological background about tea-drinking behaviours, the tea trade and tea culture. Although the description heavily draws upon Chinese archives, the discussions are intended to cover a more generic global spectrum. This chapter is subdivided into three major components: the origin of the tea-drinking behaviour; the exportation of tea and tea drinking from China to the rest of the world; and the development of a contemporary tea culture.

The Origin of Tea Drinking

There are several theories about the origins of tea. According to Indian mythology, tea originated in northern India and was transplanted into the Sichuan Province of China in the 1600s (Pettigrew, 2001). The Chinese legend, however, suggested that the origin of tea drinking can be traced 5000 years back in China, when tea was first discovered by Emperor Shen Nung, who lived between 2737–2697 BC. Shen Nung, who is credited with the invention of an agricultural system and writing the 'Medical Book', is nonetheless a mythical figure. In other words, there is no written record to prove his existence and, by the same token, his discovery of tea. However, there is documentation of the use of tea as a tribute to emperors during the Zhou Dynasty (1100–771 BC), which suggests that there were tea plantations in China as early as 1100 BC (Ruan, 1995). There is also evidence suggesting that tea drinking has its origin in south western China, especially the Sichuan and Yunnan Provinces. According to an anthropological account by Gou written during the Tsing Dynasty (AD 1644–1911), tea drinking was bought to central China when Qin conquered Sichuan in 316 BC. There are, however, other documents suggesting that tea leaves were already used for cooking and religious purposes around 547–490 BC. In a slavery contract written during the West Han Dynasty in 59 BC, there were clear descriptions about tea-drinking behaviours. The document also indicated that there was an organized tea trade and tea market during the time. The argument that tea was brought to China from India in the 1600s therefore appears to be unfounded.

Tea drinking was very much a hobby of the social elite until the Jin Dynasty (AD 265–420). During that time, there were already commercial tea plantations in certain provinces, including Yunnan, Sichuan, Hubei, Hunan, Henan, Jiangsu, Anhui and Zhejiang. Tea gradually became a popular commodity among the general public. The price of tea, due to the large-scale commercial plantations, also dropped drastically. Drinking tea became a more popular hobby and gradually become a custom or ritual. Although tea drinking is generally regarded in Chinese society as a more modest or thrifty behaviour than wine drinking, the level of sophistication in tea selection, consumption and rituals is by no means less than wine.

By the Tang Dynasty (AD 907–60), large-scale tea plantations can be found in 8 regions, 43 provinces and 44 counties. In the early Tang period, the annual tax revenue from tea exceeded 40 million currency units. Given that the regular tax rate was 10%, the annual tea trade exceeded one billion catty (a Southeast Asian unit of measurement equal to about 600 grams), excluding the private and smuggling trade. At the same time, the Tang government established the system of tribute tea, which identified 10 different species as tribute tea. It is very common in Chinese history to identify top quality species of certain commodities as tribute products. The identification indicated the quality of the product and also the preferences of the emperor. Goushiu tea is among the top of the tribute tea list. In AD 770 (?), the Tang authority established a tea plantation in Goushiu employing 30,000 workers and producing 18,400 catties per year.

Widespread tea-drinking behaviour in China is also a result of the popularization of Buddhism. Civitello (2004: 81) observes that 'just as Christianity spread on the roads in the Roman Empire, tea spread on the Silk Road, often with Buddhism'. During the Tang Dynasty, tea was largely used as praise to Buddha and as an official drink in ceremonies. In the *Rule of Monks*, edited by Weihai, there are precise rules on tea-drinking and other drinking behaviours. These rules established the official position of tea in Buddhism and among general Chinese communities.

In the Tang Dynasty, the famous poet and philosopher Lu Yu (AD 723–804) published the famous *Cha Jin* ('The Bible of Tea') in AD 780. His publication made critical contributions to the establishment of the social status and values of tea and tea drinking among the Chinese community.

Tea was bought to Tibet around the 7th century AD. It was about two centuries later when the Korean embassy in China bought a tea-tree back to Korea and initiated the tea plantation business in the southern Korean peninsula. In the early 9th century, tea was introduced to Japan from Korea. Within a few years, tea gained a certain level of public recognition. Tea, however, lost its popularity as the Sino-Japanese Trade agreement ended in AD 894. It was more than 300 years later when tea was reintroduced to the Japanese community in the 12th century.

Although there are debates on where and when tea drinking first started, it is a generally accepted belief that the tea drinking originated in China and was disseminated to other regions through trade via the Silk Road and marine routes and also by military movements.

The Different Types of Tea

Tea classifications are based on various criteria, such as origin, species and production methods. Ancient teas are mainly dominated by pressed tea. They take the form of brick, bowl or smaller lump tea. Harvested tea leaves were steamed, pressed into specific shape, dried and fermented. Fermentation is caused by the oxidation of enzymes. The dark colour of red tea is caused by a full fermentation process, where as *oolong* tea is half fermented. The geographical isolation of Yunnan, where tea plantations were concentrated in ancient China, and the difficulty of transportation promoted the development of fermentation as a production format and technique. As in the Tang Dynasty, the trend of loose tea started to emerge along the lengthy evolution of the production technique. New production methods added new versions to the traditional, resulting in fermented red (black tea), versus green, semi-green (*oolong*) and white tea. The variation in colour of red, semi-green and green tea is caused by the different levels of fermentation.

The reddish colour of red tea is the result of complete fermentation. Red tea, from traditional Yunnan Puer to the Indian Darjeeling tea, still accounts for the majority of tea output and consumption in the modern world. In the West, red tea is known as black tea. Green tea is prevented from fermentation and thus retains its green colour. Japanese teas, for example, are mainly green teas, and include *bancha, sencha* and *gyokuro* (Graham, 1998). Semi-green tea, better known as *oolong*, is partially fermented. Taiwan, for example, is well-known for its expensive varieties of *oolong* tea.

White tea, which is derived from the buds of the tea plant, is rare and mostly expensive. In terms of variety and quantity, its production is much less than its green and red counterparts.

Tea is continuously undergoing a metamorphosis. While traditional tea forms and customs are preserved as ritual enjoyment, new forms and customs, new species and new blends of tea create a new platform for tea consumption and a new marketing landscape. Taking the Taiwanese flora and fruit teas as an example, consuming and experiencing these teas has become a fashion and a motive for some travellers to visit Taiwan.

The Tea Industry in China

China started to develop foreign trade during the Zhou Dynasty (1100–771 BC). The exploration of the silk trade route, the development of the Tea and Horse Trade Route and the sea route to the Gulf of Persia further enhanced trade activities. Together with silk and pottery, tea was disseminated to central Asia and the Middle East. At about the same time, Buddhism arrived in China and started to spread. Coincidently, tea was adopted as the official drink for the Buddhist religion and as Buddhism was promoted by various emperors, tea drinking became a very popular leisure, social and religious behaviour.

A major tea-trade activity was the tea–horse trade, which commenced in about AD 756. When a riot broke out in November 755 in China, the Chinese government urgently needed horses for its soldiers. This barter trade was an important source of warhorses for various dynasties. Markets for trading tea for horses and the tea–horse trade routes were established at the western boundary of China. In the next 300 years, tea became one of the most prominent trade items. Chinese tea arrived in Africa in 1433. Since then, the tea-trade territory has expanded to cover the whole of Southeast Asia, North Asia, the Middle East and Africa. The transplanting of tea to India and Sri Lanka, and the development of a tea-drinking culture in England took place during a later period in history.

Although the general price of tea was deflated owing to large-scale commercial plantations, tea was still a very precious commodity. For example, in AD 1368, the finest horses could at most trade for 120 catties of tea each, and on average a horse was worth less than 40 catties. This trade practice, operated as a state-owned business, lasted for almost 1000 years. With the exception of the Yuen Dynasty (AD 1271–1368), tea–horse trade did not cease its operation until AD 1735.

The tea industry in Sichuan had already gone through specialization and an entrepreneurial revolution around AD 1068. As the scale of production grew, many plantations had to become specialized in their selection of tea species, production methods and the extent to which the production process was integrated. Many large plantations during this time failed to process all their harvest and thus subcontracted tea processing to specialized factories. By the Sung Dynasty, as the number and scale of state-owned plantations continued to grow, the authorities decided to privatize some state-owned enterprises. Privatization, to a certain extent, promoted the development of the private tea trade and the exploration of export trade routes beyond China.

Tea was also promoted in Islamic society as a substitute for wine since wine drinking is prohibited by Islamic religion. Tea became Islam's official drink. Tea drinking, along with the spread of the Islamic movement, became very popular among Arabian societies.

In 1867, tea was China's biggest export commodity, accounting for about 60% of the country's total export. The annual export recorded 1.31 million 'dam' (local currency), which accounted for over 90% of world total tea trade. After the Opium War, Chinese tea trade peaked in 1886 and recorded a total export of 268 million dam. After 1876, tea from India, Ceylon (Sri Lanka), Indonesia and Japan posed serious competition. In 1890, the Chinese exports dropped to about 50.9% of the world total (see Table 2.2). Another key point of consideration is that, from 1885 until 1950, many tea plantations and manufacturers were operating at a loss. The sluggish tea business in China, however, does not reflect a decline of demand, but results from the marginalization of world trade. During this dark age for China tea, trade was largely controlled by foreign trade companies and prices were manipulated by the international market in London. According to Ruan (1995), every year when new teas first appeared in the market, the market prices were driven up to attract tea gardens to increase production, but soon after the price would drop drastically. By the time of harvest, the traders purchased in bulk at a much lower market price and plantations would frequently find their businesses operating at very low margins or even at a loss.

By 1950, the total area of tea plantations in China was 160,930 hectares, harvesting 65,200 tons and exporting 8500 tons of tea. Given the difficult and chaotic situation of the tea industry in China, the government of the People's Republic of China centralized all tea operation and planning. The Great Leap Forward movement in 1961, however, decimated the industry. Total exports in 1961 had fallen to the level of 1951. In 1965, production rose to 120,500 tons and exports to 40, 800 tons. After eight years of redevelopment, the export of 1969 still only amounted to the level of 1956. However, the China tea industry in the 1970s and 1980s featured rapid growth and development. In 1976, annual production reached 233,500 tons. The exports of 1984 and 1989 were 145,000 and 205,000 tons respectively.

Table 2.1 Tea products from major tea production provinces in China

Anwei (Anhui) Province	Keemun Ching-Wo Maofeng Chunmee Green Young Hyson
Fukien (Fujian) Province	Oolong Ti Kuan Yin Jasmine White Tea Wu-Yi Oolong Lapsang Souchong
Kwangtung (Guangdong) Province	Feng Huang Oolong Lichee Congou Rose Congou
Hubei Province	North China Congou Tea Bricks
Hunan Province	Gu Zhang Maojian Yellow Tea Silver Needles
Kiangsu (Jiangsu) Province	Pi LoChun Yu Hua Cha
Szechuan (Sichuan) Province	Oolong Orange Pekoe
Yunnan Province	Yunnan Black Yunnan Golden Pu-er
Chingkiang (Zhejiang) Province	Lungching Gun Powder Tian Mu Qing Ding Puan Lung Yin Hao Jasmine Ping Suey
Formosa (Taiwan)	Black Dragon Oolong Tungting Oolong Formosa Oolong Pouchong

Table 2.2 China's share of tea exports

Year	Quantity	Share (%)
Annual average before the outbreak of Opium War	450,000	
1867	131	90
1886	268	
1890		50.9
1900		31.3
1913		21.3
1919		10.8

Source: Ruan (1995)

The specialization and level of sophistication regarding tea drinking among Chinese communities can be traced by the number of available related publications. *Cha Jin* ('The Bible of Tea') by Lu Yu (AD 733–804) is the original and probably the most important publication for the Chinese tea community. *Cha Jin* was divided into ten chapters, which focus on origins and characteristics of different tea species, tea equipment, production, tea wares, preparation, drinking methods and customs, and tea-related issues. Since *Cha Jin*, there have been an enormous number of publications about tea. Some of these are very specific, such as *Jian Cha Shuigi* (814 AD), which was about the specific requirements of water for making tea. Another publication worth mentioning is a book called *Daigui Cha Lun*, which was written by the eighth emperor of the Sung Dynasty. In addition to the contribution of its sophisticated research and detailed discussions, the social status of the author verified the importance of tea and tea drinking among the Chinese. According to Ruan (1995), there are a total of 31 different categories of tea publications in the Sung Dynasty. During 250 years of the Ming Dynasty, this increased to 68 categories. In the Qing Dynasty, the number reduced to 17 categories, although the scale and volume of publication increased tremendously. For example, the biggest book has more than 100,000 words. Today, owing to the importance of tea as an export, more scientific research has been published. The national authorities also published guidelines and technical advice on tea planting and production. Tea publications, therefore, have extended tea beyond its cultural dimension into various domains, including economic and ecological perspectives.

Yunnan, Sichuan and Fujian are among the important tea-producing zones in China. (See Table 2.1 for details of the tea products from different provinces in China.) Yunnan and Sichuan are believed to be where tea originated and both have very long histories in tea planting and customs. Fujian, in south China, has a shorter history of tea plantations, but its relatively short history does not lessen its importance. Since the first royal plantation was established there in 1302, the tea industry grew rapidly. By 1392, its annual output increased to over 900 catty and accounted for a quarter of all tribute tea at that time. Its major outputs can be subcategorized into seven classes, which suggests the high level of sophistication. In 1557, the local governor pleaded with the emperor to lift the tribute requirements and this ended its tribute history of 255 years. From then on, Fujian tea became more accessible to the public and successfully developed into a new branch of Chinese tea culture. Today, the province leads China in tea production (*People's Daily*, 2002).

Tea in Japan

There are records of tea drinking and ceremony in Japan in the 8th century. During that time, all tea was imported from China. It was around AD 805, when a Japanese monk named Eichu (AD 713–816) brought seeds back to Japan, that tea was planted on Japanese soil for the first time. Eichu planted tea only for his own consumption, but after he served emperor Saga (reigned 810–23) with boiled tea in AD 810, Saga ordered widespread tea planting, and popularized tea drinking. Graham (1998) asserted that Saga's enchantment with tea was largely driven by his fascination with Chinese literati culture. No matter what the exact motives, his interest in tea resulted in five provinces around Kyoto establishing a tea industry. Although the relationship between China and Japan deteriorated after Saga, tea custom still persisted in Buddhist temples (Graham, 1998; Pettigrew, 2001). Tea was reintroduced by Zen priests in the early 11th century and more species of tea, including powdered green tea, which later became the mainstream of Japanese tea (*matcha* and *tencha*), were introduced. The flourishing of tea in Japan was largely promoted by the use of tea in religious rituals (both Buddhist and Shinto). Tea, as a foreign trade, however, was largely affected by the political relationship between Chinese and Japanese governments. Although political tension between the two countries on and off suspended the tea trade and the diffusion of tea cultures, it facilitated the development of the unique tea custom and culture of Japan. As of the 17th century, *sencha* became very popular and widely accessible by the Japanese public. By 1658, *Sencha* is reported as being sold by peddlers in Edo (Graham, 1998).

Today, *sencha* is still the most popular beverage among Japanese communities. It has, as asserted by Graham (1998), enriched the Japanese cultural landscape immeasurably. Japanese tea such as *sencha* and tea ceremonies such as *chanoyu* ('the way of tea') have become an inseparable part of Japanese culture and provide attractions for tourists to explore and experience. *Chanoyu* classes are offered in many foreign countries and have become a very sophisticated hobby with a sizeable market segment. Places such as Kyoto and Nara have emerged as well-known destinations with tea and tea cultures being critical parts of their attractiveness.

Tea in Europe

It is not known whether the Portuguese or the Dutch first brought tea to Europe in the early 17th century. The Dutch East India Company played a critical role in planting and importing tea from Indonesia. Pettigrew (2001) asserted that the Dutch started to import tea from Java in 1610. A letter dated 1637 from the director of the Dutch East India Company to the governor the Netherlands revealed the popularity and increasing demand for tea. At the same time, tea and tea-drinking behaviours were spreading to other European countries. In response to increasing demand, commercial tea gardens were introduced in Indonesia in 1728. Farm workers were recruited from China to adopt the Chinese way of tea production.

Tea first arrived in Russia in 1618 as a gift from China to Tsar Alexis and in 1689, a trade agreement was signed between China and Russia. After that date, merchants with as many as 200 or 300 camels travelled along the Usk Kayakhta border trading fur for tea. According to Pettigrew (2001), each camel had to carry some 270 kilograms of tea, and it took them between 16 to 18 months to reach the Russian marketplace. Prices, due to logistic difficulties, were so high that tea drinking was a luxury of the social elite. By 1796, Russian's annual consumption of tea, despite the high price, grew to 6000 camel loads (Pratt, 1982; Pettigrew, 2001). Around the turn of the century the Trans-Siberian railway replaced the camel cavalcade and brought the prices down. This change in transportation mode promoted tea's popularity in Russia. Today, tea remains as one of the most popular drinks in the region.

No one would question the popularity of tea in England. Tea first appears in English documents in 1658 (Pettigrew, 2001). The first tea advertisement in England was published in the *London Weekly*, 23–30 September 1658 by Thomas Garraway. Despite Garraway promoting tea as an herbal medicine for various diseases, it was a Portuguese princess who successfully introduced tea to the higher social echelons in England after she married

Charles II. At that time, tea was a very expensive commodity. Its price ranged from 16 to 60 shillings a pound. The high retail price of tea was partially due to heavy taxes levied on it, as well as coffee and chocolate. By 1687, the price of the cheapest tea was about 7 shillings per pound, which was equivalent to the weekly wages of an ordinary worker at the time. The high price of tea also encouraged significant smuggling activities, and the blending of other types of leaves with tea. Since most of these counterfeits were green tea, they led to black tea dominating the market.

Tea became the most popular beverage in England in the 18th century, replacing alcohol in the leading position. The annual consumption increased from 30 tons in 1701 to 2229.6 tons in 1781 and further increased to 6847.8 tons in 1791 (Pettigrew, 2001). In the 19th century, afternoon tea became a part of English daily life. The mass demand for tea, however, created a substantial trade deficit. With the failure of promoting cotton to China, the British and Portuguese started to export opium to China in exchange for tea (Pettigrew, 2001). Although opium was prohibited by Chinese law, smuggling activities and the black market had never been so vibrant. In 1839, a Chinese official, Lim, destroyed 20,000 cases of British opium in Guangdong, which directly led to the outbreak of the Opium War in 1840.

In response to the assault of the British army, China imposed an embargo on tea shipments to England. The English merchants, therefore, began to investigate the possibility of planting and producing tea products in other parts of the British Empire. For their first test plantation, they identified north India. In 1849, commercial plantations were established in Darjeeling, Cachar, Sylhet and other areas in north India. Tea plantations were also established in Ceylon in the 1870s when coffee beans failed there as a crop. After that, north India and Sri Lanka became the most important tea-growing areas for the British market.

James Taylor and Thomas Lipton, who founded the Indian and Sri Lankan tea industry, are the most important pioneers. In the 1870s, Lipton directly exported tea from his tea gardens in Sri Lanka to his retail shops in England. His direct marketing channel increased his control over the business and the profitability of his trade. Gradually, India and Sri Lanka took over the leading position from China as the exporters of tea to England. Despite the end of the colonial era of the British Empire and its various impacts on former colonies, tea had by then established its critical position in the Indian and Sri Lankan economy.

Ireland is the heaviest tea-drinking country with per capita consumption of 3.6 kg per year. It is followed by England, New Zealand and Canada (Manil & Zbinden, 2001). Although tea was once very popular in France and Germany, it was replaced in popularity by coffee in the late 17th century. The annual per capita tea consumption for these countries is 230 kg and 1 kg respectively (Manil & Zbinden, 2001).

Tea in South Asia, Africa and the Middle East

India has a very important role to play in the development of the modern tea industry. According to Eden (1965), the modern form of the tea industry is an extension of the development in India in the 18th century. The investigation of the possibility of tea plantations being developed in northeast India between 1818 and 1834 became the cornerstone of the Indian tea industry. Under threats of the frequently disturbed tea trade with China, the English traders were eager to establish a new source of tea. The 'Committee of Tea Culture' was, therefore, formed in 1834 in Calcutta to experiment with tea growing in the Calcutta Botanical Gardens. Since then, India has developed into a major tea-exporting region.

Following the footsteps of the Indian tea industry, commercial tea planting in Ceylon took off in the 1870s. Although there were only 10 acres recorded in 1867, 14,226 acres were reported in 1880. In 1895, tea growing expanded to 305,000 acres (Eden, 1965). The rapid development was largely due to the government's encouragement, the huge market demand and the failure of the coffee plantation owing to a blight known as 'Coffee Rust fungus' (Pratt, 1982). Tea is still among the most important trade commodities in India and Sri Lanka. India tea exports (173.1 million kg) experienced a 14% decrease in 2003, which is by and large offset by the increase for Sri Lanka (11.3 million kg) and China (8.3 million kg) (Tea and Coffee Trade On-line, 2004).

In Africa, tea was first grown at the Durban Botanical Gardens in 1850 and extended to Natal in 1877 after the coffee failure (Morrison, 1943). In the early 19th century, tea specimens were planted in eastern Africa at Limuru (Kenya), Entebbe (Uganda) and Amani (Tanganyika). Kenya remains the second largest tea-exporting country with a total export of 237.5 million kg. The oldest continuing tea plantation in Africa is that of Malawi, which was established in around 1887 (Eden, 1965; Denham, 1954).

For religious reasons, tea is a very common drink among Middle Eastern countries. Iran and Iraq, for example, imported 40,200 and 57,000 metric tons of tea for consumption in 2001. Table 2.3 illustrates the annual production and exports of tea and Table 2.4 illustrates some of the latest tea trade statistics in terms of annual imports of tea for consumption for the year 2002.

Table 2.3 Annual production and exports of tea for selected countries (metric tons)

Country	Production		Exports	
	2001	*2002*	*2001*	*2002*
India	*853,710*	*826,165*	*179,857*	*196,914*
Bangladesh	*57,341*	*52,863*	12,925	13,653
Sri Lanka	296,301	310,604	287,503	285,985
Indonesia	172,897	172,792	99,721	100,185
China	701,699	745,374	249,678	252,273
Iran	*59,000*	*53,000*	*4,000*	*3,000*
Japan	89,809	84,200	760	806
Turkey	142,900	*142,000*	4,809	5,160
Vietnam	*80,000*	*84,000*	68,217	74,812
Kenya	294,631	287,044	258,118	267,721
Malawi	36,770	39,185	38,261	39,385
Uganda	33,255	33,831	30,427	31,073
Argentina	*59,000*	*58,000*	*56,645*	*57,107*
World total	*3,046,121*	*3,062,665*	*1,392,140*	*1,427,974*

Note: Figures in italics are provisional

Source: International Tea Committee (2002)

Culture and Tea Culture

As discussed in the previous section, tea drinking has spread into various cultures. Although not all of them take tea and tea-drinking to the same level of importance and seriousness, tea is certainly an important part of modern culture. This section discusses the role of culture in tea-drinking behaviours, tea-drinking's role in both Oriental and Western culture, and the development of a tea-drinking culture. The earlier sections have defined tea culture in its political, cultural, social, economic and religious contexts. This section will also focus on the utilization of tea as an attraction for cultivating cultural tourism.

Tea drinking is a cultural event. It is interesting to notice how tea drinking has blended into the drinkers' cultural arena and thus unique tea cultures have emerged. Modern literature features tea and tea drinking in its stories. This has two important implications. First, literature became an important

Table 2.4 Annual imports of tea for consumption in selected countries
           (metric tons)

	2001	*2002*
Russian Federation	153,718	162,601
Other CIS	*57,000*	*53,000*
United Kingdom	136,558	136,598
Pakistan	106,822	97,827
USA	96,668	93,474
Egypt	56,403	78,942
Japan	60,056	51,487
Iran	*42,200*	*41,600*
Iraq	*62,000*	*81,000*
Morocco	*37,701*	*42,000*
Poland	33,102	31,000
World total	*1,316,200*	*1,353,500*

Note: Figures in italics are provisional

Source: International Tea Committee (2002)

source of information for the study of tea. Second, tea's cultural importance
has been enhanced by this literature. The processes of adaptation and
acculturalization occur simultaneously. Although tea drinking has perhaps
over 400,000 years of history, tea culture is still evolving. On the other hand,
tea also tells stories about destinations and localities. No matter if it is
Darjeeling in north India; Kyoto in Japan, or Yunnan in China, tea plays
a critical part in each region's history and forms an inseparable part of
the local culture. The mythical stories, the legends, the sites and history, the
antiques and aretfacts come into the formation and presentation of the
exotic theme of a particular locality for communication and consumption.

Tea drinking is a social event. Although the existence of tea classification
and grading was confirmed in the Tang Dynasty, it was only used to
facilitate trade. By the Sung Dynasty, however, tea was associated with the
social status of drinkers. Tea became collectable and a symbol of wealth. Tea
competition emerged as an organized social event among the elite. They
would prepare and present their collections – evaluations were based on the
tea's colour, taste, scent, and formation. By then, tea had gained equal status
with chess, music and calligraphy as one of the most important forms of art
in the Chinese community. Today, many Chinese families still regard going

to tea houses at the weekend as an important family activity. It is also a very common way of gathering with friends and relatives. There are many types of tea houses with very different operating modes. Furthermore, there are different types of cultural activities associated with different types of tea houses and the behaviours of visiting tea houses. Combining cultural and social dimensions of tea drinking, visiting tea houses and experiencing tea-drinking customs can be a very attractive sociocultural activity for tourists, and may also help them to understand a particular locality.

As mentioned earlier in the chapter, religions such as Buddhism, Taoism and Islam have designated tea as their official drink and tribute to the gods. Followers might have to adapt to a set of specific tea-drinking habits and behaviours. Hence, tea-drinking behaviour can have a religious dimension. Whether this can be utilized as an asset for capitalizing on tea as an attraction, however, is yet to be established. A great deal of creativity and innovativeness can be expected for the development of such a dimension. It is still a question of whether or not the religious sector is willing to cooperate in commercialization of their customs.

Today, tea is still one of the most popular beverages among Chinese communities. In 2004, China's tea plantations exceeded 1.6 million acres with an annual production of more than 745,000 metric tons. Although statistics on the annual consumption of tea are not available, over two-thirds of the annual outputs are for domestic consumption. Tea and tea drinking is a critical part of contemporary Chinese culture.

Tea Tourism and Attractions

The relationship between tea and tourism may initially seem remote, yet it is not. The sophisticated tea-drinking and consumption patterns suggest that there is potentially a large consumer market segment that might demand a customized experience in conjunction with tea, tea origins, tea products and tea customs. It could be an intercultural interaction and exotic pursuit or simply a quest for a higher level of tea enjoyment. Either way, tea can be capitalized upon as a theme for developing tourist products and attractions. Using mainland China as an example, there are at least six major tea-exporting provinces that can develop tea-related tourism activities to enhance their attractiveness as destinations and to improve their incomes. Using Taiwan as another example, the new emerging fruit and flora tea fashion has become an additional attraction for tourists. Tea and utensils are largely purchased as souvenirs and gifts. Malaysian milk tea, horse-milk tea in Tibet and apple tea in Turkey are generally regarded as tourist attractions. Tea growing bases, such as Darjeeling, have started to develop their tea-tourism products including visits to and lodgings at tea plantations, tea festivals and other activities. Although tea is not yet fully exploited for tourism purposes, its potential is anything but small.

References

Civitello, L. (2004) *Cuisine and Culture: A History of Food and People*. Hoboken, NJ: Wiley.

Denham, G.C. (1954) *World Corps*. 6, 314.

Eden, T. (1965) *Tea*. London: Longmans.

Graham, P.J. (1998) *Tea of the Sages: The Art of Sencha*. Honolulu, HI: University of Hawaii Press.

Manil, C. and Zbinden, M. (2001) *Tea Time*. London: Cassell & Co.

Morrison, R.D. (1943) *Memorandum Relating to the Tea Industry and Tea Trade of the World*. London: International Tea Committee.

People's Daily (2002) China's special teas promise rosy future. Online document: http://english.peopledaily.com (19 September 2002).

Pratt, J.N. (1982) *The Tea Lover's Treasury*. San Ramon, CA: 101 Productions.

Pettigrew, J. (2001) *A Social History of Tea*. London: National Trust Enterprises.

Ruan, H. (1995) *Cha zhi wen shi bai ti*. Hangzhou: Zhejiang (in Chinese).

Tea and Coffee Trade on-line (2004) Online document: http://www.teaandcoffee.net/0604/world.htm (accessed 27 July 2004).

Chapter 3

Tea and Travel: Transforming the Material Culture of Tea

LEE JOLLIFFE

This chapter identifies the material culture associated with tea, highlighting the history of tea and travel that has played a role in transforming this culture into one with related souvenirs, collections and exhibitions. The transfer of tea-related objects from one function and owner to another, and the changes in associated meanings that accompany this process form a central theme to the chapter. This work is informed by the literature on the history of tea and its traditions (such as Shalleck, 1972; Smith, 1986), as well that reflecting tea and travel (such as Goodwin, 1991; Hamel, 2001), and by related material culture and museological studies (for example, Hitchcock & Teague, 2000; Kreps, 2003; Whitcomb, 2003). Conclusions are made about the cross-cultural and intercultural transformation of tea's material culture resulting from travel, and its implications for tea-related tourism.

The Tea and Travel Connection

History shows a rich connection between tea and travel. The first English language reference to tea appeared in a 1598 translation (from Dutch) of Linswchoten's edited volume of stories of his foreign voyages (Shalleck, 1972). This account included a description of the utensils used in the serving of tea in Japan, including the pot and the earthenware cups. Samuel Purchas, writing in 1625, described the preparation of tea noting the porcelain cups used in both China and Japan (Shalleck, 1972). By 1678 the East India Company was importing tea into England and a number of tea traditions were subsequently introduced. This includes the rituals of afternoon tea, high tea and evening tea as a meal.

Following initial discoveries in the culture of tea by travellers, tea trade routes were established and traders travelled to negotiate the purchase of tea, returning home with not only tea, but often souvenirs of their tea-related travel. Westerners travelled to the East in search of the secrets of tea, its origins and production, sometimes gathering mementos of their experiences with tea along the way. International exhibitions held in London, England, beginning with the Great Exhibition of 1851, exhibited the wares of exotic countries, including tea and tea-related goods, for an eager Victorian public (Barringer, 1998). These exhibitions led to the foundation of the South Kensington Museum (later renamed the Victoria and Albert Museum). It is reported that in 1859 the museum held a special display of Chinese food and also exhibited Chinese and Japanese porcelain. Museum collections thus naturally included objects related to the tea trade and tea consumption. This is also reinforced by the fact that the Museum at that time aimed to display a comprehensive range of goods from India and dispatched representatives to collect these materials in 1883 (Barringer, 1998). Missionaries during their travels also acquired tea-related artefacts. For example, in 1915 the author's grandparents (Canadian missionaries serving in China) were given a ceremonial Tibetan teapot as a wedding present.

In more recent times those interested in tea have travelled in search of authentic tea experiences related to the origins of tea in locations such as India and China (Goodwin, 1991). As tourists they have also retraced the old tea trade routes, such as the Silk Road connecting Xian in central China with the eastern Mediterranean (Hamel, 2001) and the Tea and Horse Trade Route connecting Tibet, Yunnan Province, China and Southeast Asia (Duangmee, 2003). During such forays travellers have acquired objects that serve as a reminder of their tea experiences. These souvenir items represent aspects of the rich material culture of objects that relate to the tea cultures of a number of cultures and societies.

Today, in China, tea services and accessories are available in tea shops and tea markets (as at the tea market in Fuzhou, China) for tourist purchase, and in Japan the 'tea ceremony' forms a major attraction for cultural tourists visiting the country. In England, for example, tea rooms and shops serving tea and selling tea souvenirs have an important role in creating a social reality of a country where many still enjoy the afternoon tea ritual, recognized by some as an important symbol of heritage in Britain (Howard, 2003). Boniface (2003: 116) indicates that 'in their colonization of tea, the British scooped it up and made it their own identity'.

The miniaturization of everyday objects and their presentation as mementos of experiences (Hitchcock & Teague, 2000: 13) is reflected by the miniature teapots and teasets widely available in a number of countries. These teapots are usually produced solely for the tourist trade, for tourists may not be able to carry home full-scale items. This is an example of the threat that tourism poses to the authenticity of 'tourist arts' in general, and specifically those related to tea. In many cases the tourist is purchasing a 'reminder not even of what has been seen but of the idea of the souvenir itself' (Horne, 1984: 248). The souvenirs of tea travel are thus objects derived from the rich material culture of objects associated with tea. Purchased as mementos of tea experiences in one culture, they can, through travel, be imported into other cultures and subsequently adopted by them.

Material Culture Associated with Tea

Material culture consists of objects, both man-made and natural, that take on particular meanings and carry messages when used. In many cultures objects with special value and meaning are used and kept by individuals and are often collected and stored in institutions such as museums (Kreps, 2003). Pearce (1992: 4) refers to museum objects as 'selected lumps of the material world to which cultural status has been ascribed'. Such objects are frequently known as artefacts, defined by Burcaw (1975: 4) as 'an object [objects] produced or shaped by human workmanship or, possibly, a natural object [objects] deliberately selected and used by a human being'. Because of the meanings associated with them, objects of material culture play an important role in the transmission and transformation of cultural knowledge.

Tea's material culture has its roots in the agricultural tea gardens and tea plantations where tea, the leaves of the _Camellia sinensis_ plant, is cultivated and harvested. Objects associated with tea at this stage include the baskets worn on the back and used during the picking or the plucking of the bud together with the top two leaves (Smith, 1986). At the factory or production area the tea leaves are withered, often being spread out in larger shallow baskets. Tea was traditionally shipped from the tea gardens in India, China or Ceylon in large aluminium-lined wooden chests labelled with the estate name, the grade of the tea, the year it was processed and the weight of the contents etc. (Smith, 1986). While tea is no longer shipped using this method, these chests remain as a reminder and souvenir of the traditions and culture of the tea trade.

There is also a rich variety of objects related to the serving and consumption of tea, referred to by Pratt (1982) as 'tea things' and by Smith (1986) as 'tea impedimentia'. The origins and adaptations of these objects encompass not only the tea-producing countries (such as India, China, Sri Lanka, Kenya and others) but also the tea-consuming countries, which includes most of the globe, tea being, after water, the most widely consumed beverage in the world (Walker, 1996). These accessories include the teapot, the tea kettle, the teacup and the tea service. Each country has adapted these objects and there are particular ones associated with the tea traditions of individual nations, as illustrated later in this chapter.

The material culture associated with tea includes historic buildings and sites associated with tea gardens, tea trading and tea consumption, as well as geographical areas or districts related to tea production and consumption. An example of a site associated with tea production is the Tea Factory Hotel (a former tea factory) in Sri Lanka, profiled in Chapter 6 by Gunasekara and Momsen. Examples of sites associated with the retailing and serving of tea, are the original shop in the Strand, London of the Twinings Company (purveyors of tea) (Twining, 1956) and the Willow Tea Rooms in Glasgow (designed by Charles Rennie McIntosh) (Pettigrew, 2001). In South London, in an area that was once the centre of the tea trade in England, two sites are now the only remnants of the area's rich tea history. The first, the Bramah Tea and Coffee Museum, documents the built heritage of the area in which it is situated, in particular in relation to tea. It includes the former headquarters of tea companies and the location of the London Tea Auctions as well as the former docks where the tea clippers unloaded their shipments of tea. At the second site, in nearby Greenwich, the *Cutty Sark*, the last of the clippers is docked and can be visited. Exhibits at the ship document the life of the ship as a 'tea clipper' carrying tea from China to London.

In addition objects with artistic merit associated with tea such as collectors' teapots, works of art incorporating the tea theme, and artists' interpretations of tea utensils, accessories and rituals are representative of tea cultures and their adaptations. An example is 'The New Way of Tea' exhibition, held by the Asia Society and Museum in New York in 2001 (see http://www.asiasociety.org). This exhibit contained tea-gathering utensils and installations of tea rooms by different artists and designers, reflecting the traditions behind the Japanese tea ceremony. Another collection of art objects relating to tea is reflected in the Kamm collection of teapots and teapot images created by artists, exhibited as part of the circulating Artful Teapot Exhibition, which included both teapots made for use and those made for art (Clark, 2001). Objects produced by tea companies related to the marketing of tea, such as collectors' items, may also become mementos of tea experiences. These items are often packaged with tea at the retail level, for both resident consumers and tourists. An example is the small porcelain animals made by the Wade Pottery in England, which were inserted into tea boxes produced under the Red Rose Tea brand in Canada, and have now become collectors' items.

Tea and its packaging (such as metal tea tins (caddies) that are kept for use after the tea is consumed), when purchased for consumption by the tourist once home, might also be considered to be a souvenir of travel in search of tea. The travel associated with acquiring tea and souvenirs associated with it has now taken on another meaning, with the advent of both mail order tea enterprises and tea companies that do business through the Internet. So now one does not have to travel to acquire the souvenirs of tea. In this form of 'armchair travel', the consumer can order tea and all of the associated equipment and accessories, including books about tea. For example the Stash Tea Company based in Oregon, USA in their 1994 mail order catalogue included: an Assam teapot by Bodum, developed in conjunction with the British Tea Council; a stoneware teapot, made by the Pristine Pottery in Stoke-on-Trent, Staffordshire, England; and an Osiris tea kettle by Bodum, based on an original design for the Museum of Modern Art in New York. The Internet sites thus act somewhat as virtual department stores, displaying tea wares for purchase. The ready availability of these items demonstrates how both mail order and Internet ordering is changing the nature of the potential acquisition of tea-related objects. Physical travel to acquire these items is no longer necessary. The origins of the items sold shows how tea traditions are carried and transformed from one culture to another.

Collecting Souvenirs of Different Tea Cultures

Each country that has adopted tea has developed its own customs related to the serving of tea and the objects necessary for this service. For example, tea is said to have originated in China (Shalleck, 1972), was imported into Japan (there developing into a uniquely Japanese ceremonial drinking of tea (Sadler, 1962)), and was adopted by the British as a national drink (Boniface, 2003). This section briefly reviews the concept of tea souvenirs, as well as the tea histories and traditions of these three tea cultures, observing the importation and adaptation of tea and its material culture from one society to another and noting the different resulting forms of tea souvenirs (Table 3.1).

China has rich traditions related to the origins and consumption of tea. Lu Yu writing in AD 780 celebrated the beverage of tea, outlining its preparation, listing its varieties, cataloguing its utensils and providing a synopsis of tea history (Shalleck, 1972). The utensils, the early material culture relating to tea in China included: the basket for firing tea; the anvil and mallet for moulding teacakes; the tea-grinding mill; dust brush; lacquered wooden cup holder; porcelain teacup; bamboo scrubbing brush;

Table 3.1 Typology of tea souvenirs

	Historic sites and architecture	*Objects related to tea trade*	*Items for the preparation of tea*
China	Tea gardens Tea houses Tea docks	Tea processing equipment	Kettles Tea vessels Tea tables
Japan	Tea houses Tea gardens	Tea whisk Teacloth Teaspoon Tea kettle	Tea caddy Tea bowl
England	Tea trading shops Tea rooms Tea docks Tea clippers	Tea signs Tea chests Tea posters	Teapots Teacups Tea tables Tea caddies Tea services

and teapot. Tea formed a central part of Chinese culture, 'The tea house in the town or village was Old China's universal meeting place for friends' (Spencer, 1960: 103). During the Cultural Revolution in China there was a suspension of many of the traditions associated with tea, including the closing of tea houses. Today China's tea culture is once again celebrated in contemporary 'tea arts' performances, such as those discussed by Huang and Hall in Chapter 7, and by Dewar and Li in Chapter 12. The equipment used in preparing the tea is an important part of these ceremonies. For example, in Fujian Province, China tea tables and tea trays made from the burls of trees are traditional and are still used today. In addition to purchasing tea as a souvenir the visitor to China is likely to purchase equipment for the preparation of tea that might include teapots, tea vessels, tea utensils, tea trays, etc. These accessories can vary by region, and individual areas of China are known for the production of specific wares associated with tea. For example, noted tea expert James Norwood Pratt, writes of his travels with San Francisco-based Imperial Tea Court's China Tea and Culture Tour documenting a visit to a teapot production facility (2002):

> The next morning I headed south of Shanghai on the road to Xi-xing, home of China's famous purple sand clay earthenware teapots. Teapots have been made since about the time of Christopher Columbus, which

makes the teapot a fairly recent development in the history of China tea, if anything in China may be considered to be recent. To watch these master potters was to witness antiquity alive and vibrant in the present moment.

In earlier writing Pratt (1982) referred to the official history of the teapot as beginning in AD 1500 with the production of these unglazed teapots. The process of watching the production of the object and the potential souvenir thus becomes an attraction in itself. Pratt refers to the underlying tea theme for the tour as 'a thread we will follow through all of the aspects of Chinese culture we will experience' (Pratt, 2002). The souvenirs of the material culture of tea, acquired on tea tours such as this, are important reminders of the tea experience.

The existence of Japan's tea ceremony is the direct result of tea travel. It is reported that a Japanese monk brought tea from China to Japan in AD 804, leading to the introduction of the tea tradition in Japan (Civitello, 2004). The traditions in the Chinese ceremony were refined and adapted, resulting in a ceremony unique to Japan. This demonstrates the intercultural and cross-cultural exchanges of knowledge that relate to tea arts and tea artefacts. The Japanese tea ceremony is as much a way of life as a tea ritual – a ritual of serving and drinking tea as an expression of Zen Buddist philosophy (*Oxford English Reference Dictionary*, 2002). Civitello (2004: 85–6) reflects on the creation of the tea ceremony in Japan, clearly citing it as an example of the transformation of tea and its traditions from one culture to another:

> In the tea ceremony we can see a cultural shift, where old traditions are replaced by something that is completely new, which becomes the tradition. The tea ceremony is a flawless execution of the combination of art, food and religion that began in cave paintings 35,000 years ago.

The space in which the Japanese tea ceremony was conducted evolved from a room in one's own house, to an attached room, to a separate tea house (Shalleck, 1972: 21). Smith (1986) describes these tea houses as special wooden houses constructed in the corner of a garden for the tea ceremony. The tea gardens thus became important spaces for the location of the tea houses and the staging of the tea ritual. Sadler (1933) writing on the tea ceremony recorded a rich material culture that includes not only the tea house itself and the order of the tea ceremony, but in addition an elaborate system of utensils necessary for the ritual. The ceremony requires utensils that include: a fresh-water vessel and tea caddy; a tea bowl, tea whisk, tea cloth and teaspoon; a waste-water receptacle, a dipper and a stand for the kettle and dipper. In his 1906 classic on the tea ceremony, Okakuro observed that the tea room was an oasis in the dreary waste of existence and a place where weary travellers could meet to drink with a common appreciation of tea. Today the tea ceremony is a part of the cultural experience of tourists visiting Japan (Smith, 1986) and contemporary items related to the tea ceremony are available for acquisition by visitors as souvenirs of their tea experiences. In Japanese culture the gift of tea itself is also an important souvenir, as indicated by Graburn (2003): 'Tea from different regions has different qualities which one is supposed to appreciate and some of them are known throughout Japan, thus a buying a package from that place would constitute a proper *omiyage*, i.e. place related souvenir gift.'

In England the service of tea has spawned a range of accessories that Michael Smith (1986) refers to as 'tea impedimentia' and Edward Bramah, founder of the Bramah Tea and Coffee Museum, refers to as the necessary 'equipage' to make tea. These objects have their functional origins in China and other countries but have been adapted to fit the needs of the West. As identified by Smith this equipment includes the teapot, the tea caddy, caddy spoons, the mote spoon, tea urns, tea kettles, tea trays, tea tables, teacups, teapots and tea services. The teapot is described as: a covered pot with a spout in which tea is steeped and from which it is served (*Canadian Dictionary of the English Language*, 1998). Clark (2001: 11) refers to the teapot as 'the grande dame of [tea] paraphernalia – that spouted steaming engine of hospitality'. The design and use of most tea accessories evolved along with the development of the tea trade. For example the teacup, initially small because of the high cost of tea, became larger as prices fell. The necessary equipment to serve tea also increased, according to Goodwin (1991: 266):

> By the early nineteenth century the drawing room of a well-to-do British household could be furnished with a lidded table containing the paraphernalia for 'teaing', knowing as a teapoy, or teapoise . . . Out of the teapoy came the tea-pot and the tea-caddy – a box usually with two compartments lined in lead to seal in the aroma, which may have originally held a catty or so of tea, and a small tea-shovel or tea-spoon.

As the serving of tea became popular, tea services were introduced. These consisted of sets of a teapot, sugar bowl and cream jug and later included cups and saucers, first made in silver, later in porcelain (Smith, 1986). Boniface (2003) discusses the evolution of the tea room, as a place where people went to take tea. She indicates that the tea room has taken on some of the attributes of the English afternoon tea ceremony. Key components of the tea room are the physical surroundings as well as the china teapots for serving the tea and the teacups for drinking the tea. These are yet more artefacts with which we associate special meanings as part of the culture of tea.

The souvenirs collected, the material culture of tourism is referred to by Graburn (2000) as the material counterpart of travels, events, relationships and memories of all kinds. Graburn goes on to note that the meanings associated with souvenirs change according to ownership and this is an important note for the formation of collections related to tea – as objects become divorced from their original use and function, they take on new meanings. Furthermore, objects assembled together away from their owners and exhibited are imbued with yet other meanings through the curatorial process, as noted by Graburn (2000) – the institutional possession of formerly private souvenir possessions illustrates the creation of public culture. For tea-related tourism, the formation of the massive collection of some 3000 teapots at the Norwich Museum in England illustrates this phenomenon (Jolliffe, 2003). Other museums in the United Kingdom holding significant collections of teapots include the Museum of Worcester Porcelain in Worcester and the Potteries Museum and Art Gallery in Stoke-on-Trent (Thorp, 2004).

In their work on souvenirs, Hitchcock and Teague (2000) explore the issues of authenticity, identity, consumption, commodification and development of what Graburn (2000) refers to as 'tourist arts'. Hitchock and Teague (2000: 4) observe that souvenirs are intimately connected with the idea of a pilgrimage (and thus the tourists' quest for authenticity), noting that: 'Souvenirs are mementos of the out of ordinary experience of the holiday.' As shown in this chapter, tea plays a role in the identity of societies. For example, China is known as the 'homeland of tea' (Pratt, 1982); Japan is known for its 'tea ceremony'; and England is known for 'afternoon tea' (Smith, 1986). In each of these societies, objects and traditions are associated with and represent tea cultures. What had once belonged to individuals, once collected, grouped and exhibited becomes culture in the public domain.

Tea Collections and Tea Museums

It is evident that travel has directly contributed to the collections of tea-related items and to the creation of tea-related collections. Specialist museums relating to tea include: the China Tea Museum in Hangzhou, China; the Ping Lin Tea Museum in Ping Lin, Taiwan; The Tea Museum in Shizaku Prefecture, Japan; the Bramah Tea and Coffee Museum in London,

Table 3.2 Tea museums

Name	Location	Opened
China Tea Museum	Hangzhou, China	1991
Ping Lin Tea Museum	Pin Lin, Taiwan	1997
The Tea Museum	Japan	1998
Bramah Coffee & Tea Museum	London, England	1992

Source: adapted from Jolliffe (2003a)

England; and the Flagstaff House Museum of Tea Ware in Hong Kong. The first three museums have been established in China, Taiwan and Japan, in areas with a rich tea history, culture and both historic and contemporary production of tea. The last two museums have been established in London and Hong Kong, both locations that have a rich connection to the historic tea trade.

The transformation of tea-related collections into museums and exhibitions is a relatively recent phenomenon, as is reflected by the establishment dates of the relevant museums. This could indicate a growing awareness by destinations with tea history of the power to transform tea collections and their story into destination attractions. All of these museums transform the material culture of tea into exhibitions, which pass on the meanings associated with tea cultures and offer visitors the opportunity to experience tea cultures. The presentation of objects in museum exhibitions can change their message, as both the museum curator and the museum designer play a role in determining the story to be told (Graburn, 2000; Hudson, 1977). One observer has seen these museums as a metaphor for the activity of travel, in that museums are a destination for travelers and can be compared as a form of travel (Kirschemblett-Gimblett, 1998).

Tea Exhibitions

At these museums, tea-themed exhibits normally present the material culture in a linear manner, grouping objects and information chronologically, stylistically or thematically. For example in the Artful Teapot exhibition and accompanying catalogue (Clark, 2001) collections were grouped thematically according to the materials and form represented by the artefacts. Museum exhibitions thus present a kind of diorama of tea cultures for the visitor, or a 'touristic panorama', as referred to by Morris (1988), a space through which the tourist passes. The curatorial process, by grouping tea-related collections thematically, is controlling the messages presented to the tourists as they pass through this space. The differences in thematic approaches can be seen from the titles found in the sample listing of tea exhibitions shown in Table 3.3.

In addition to the influence of museum curators and designers, sponsors can also have some control over the message delivered. In the case of exhibitions about tea, it is evident that individual tea companies have played a significant role in the sponsorship of such exhibitions and their accompanying catalogues. The trade may be involved in this process because it assists with branding and promotion, providing valuable marketing opportunities. For well-established tea companies, such as Twinings, exhibition and catalogue sponsorship (as well as an ongoing association with a pre-eminent teapot collection shown at Norwich Castle Museum) reinforce the branding of their 'tea products' and perpetuate their apparent dominance in the market. Many tea exhibitions circulate from one museum to another, thus bringing their interpretation message to a

Table 3.3 Examples of tea exhibitions

Yixing Teapots, TeaCup, Seattle	21 October– 21 November 1994
Winter Whimseyland, The Perennial Tea Room	1–23 November 1994
Teapotmania: The Story of the British Craft Teapot and Tea Cosy, Norwich Castle Museum	30 September– 26 November 1995*
Tea Trappings: Silver Strainers and Infusers from the Nowell Collection, Brandywine River Museum, Chadds Ford, Pennsylvania	26 May–29 July 2001
The New Way of Tea, Asia Society and Museum, New York	6 March–19 May 2002
Traditions in Excellence: 100 Teapots from the Norwich Castle Museum, Concord Museum, Mass. USA	25 January–27 May 2002*
The Art of the Teapot, Gardiner Ceramic Museum, Toronto	6 February–25 May 2003*
Chocolate, Coffee, Tea, Metropolitan Museum of Art, New York	3 February–11 July 2004
World Tea Party: Art Gallery of Victoria	25 June–29 August 2004

*Also shown at other venues as part of an exhibition tour

Various sources

larger audience. The travel costs associated with such exhibitions is often borne by sponsors. For example, the Artful Teapot exhibition circulated to museums in: Napa, California; Montgomery, Alabama; Toronto, Ontario; Long Beach, California; and Charlotte, North Carolina. The World Tea Party had its first exhibit at the Art Gallery of Victoria in 1993 followed by an exhibit in summer 2004: 'Since 1993, the World Tea Party has been a continually evolving international celebration of the art and culture of the world's most-loved beverage – tea!' (Art Gallery of Victoria, 2004). According to exhibit curator Dr Judith Patt, tea, the subject of the exhibition, has had a wide-reaching effect on the visual arts, the decorative arts, architecture, social ritual and contemporary cultural production (*Globe and Mail*, 2004). The exhibitions are a focal part of the World Tea Party and, as with other tea exhibitions, are complemented by interpretative activities and a catalogue.

Specialty tea shops also sponsor exhibitions or special showings of tea-related wares, for example the TeaCup and the Perennial Tea Room in Seattle have respectively exhibited Xixing teapots and collectors' limited editions of novelty teapots (see Table 3.3). In the latter exhibition, the novelty teapots are representative of a genre of whimsical and fanciful teapots that have been produced from the 16th century (Xining pots made to resemble bundles of bamboo, tree trunks and gourds) to more recent times when teapots have featured both animal and human forms (Miller, 1996). The postcard advertising this exhibit at the Perennial Tea Room featured a collectable teapot. These exhibitions thus also form an opportunity for locals and visitors to acquire tea-related collectables.

As well as the opportunity to acquire tea-related collectables, these exhibitions also provide the opportunity for both locals and visitors to experience the culture of tea associated with the useful as well as the artistic objects produced for its consumption and appreciation. The enthusiasm related to the collecting of tea-related objects was reflected in the 1995 exhibition Teapotmania sponsored by the Norfold Museums Service and R. Twining & Company. Dedicated teapot collectors are now served by their own UK-based club called Totally Teapots (http://www.totallyteapots.com).

An important part of the tea-related exhibitions in public museums is the associated public programming. This may consist of guided tours, special lectures and events that will allow the visitor to gain a more in-depth knowledge of the subject matter. For example when the Artful Teapot exhibition was hosted in Toronto in 2003 at the Gardiner Museum it was accompanied by public programming that included a symposium, a collectors' talk with slide show, curator tours, lectures, and a family day with a 'Mad Hatter's Tea Party'. During the period of the exhibition the Gallery Shop sold related publications and Twinings tea (Twinings was one of the exhibition sponsors), and also exhibited teapots handmade by Canadian potters. Additionally, the museum café served teas.

Exhibitions such as the Artful Teapot serve as attractions for tourists interested in tea. The exhibition also demonstrates another role for tea in inspiring artwork that in turn provides another product for tea tourism. During its time at the Gardiner the exhibition served as an attraction for those interested in tea, providing a tea experience for visitors. Exhibitions like this, when combined with other activities, contribute to the development of tourism related to tea. A circulating exhibition such as this one would also have stimulated an associated roster of public programmes at the other museums where it was hosted.

Conclusion

This chapter has examined the influence of travel in transporting and transforming tea cultures from one society to another. It has also explored the pivotal role of collections of tea-related objects in that process. In profiling and examining the material culture of tea, it is evident that the cross-cultural and intercultural transformations undergone play a significant role in providing products and experiences for tea tourism. Through mail order and the Internet people are now also able to obtain tea-related collectables without travelling, in a modern day form of 'armchair travel'.

Furthermore, the collection process facilitates the use of objects imbued with meanings, which are transformed as they are acquired as souvenirs, formed into collections, and transformed into exhibitions, which, in turn, provide tea experiences for visitors. The roles of both the museum curator and museum designer, and the tea trade itself, in influencing the messages delivered as part of this experience are noted. Artists also play a role in creating artistic expressions that reflect tea cultures and that are exhibited as part of a tea-related public culture. Museums, by hosting tea-related exhibitions and creating associated public programming, create opportunities for tourists to experience tea. And the conservative tea industry is inadvertently involved in nurturing tea-related tourism through the creation of tea mementos and through the sponsorship of exhibitions and related catalogues (particularly true of the Twining Company). The Internet is also increasing the availability to ordinary people of the material culture related to tea and this in turn may have an influence on nurturing new travel for tea. Individual collectors such as the Kamm (Clark, 2001), tea shops, such as the TeaCup, and public museums, such as the Norwich Castle Museum, have assembled together the mementos and artistic interpretations of tea and play a role in sharing them with an eager public.

A number of influences make the transformation of tea cultures possible. First and foremost, both in a historical and contemporary sense, is trade and the travel associated with it. Second is travel itself, whether undertaken for the purposes of tea tourism, or undertaken for a leisure or business experience, which might happen to include the acquisition of tea-related material culture. Third, individual collectors, public museums and collecting institutions also make the transformation of tea cultures possible by collecting and preserving objects that represent these cultures. Collections are further transformed into public exhibitions and invested with the meanings attributed to them by collectors, curators and exhibit designers. These exhibitions in turn provide opportunities for the public to experience an adjusted set of meanings associated with the material culture of tea being exhibited. Imbued with meaning, the artefacts related to tea are an essential and symbolic part of the process of inventing and reinventing tea from one culture to another; a process that ultimately provides experiential products for tea tourism, including both traditional exhibitions and contemporary interpretations of tea cultures.

References

Art Gallery of Victoria (2004) Online document: http://aggv.bc.ca/exhibitions.asp (accessed 30 July 2004).

Asia Society and Museum (2004) *The New Way of Tea*. Online document: http://www.asiasociety.org/arts/newwayoftea/ (accessed 14 June 2004).

Boniface, P. (2003) *Tasting Tourism: Travelling for Food and Drink*. Aldershot: Ashgate.

Barringer, T. (1998) The South Kensington Museum and the colonial project. In T. Barringer and T. Flynn (eds) *Colonialism and the Object; Empire, Material Culture and the Museum* (pp. 11–27). London: Routledge.

Burcaw, G.E. (1975) *Introduction to Museum Work*. Nashville, TN: The American Association of State and Local History.

Canadian Dictionary of the English Language (1998). Scarborough: ITP Nelson.

Civitello, L. (2004) *Culture and Cuisine: A History of Food and Peoples*. Hoboken, NJ: Wiley.

Clark, G. (2001) *The Artful Teapot*. London: Thames & Hudson.

Dungamee, G. (2003) Tea horse trade route. *Bangkok Post*, 11 December.

Goodwin, J. (1991) *A Time for Tea: Travels through China and India in Search of Tea*. New York: Knopf.

Globe and Mail (2004) Art steeped in social ritual. 8 July 2004.

Graburn, N.H.H. (2000) Preface. In M. Hitchcock and K. Teague (eds) *The Material Culture of Tourism* (pp. xii–xvii). Aldershot: Ashgate.

Graburn, N.H.H. (2003) Personal correspondence.

Hamel, D. (2001) Tea: A Silk Road Odyssey. *The Student Traveler* (24) 2, Fall 2001, pp. 10–11.

Hitchcock, M. and Teague, K. (eds) (2000) *The Material Culture of Tourism*. Aldershot: Ashgate.

Horne, D. (1984) *The Great Museum: The Re-Presentation of History*. London: Pluto Press.

Howard, P. (2003) *Heritage: Management, Interpretation, Identity*. London: Continuum.

Hudson, K. (1977) *Museums for the 1980s: A Survey of World Trends*. Paris: Unesco.

Kirschenblatt-Gimblett, B. (1998) *Destination Culture: Tourism, Museums and Heritage*. Berkeley, CA: University of California Press.

Kreps, Christina, F. (2003) *Liberating Culture: Cross-Cultural Perspectives on Museums, Curation and Heritage Preservation*. London: Routledge.

Miller, Joni (1996) *The Collectible Teapot and Tea Calendar for 1996*. New York: Workman Publishing.

Morris, M. (1988) Panorama: The live, the dead and the living. In P. Foss (ed.) *Island in the Stream* (pp. 160–227). Sydney: Pluto Press.

Oxford English Reference Dictionary (2002) Oxford: Oxford University Press.

Pratt, J.N. (1982) *The Tea Lover's Treasury*. San Ramon, CA: 101 Productions.

Pratt, J.N. (2002) *Pilgrimage to the Holy Land of Tea, Imperial Tea Court/China Tea Tour Essay*. Online document: http://www.imperialtea.com/tea/tours/TheTour.html (accessed 20 March 2002).

Pettigrew, J. (2001) *A Social History of Tea*. London: The National Trust.

Pearce, S.M. (1992) *Museums, Objects and Collections: A Cultural Study*. Leicester: Leicester University Press.

Sadler, A.L. (1962 [1933,]). *Cha-no-yu: The Japanese Tea Ceremony*. Rutland, VT: Charles E. Tuttle Company. Reprint of first edition.

Shalleck, J. (1972) *Tea*. New York: Viking Press

Smith, M. (1986) *Michael Smith's Afternoon Tea*. London: Macmillan.

Spencer, C. (1960) *The Land of the Chinese People*. New York: J.B. Lippincott Company.

Stash Tea Catalogue (1994) Tigard, OR: Stash Tea Company.

Thorp, L. (2004) Seduced by teapots. *BBC Finest Antiques*, May, 52–62.

Twining, S. (1956) *The House of Twining: 1706–1956*. London: R. Twining & Co. Ltd.

Walker, J.R. (2002) *Introduction to Hospitality*. Upper Saddle River, NJ: Prentice Hall.

Whitcomb, A. (2003) *Re-Imagining the Museum: Beyond the Mausoleum*. London: Routledge.

World Tea Party, Art Gallery of Victoria (2004) Online document: http://aggv.bc.ca/exhibitions.asp (accessed 14 June 2004).

Chapter 4
Tea Traditions in Taiwan and Yunnan

PAUL LEUNG KIN HAN

This chapter is about the development of tea and tourism in China, making use of Yunnan in mainland China and Taiwan as subjects for discussion. Tea and tourism are two critical trade commodities for China, both now and in the past. Tea drinking and travelling are the two most popular leisure activities among the Chinese. Tea, trade and travel are intertwined in the history of China. One the one hand, tea is one of the major trade commodities that promoted the development of ancient trade routes, which in turn facilitated the development of travel and tourism in ancient China. On the other hand, the establishment of these trade routes and activities promoted the spread of tea culture.

The Tea Trade

Since the discovery of tea, its development has never ceased. Today, there are more than 1.6 million acres of tea plantations in China, accounting for 45% of the total tea-growing area of the world. Commercial plantations can be found in 57 countries. Tea's importance as a commodity cannot be underestimated. India, Sri Lanka and China produced 1851.7 metric tons of tea in 2001, which accounted for 61% of the world's total (International Tea Committee 2002). These data do not merely illustrate the economic importance of tea as a commodity, but also suggest that tea drinking itself is both a serious subject and a sophisticated hobby. The tea industry argues that tea drinking can be at the same time a form of leisure, a pursuit of personal enjoyment, a taste of an exotic culture, a quest for health and relaxation, a family activity, and a social event. Many of these descriptions can be seen to be very similar to those for tourism. In other words, tea might have some potential to be developed as a tourism theme and a motive to travel.

While many details regarding the importance and development of the tea trade have been given in Chapter 2, it is useful to briefly review the related development of tourism in China. Tourism has become a critical trade and foreign exchange earner in the greater China region. Modern tourism in China sprang up in the 1950s. The establishment of the China International Travel Service in 1954 and the State Tourism Administration of China in 1964 formally avowed the status of tourism. Although tourism did not receive a lot of attention at that time, the development in travel activities, both in terms of domestic travel and foreign visitors to China, suggested the importance of tourism to China's future development. The Open-door Policy in 1978 marked a new era of development. Since then, the tourism business has grown rapidly with the number of tourists in 1999 reaching 72.8 million, 40 times the figure for 1978. Foreign tourist arrivals for 1999 were 8.43 million, generating a foreign exchange income of US\$14.1 billion, 54 times that of 1978. This growth momentum continues. China's tourism administration reported 8.7747 million tourists from outside the Chinese mainland visited mainland China in May 2003, registering an increase of 61.42% year-on-year, and 11.37% over the same period in 2002. Currently, China is one of the top destinations in the world. The World Tourism Organization estimates that, by 2020, China will be the world's number one tourism destination and the fourth largest nation of tourists. With the improvement in their living standards, the Chinese people have an increasingly strong interest in travelling. In 1999, domestic tourism reached 719 million with a total spending of 283.2 billion yuan – 14.3% and 105.9% increases respectively over 1995.

China is a gifted destination. It embraces a large collection of touristic resources, which include scenic spots and historical sites, spectacular landscapes, and colourful and varied ethnic customs and culture. Chinese paintings, native products, handicrafts, rare medicinal herbs and tea are all popular with foreign visitors. Among all these resources, tea is a tourism alternative that has not been fully explored.

Tea tourism is the product of the marriage between these two critical sectors of trade and cultural events in China. As an alternative tourism product, it is, however, a relatively new concept. While there is wine tourism literature (for example, Charters & Ali-Knight, 2002; Charters & Ali-Knight, 2000; Hall *et al.*, 2000; Dodd & Bigotte, 1997; Frochot, 2000), literature on tea tourism, to the knowledge of this writer, is scant. The chapter by Jolliffe in Hall's book on food tourism (Hall *et al.*, 2003) is in fact the only piece of work that can be found in the existing literature. Although tea tourism is not and should not be restricted to the Chinese community, this chapter investigates and explores the potential of this new product in

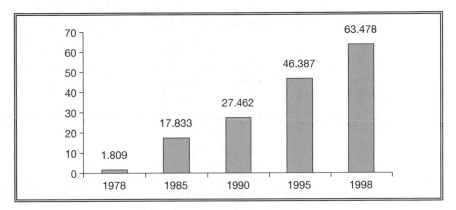

Figure 4.1 Development of tourism in China (arrivals in millions)

Source: Adapted from China National Tourism Administration
(http://cnta.gov.cn)

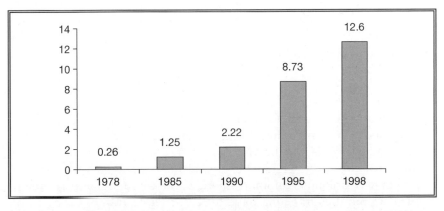

Figure 4.2 Development of tourism in China (receipts in billion US$)

Source: Adapted from China National Tourism Administration
(http://cnta.gov.cn)

the greater China region by studying two different forms of tea tourism in Yunnan and Taiwan. It also examines the extent to which tea affects place identity, thereby contributing to destination promotion and marketing. Special attention is given to characteristics, development, and encouraging and impeding factors, as well as to the advantages and disadvantages of developing tea tourism.

Tea Traditions: From Tea Appreciation to *Yum chea* ('Tea Party')

Choosing Chinese communities as the subject for discussion in relation to tea and tourism has specific reasons. First, China is commonly regarded as the origin of tea-drinking culture, although there is no official record of when and where tea was first served and consumed. According to Chinese legend, tea was discovered by the Emperor Shen Nung at some time between 2737 and 2697 BC. At the very beginning, tea was regarded as a herbal medicine and as an appreciation to the god(s). During the Chow Dynasty (11th century BC–771 BC), tea became a popular drink among the social elite. In the West Han Dynasty (206 BC–AD 8), tea had already emerged as a custom. Various documentation has also indicated that there already existed well-organized tea markets during that time. Given this historical background, selecting Chinese communities for investigation has much symbolic value.

Second, China is regarded as one of the largest exporters and markets for tea. In 2002, mainland China exported US$ 342 million worth of tea (International Tea Committee, 2002). Although the annual importation of tea is only about US$ 3 million, this by no means indicates that the Chinese consume less tea than another other major tea markets. Besides enjoyment and health considerations, tea's popularization or mass consumption is associated with the spread of Buddhism, Taoism and Muslim religions. These religions designated tea as an official drink for monks and followers. The expansion and spreading of these religions, therefore, promoted tea drinking all over Asia and the Middle East.

Third, tea culture in China is exotic, attractive and rich in diversity. Although tea drinking is common among various ethnic groups, different ethnic communities in China have different tea traditions. They drink different tea, at different times of day, on different occasions, with different customs, and accompany it with different foodstuffs. Tea drinking is a social event as well as something carried out for personal enjoyment. Travellers who would like to engage in and have a taste of the local culture, therefore, cannot avoid the consumption of tea and exposure to tea events.

Yum chea, for example, is a traditional tea party and a family gathering that takes place in a commercial catering outlet. Different styles of small dishes, called *dim sum*, are to be served alongside the drinking of tea. Traditional *yum chea* activity takes place from the early morning until the lunch hour. More recently, however, the *yum chea* hour has extended throughout the day and night. Night tea, which normally starts at 9:00 p.m.

and extends beyond midnight, is gaining popularity in many provinces in China.

Although the *yum chea* culture, customs and even the catering outlet has changed substantially over the years, *yum chea* as a form of leisure and social activity has never ceased in its importance. Besides maintaining its popularity among the local people, it has gained the attention of foreign tourists. It has evolved and is being promoted as a unique cultural tourist attraction for those who visit Hong Kong and Guangdong.

Tea Tourism: The Consumption of Tea Culture

There is no official definition for tea tourism yet. Although there are small-scale tea garden visits and farm stays in India, especially in Darjeeling, tea's potential as a tourism product has not been fully recognized. Tea tourism remains a vague term. As a working definition, tea tourism can be defined as any activity organized by a travel- and tourism-related entity, including individuals that utilize tea, tea drinking and related aspects, and offer them as products to tourists for consumption. This pursuit, as with other cultural pursuits, can be anything ranging from a passive consumption of something unfamiliar in an alien setting as 'just another item' on the itinerary to a serious 'career-like', self-enhancing systematic pursuit (see also Prentice & Andersen, 2003; Richards, 2001). Tea tourism is still at an early stage of development and whether it can be developed into a mainstream tourism alternative has yet to be confirmed.

Readers might question why tea tourism should be in the limelight. The rationale is multidimensional. First and foremost, tea drinking is probably one of the most popular hobbies and pastimes, especially in the Chinese market. One trader told this author that the Chinese drink more tea than water on a daily basis. As well as sheer volume, the level of sophistication in tea consumption has advanced throughout the history of tea drinking. Some tea drinkers are willing to invest thousands of US dollars on tea wares for usage and collections. Though tea drinking is a form of leisure, it can have very precise rituals and procedures. Drinking a few cups of tea after dinner can last for an hour or two. Even ordinary tea drinkers will pay attention to the detail of the tea wares and water they use, let alone the selection of tea. If tea drinking is a serious hobby, it would be reasonable to suspect that there is a potential market of tea drinkers who would like to travel in order to see and experience more about tea. This is not to say that all tea drinkers will be motivated to engage in a tea pilgrimage or tour, or be interested to search out the origins of different teas. However, the spending pattern, the quest for quality and the level of sophistication of serious tea drinkers suggests there is potential for development.

Second, increased tea tourism can lead to economic development and the related betterment of living standards for the peasants involved in tea production. Unlike many other agricultural products, tea has a high commercial value. And its yield can critically improve the living standards of rural agricultural communities. At the same time, bringing tourists to tea plantations and factories can directly bring economic benefit to the local community. The kind of 'buy-direct' arrangement facilitated by tourism activities can break the manipulation and marginalization of international tea trading practices. This 'pro-poor' concept is, of course, not a new one. Oxfam, for example, has been actively promoting their 'fair-trade coffee' programme in order to help coffee farmers to combat poverty. The programme, however, faces numerous obstacles and has not been very effective in expanding its market coverage. And as the funding diminishes, the programme has difficulties sustaining itself. Whether the gap in funding can be filled with and bridged by tourism has yet to be tested, although Tourism Concern has experimented with a form of tea tourism in the tea gardens of Sri Lanka. In other words, if tea tourism is successful, it may well show the potential that exists for other forms of folk economy.

Furthermore, tea tourism has the potential to promote the development of small-scale village industries (SSI). Accommodation establishments, tea houses and restaurants, tea wares and souvenirs are few of the more usual examples. No matter whether we are interested in revitalizing villages, as Gandhi prophesied, or not, tourism and the augmented SSIs enable the creation and dissemination of economic benefits to different segments of society.

Tourism is deemed to be eco-friendly. Tea tourism, as a sub-sector of tourism, also embraces the same merit. There is a trend in China towards the production of organically certified tea. Although the development of tea plantations affects the use and transformation of the landscape, it is relatively environmentally friendly and any damage to the environmental can be limited or rectified by careful planning. For example, the government can regulate the scale and development of new plantations. Not all tea species need to be grown on plantations. Some tea leaves are picked from wild tea-trees. Some of these tea-trees in the southwestern part of China are over a thousand years of age. These resources, i.e. tea leaves, give economic value; in turn this value gives a reason for the local communities to protect and look after the health of the trees and the surrounding wildlife.

Two Approaches to Tea Tourism: Taiwan Tea Houses and Yunnan Tea Tours

Tea tourism, like many other types of tourism, is not homogeneous. It covers a wide range of possibilities. In this chapter, two different examples illustrate the different ways that tea tourism can be developed. Some of the products and approaches to development are featured for discussion, however this is by no means an exhaustive list. Rather, the examples show just a few options at the introductory stage of a life cycle. There is no limit to the development potential other than the creativity required.

For discussion, Taiwan and the Yunnan Province of mainland China have been deliberately chosen as subjects. Both of them have started to develop tea-tourism products. Although both locations share the same origin and culture, and both plant and export tea, the development of their tea commodities and services is divergent. While a large-scale programme and systematic plan for collaborative development of tea tourism is still not available, tea museums, trips, and tourism products are already available for consumption. This chapter pinpoints two relatively unique areas for discussion: modern tea houses in Taiwan and tea tours in Yunnan.

Taiwan

Taiwan, the biggest island in the greater China region, is separated from the mainland by the Taiwan Strait. It is bordered on the north by the East China Sea, on the east by the Pacific Ocean, and on the south by the South China Sea. The government of Taiwan also administers the P'enghu Islands (Pescadores), the Chinmen Islands (Quemoy Islands), and the Matsu Islands. The total area administered by the government of Taiwan is about 36,000 kilometres (about 13,900 miles). Taiwan Island is about 390 kilometres (about 240 miles) from north to south and about 140 kilometres (about 90 miles) from east to west.

Although tourism is a prominent economic sector in Taiwan, the government of Taiwan is now giving more attention to the development and promotion of tourism (Kuo *et al.*, 2005). In recent years, tourism has become more important to the Taiwanese economy. Tourist arrivals and receipts for 2001 were 2.62 million and US$ 3,991 million respectively. Development, however, was clouded by natural disasters, regional economic downturn and competition. The Taiwan Tourism Bureau, therefore, launched a series of strategies including: the relaxation of visa restrictions on the arrival of Hong Kong Chinese; active product developments; and intensive marketing communication programmes to attract new target groups.

Among the various tactics, the development of cultural tourism products is one of Taiwan's major directions and tea is one of the most important cultural assets of the Taiwanese.

Taiwan's tea industry started with the early Chinese settlement in the 17th century. *Oolong* tea is one of the few featured products of Taiwan, however, owing to its limited annual output, prices are high. Economic prosperity in the 1960s largely improved the livelihood of the local people and promoted domestic demand for tea and it is now among the most discriminating and dynamic tea markets in the world (Wicentowski, 1999).

Rather than focusing on this traditional form of tea product, however, this chapter looks at the development of contemporary tea houses. To place the discussion in context, it is also essential to briefly review the development of tea houses in Taiwan. Tea houses were originally brought to Taiwan by Chinese immigrants. Tea houses have a long history in China and their form has changed tremendously over the years. Wicentowski (1999) asserts that the unique historical experience of Taiwan has provided the conditions for a fascinating and diversified development of tea houses. The modern Taiwanese tea house is a combination and improvisation of the traditional tea house, the English tea house and other innovations.

The traditional tea houses in Taiwan, an endangered species, largely appeal to the elderly segment of the market. Visiting a tea house is a leisure and social event. Wicentowski (1999) noted that everyone in the tea house would usually know everyone else. The act of patrons chatting with one another forms a critical part of the occasion. The 'tea art house' is the new version of a traditional Chinese tea house, which emerged in the 1970s. These tea art houses focus on the quality of tea leaves, serving utensils, and water for boiling tea, paying attention to every detail of the ritual. Their customers are willing to pay high prices for quality. The Lu Yu Tea Art Centre is an example of these tea art houses.

The modern tea culture and tea houses emerged in the mid-1980s. The development of modern Taiwanese tea houses can be subdivided into two phases or streams. The first stream is also known as the 'bubble tea craze', which emerged in the late 1980s. The concept started to be exported to other countries including Hong Kong and mainland China in the early 1990s. According to Lee Jolliffe (the editor of this book), the bubble tea stream has been introduced to Canada as well. The second stream is the combination tea and tea houses that emerged in the late 1990s. The main differentiation between the two streams is the ambience of the outlet and the style of the beverage. The service quality, the selection of tea wares and the consumption behaviours of the second stream are more sophisticated than those of the bubble tea outlets. Compared to traditional tea houses, commonly called tea art houses, the two modern streams can be regarded as completely different commodities for completely different markets. The three streams of tea houses still co-exist today and diversity is one of the major characteristic of the Taiwanese tea market.

Following the success of chain cafés, such as Starbucks and Dante, English-style tea houses, such as the Rose House and the London Tea House, with dainty English-style teasets and an English-style atmosphere, gained popularity in the mid-1990s, especially among female consumers (Euromonitor, 2004). These so-called English-style tea houses have very little to do with traditional English tea, however. The Taiwan tea industry innovatively developed a series of alternative tea products, for example, floral, herbal and fruit teas. Through mixing and matching, a range of combination or blended teas was launched into the domestic market in Taiwan. Since then, modern tea houses started to grow in terms of number, coverage, market share and diversity. These tea houses are directly competing with coffee shops. In order to maintain their competitiveness, tea houses excel by creating unique tea offerings, improving interior decoration and ambience, and further developing their menus.

The consequence is a departure from the traditional quest for high quality leaf tea to the marketing of variety. These tea houses proactively identify and innovatively incorporate new materials for making tea and tea-related drinks. Citrus, berries, nuts, flowers and dairy products are mixed and matched to produce novelty flavours. Heavy investment and special attention have been paid to interior design in order to attract a younger age group. The ambience of the shop is regarded as an important part of the augmented product.

Euromonitor (2004) reported that the growth of the black specialty and fruit/herbal tea markets is unlikely to be sustained because of the strong competition from traditional Chinese tea. It also asserted that the market would be dominated by female customers. These conclusions, however, are yet to be tested. According to the observations and interviews conducted by the author, the modern tea house business is still growing healthily and the gender bias is not overwhelmingly visible. In the few visits made to Taiwan by the author between 2002 and 2004, an increasing presence of tourists was witnessed.

Although local patrons are still the major target group for these tea houses, some are being featured in travel books and literature as must-see attractions for tourists. Taiwan's contemporary tea culture is now an important part of the food and beverage culture of Taiwan and an exotic cultural attraction for tourists. In response to the emerging trend of tea houses, its supply chain has also grown rapidly. The wholesale district in the city of Taipei, for example, attracts many tourist visits. According to the merchants in the wholesale district, the importance of tourists to their businesses, though small at the moment, is clearly increasing.

In the past, Taiwan had not been actively promoting its tea houses as tourist attractions, partially through ignorance. According to a contact in Taiwan, the Taiwanese have never been aware of how important and attractive tea houses could be in promoting tourism businesses. In the 1980s, when the local economy was still booming, tourism was not taken seriously. It was regarded as a second-class business. The development of tourism and tourist attractions, therefore, has been lax. The development of tea houses and the modern tea culture is a natural evolution in the local market. Only after it took form and became a unique feature of society did the tourism authority decide to take advantage of it, in order to promote it as an additional attraction. However, it now has to face a new challenge. The successful development of modern tea culture and products induced operators to start up branches in the mainland China and Hong Kong markets. Given the fact that innovators can hardly patent their operation and products, the entry barrier is low. Imitators in the region, especially those in Hong Kong and mainland China, efficiently stereotyped similar concepts. Competitors are capitalizing on tea house culture as an attraction and therefore investing in this area has difficulties and risk.

This modern tea house phenomenon indicates an important dimension in the development of cultural tourism – the diffusion of culture. This syndrome is of particular importance when: (1) the subject culture and or cultural product does not conflict with the cultures of the tourists; and (2) the host and the tourist community are culturally and geographically close and affiliated to one another.

Yunnan

Yunnan Province is situated in the most southwest region of China. It borders the countries of Vietnam, Laos and Burma. Yunnan is known to be one of the places of origin of tea and is famous for its red tea, *Puer*. Since ancient times, red tea bricks and blocks were traded from Yunnan to other parts of China and neighbouring countries. However, if you assume that Yunnan's location can benefit the tea trade, it is not quite the case. Although Yunnan Province borders Guizhou Province and Guangxi Zhang Autonomous Region to the east, Chongqing and Sichuan to the north, and Tibet Autonomous Region to the northwest, its access is blocked by natural barriers. This isolation might have given Yunnan a perfect opportunity to preserve its unique cultural context, but it has never been an obstacle to the tea traders.

Yunnan covers an area of 394,000 square kilometres and has a population of more than 42 million people. It has a diverse topography and is well known for its natural biodiversity. Another asset of Yunnan Province is its cultural and ethnical diversity. There are 25 different ethnic minorities in Yunnan and this multiplicity of cultures has endowed the province with a rich heritage that it shares with all its visitors. Some of Yunnan's major attractions are: Stone Forest (Shi Lin), one of the world's natural wonders; Daguan Park; Black Dragon Pool; Zheng He Park; Bamboo Temple; Golden Temple; the Western Hills; Huating Temple; Taihua Temple; the Sanqing Temple; Longmen (Dragon Gate); Xishuangbanna, a tropical rainforest that is the home of the Dai people; Jade Dragon Snow Mountain; Shangri-la; and Lijiang Old Town, a world heritage location. With this cultural heritage, it is clear that Yunnan has the merits to develop cultural tourism. Tea is just one of the many possibilities. The option of tea, however, embraces unique attractiveness and specific merit that make it much more than just another attraction.

According to the tea community, Yunnan is one of the must-see destinations. Although it is well known for its black tea, it also plants and produces white, green and scented tea as well. Some of the black/red tea has become collectable. Given the various natural and cultural attractions of the province, however, tea has not been fully capitalized on as a tourist attraction. Tea tours to Yunnan were only recently introduced to the West. For example, a 14-day tour sponsored by a tea wholesaler was introduced to the US market. This US$ 4000+ tour covers tea destinations including Beijing, Wuhan, Kunming, Zhejiang and Hangzhou. Shanghai and Taipei are also made available as extra excursions for additional charges, and small-scale plantation visits can also be arranged on request. Farm stays and a tea museum, however, are still not available in Yunnan. Nonetheless, there are a few tea attractions located in Yunnan. Each attraction functions like a small museum: staff members will serve tea, demonstrate the making of tea, and disseminate information about various types of tea. These attractions are largely owned and managed by tea merchants and their main purpose is to promote and sell tea products. Since their targets are, by and large, local tourists, not much has been offered to encourage international travellers, including those from Hong Kong and Taiwan, to visit these attractions.

Although the large tea museum, the National Tea Museum, is located in Hangzhou, Yunnan in itself could be described as a 'grand museum', perhaps resembling an eco-museum presenting a living heritage of tea. Tea plantations, ancient tea-trees and forests, production facilities, tea houses, tea markets, tea trade routes and other related features could easily be capitalized and organized into attractions. There are, in fact, tea and cultural tours offered to foreigners and overseas Chinese visitors, the tours for foreigners tending to be both expensive and extensive, as take the tourists to various provinces and attractions. The duration of the tours normally lasts for 14 days or more. While these tours have the advantage of seeing many different tea origin sites in China, they have the disadvantages of tedious travelling and limited interaction with any locality and its tea culture. Trying to feature everything in one tour sometimes causes tourists to be unable to see anything in any depth.

Tea tourism in both Taiwan and China is still in an early stage of development of the products on offer. Figures 4.3 and 4.4 illustrate the different product development framework of Taiwan and China respectively. As shown in Figure 4.3, tea and tea culture are an integral part of the Taiwanese cultural context. Tea products and attractions were designed to satisfy the needs and wants of the local people. Foreign tourists

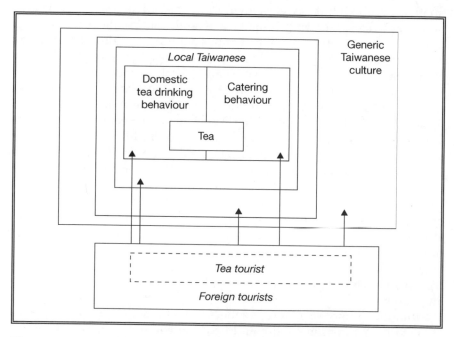

Figure 4.3 Tea tourism product in Taiwan

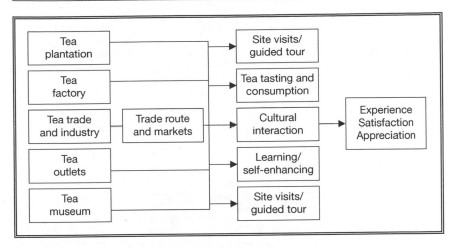

Figure 4.4 Tea tourism product in Yunnan

are sharing the facilities with the local community and the tea tourist is still very much part of an immature market segment.

On the other hand, developments in China have been taken one step further to conceptualize, materialize and commodify tea tourism. Although foreign tourists are limited in number, capitalization of tea culture and products at the travel retailing level is more mature in China than in its Taiwanese counterpart. Organized tea tours are available as well as small-scale farm visits and tea ceremony seminars. Nonetheless, tea tourism is still new to the market. The current development is very much product-related with activities and itinerary built around tea-related attractions. By using the fanning-out approach, the next step, therefore, is to evolve new directions to augment the products on offer. Such a direction is reflected in a recent report (2006) in the *Globe and Mail* (Toronto, Canada) in which author Geoffrey York indicates: 'The ancient beverage has suddenly become the latest collecting craze among China's affluent young professionals. The Chinese media are buzzing with talk of tea auctions, tea vintages, skyrocketing prices and market speculation.' York goes on to compare this trend of tea collecting and tasting to the Western trend of wine collecting and tasting.

The fanning-out approach can be adapted to the development of both product and markets. Figures 4.5 and 4.6 below illustrate the two different applications. As Figure 4.5 shows, a range of alternative activities can be developed as a spin-off from tea, though keeping tea as a theme or subject.

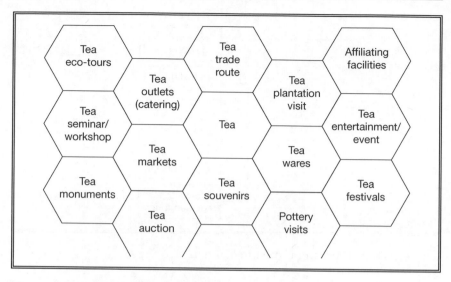

Figure 4.5 Variety of tea tourism product

These items can be developed into stand-alone tourism product alternatives or components of a bigger product consortium.

Figure 4.6, on the other hand, shows the composition of a potential market segment for tea tourism. The core targets for tea tourism might include tea hobbyists, cultural tourists and novelty-seekers. It is apparent that the tea hobbyist, owing to an interest in tea, is the prime target for tea tourism. The more serious the people in this group are about tea, the more likely it is that they will appreciate and be willing to spend time and money on a tour with tea as its central theme. Cultural tourists, on the other hand, would see tea as a form of cultural product and tea drinking as a cultural behaviour. Given the exotic nature of tea and tea rituals, this particular segment could be a potential target for cultivation. The third component of the segment is composed mainly of the variety- and novelty-seekers. This group of tourists, however, is not a stable segment. On a large-scale, both 'starters' and 'quitters' can be expected. A few, however, can be developed into more serious tea tourists in the long run. They could become tea hobbyists or tea-specific cultural tourists.

The idea presented in Figure 4.6 is a preliminary assessment of the market. More research and study is critical to provide essential information for understanding the potential market for tea tourism in Taiwan and Yunnan.

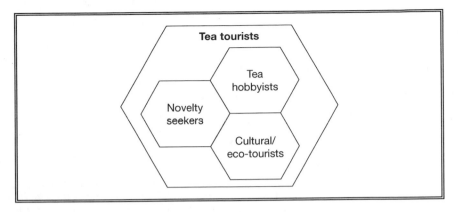

Figure 4.6 Composition of the tea tourist segment

Conclusion

This chapter has some important conclusions. First, tea drinkers and hobbyists form a unique market segment for development. Second, although the potential contribution of tea tourism has yet to be fully documented and confirmed, the author believes that it has the potential to: promote small-scale village industries; contribute to the redistribution of wealth; increase employment, which in turn will facilitate the mitigation of rural poverty; and facilitate natural environment preservation and cultural asset conservation. Third, by comparing the development of modern tea culture in Taiwan and traditional tea culture in Yunnan, traditional tea placed in its cultural context seems to offer greater merit for positioning the tea tourism product and acting as a barrier to new competitors. It might also suggest that the success of tea tourism depends very much on how well tea is featured in a more macro-cultural environment. In other words, pulling tea, or any other cultural attractions, out of the cultural consortium as a stand-alone attraction might detract from its attractiveness.

Although China is regarded as the home of the origin of tea, tea and tea tourism is now by no means unique to the Chinese communities. With 57 countries planting and producing tea as a trade commodity, tea tourism is definitely a viable option for product and market development in these countries.

References

Charters, S. and Ali-Knight, J. (2000) Wine tourism – a thirst for knowledge? *International Journal of Wine Marketing* 12 (3), 70–80.

Charters, S. and Ali-Knight, J. (2002) Who is the wine tourist? *Tourism Management* 23 (3), 311–19.

Dodd, T.H. and Bigotte, V. (1997) Perceptual differences among visitor groups to wineries. *Journal of Travel Research* 35 (3), 46–51.

Euromonitor (2004) *Hot Tea in Taiwan*. Online document: http://www.the-infoshop.com/study/eo18836_hotdrinks_taiwan.html (accessed 10 August 2004).

Frochot, I. (2000) Wine tourism in France, a paradox? In C.M. Hall, L. Sharples, B. Cambourne and N. Macionis (eds) *Wine and Tourism From Around the World* (pp. 67–80). London: Butterworth Heinemann.

Hall, C.M., Sharples, L., Cambourne, B. and Macionis, N. (eds) (2000) *Wine Tourism Around the World: Development, Management and Markets*. Oxford: Butterworth Heinemann.

Hall, M., Sharples, L., Mitchell, R., Macionis, N. and Cambourne, B. (2003) *Food Tourism Around the World: Development, Management and Markets*. London: Butterworth Heinemann.

International Tea Committee (2002) *Tea Statistics*. Online document: http://www.intteacomm.co.uk/statsframe.asp (accessed on 4 February 2003).

International Tea Trade Committee (2004) *International Tea Trade Statistics*. Online document: http://www.inttea.com/ (accessed 2 July 2004).

Jolliffe, Lee (2003) The lure of tea: history, traditions and attractions. In M. Hall, L. Sharples, R. Mitchell, N. Macionis and B. Cambourne (eds) *Food Tourism Around the World: Development, Management and Markets* (pp. 121–36). London: Butterworth Heinemann.

Kuo, N., Hsiao, T. and Lan, C. (2005) Tourism management and industrial ecology: A case study of food service in Taiwan. *Tourism Management* 26 (4), 503–8.

Prentice, R. and Andersen, V. (2003) Festival as creative destination. *Annals of Tourism Research* 30 (1), 7–30.

Richards, G. (2001) The experience industry and the creation of attractions. In G. Richards (ed.) *Cultural Attractions and European Tourism* (pp. 55–69). Wallingford: CABI International.

Wicentowski, J. (1999) *Tea Houses in Taiwan*. Online document: http://www.people.fas.harvard.edu/~wicentow/tea/ (accessed 29 June 2004).

York, G. (2006) Steep profits in tea collecting across China: Affluent young professionals spur craze in which vintages are valued like fine wine. *Globe and Mail*, 30 January 2006, A3.

Part 3: Tea and Tourism: Political, Social and Economic Developments

Chapter 5

Tea Production and Tourism Development in Assam: A Missed Opportunity?

KEVIN HANNAM

Theoretically, this chapter draws upon political ecology in order to understand the history of tea production and subsequent tourism development in Assam. Blaikie and Brookfield (1987: 17) argue that a Third World political ecology combines the 'concerns of ecology and a broadly defined political economy'. Contemporary political ecologists have examined the politics of environmental change in the Third World in terms of certain problems, concepts, socio-economic characteristics and regions, or used a combination of these (Bryant, 1992; Peet & Watts, 1996; Bryant & Bailey, 1997; Peluso & Watts, 2001). Furthermore, Bryant and Bailey (1997: 3) point out that:

> Political ecologists appear to agree on two basic points . . . Firstly, they agree that the environmental problems facing the Third World are not simply a reflection of policy or market failures . . . but rather are a manifestation of broader political and economic forces. . . . [A] second area of agreement among political ecologists is the need for far-reaching changes to local, regional and global political-economic processes . . .

Political ecologists are thus highly sceptical about the merit of concepts such as sustainable development, partly because of the way such ideas have been incorporated into the dominant discourses of global organizations, nation-states and multinational corporations without much change occurring at a grassroots level. This is largely because of the foregrounding of the political in political ecology research. Moreover, this is all the more apparent in Third World contexts where the colonial legacy of commodification and land degradation has led to the continuation of social and

71

environmental conflicts in the post-colonial era. Ultimately, a political ecology approach is grounded in a historical and material analysis of the often complex and unequal relations of power within any environmental context.

Methodologically, this chapter is based upon a range of documentary sources as well as the author's ethnographic field trip to Assam in March 2003. This is supplemented by interviews conducted at the Ministry of Tourism in New Delhi in March 2003 and January 2004.

In summary, the chapter sets the production of tea and tourism development within the historical context of the production of tea plantations in Assam from the 1820s until the present day. Tea production and tourism development is then analysed against the political backdrop of the United Liberation Front of Assam's (ULFA) increasingly violent strategies for gaining independence from what it sees as India's colonialism. It is concluded that India's contemporary tourism development strategies in Assam can be seen as a means to normalize social relations and as a continuation of internal colonial authority.

The Political Ecology of Tea in Assam

Geopolitically, Assam's location constitutes a 'frontier' region, which is of strategic importance to India as it has international borders with Bangladesh, Bhutan, China (Tibet) and Myanmar (Burma). Originally encompassing the entire north eastern region, the state of Assam is today the largest and most populated state (around 26 million), located in the north eastern region of India alongside six other states (Arunchal Pradesh, Manipur, Meghalaya, Mizoram, Nagaland and Tripura) and connected only by a narrow 20 km strip of land to the rest of India (the Shiliguri corridor). Baruah (2001: xii) notes: 'The tenuousness of this physical connection underscores the region's cultural and political distance from the Indian heartland'. The region is deemed to be one of the most ethnically and linguistically diverse regions in India, as well as one of the most politically sensitive. As such the region is also seen as strategically important to the Indian government in terms of maintaining the internal national integrity of India.

Assam as a distinct colonial province was formed in 1874 on the basis of largely accidental administrative convenience rather than historical or cultural reasoning. In the early part of the 19th century Assam had been viewed largely as an appendage of the province of Bengal. During British administrative reorganizations the name Assam was only retained because of lobbying from the British tea industry, who successfully argued that the word Assam was known in the international tea markets and thus should be retained. In this context Baruah (2001: 27) notes:

> Given the circumstances of the formation of the British province of Assam, the boundaries obviously do not coincide with those of precolonial Assam in a political, cultural, or economic sense. Certain areas that were not historically part of Assam became part of colonial Assam, while other areas that were a part of Assam did not.

In the late 18th century 'considerable discussion took place in the East India Company about the potential of tea cultivation in India' (Chatterjee, 2001: 54). The East India Company wanted to cultivate tea in India as it saw China having a monopoly on this increasingly important consumer item. In 1833, Lord Bentinck's 'Tea Committee' concluded tea was 'beyond all doubt indigenous to upper Assam, a discovery by far the most important and valuable that has ever been made on matters connected with the agricultural or commercial resources of this empire' (cited in Chatterjee, 2001: 55). In the early 19th century, the British government began to call Assam 'fine tea country', and by 1841 significant volumes of tea were being exported to Britain (Chatterjee, 2001). The East India Company designated large areas of Assam as 'wastelands', available either for tea plantations or for peasant settlers (Guha, 1991). This was the reward of conquest and, in effect, the process of enclosure involved the commodification and subsequent exclusion of the local elites as well as the peasants and tribal populations from the land (Baruah, 2001). Nonetheless, this process of enclosure met with protracted resistance (Chatterjee, 2001).

As a result of this 'green imperialism' (Grove, 1995), in many parts of Assam a villager would have to walk many miles around tea plantations as the use of the roads through plantations was restricted. Moreover, the right of way through tea plantations became a major issue in Assam's anti-colonial politics in the early 20th century. By 1901 British-owned tea plantations had enclosed 'some one fourth of the total settled area (or five per cent of the total area) of Assam proper, under their exclusive property rights' (Baruah, 2001: 48).

Furthermore, the economic transformation of Assam during the colonial period also led to a significant demographic shift. Colonial officials actively encouraged immigration into Assam because they perceived the Assamese peasantry as being lazy and of showing little interest in the waged labour on offer in the tea plantations (Chatterjee, 2001). Throughout the entire colonial period, the British treated Assam as a frontier land for population migration from the colonial province of Bengal (present-day West Bengal, Bihar, Orissa and Bangladesh). Justifying moves to combine the former areas of Assam and Bengal into a single province, an official said, 'since Bengal is very densely populated . . . it needs room for expansion and it can expand only eastward' (Baruah, 2001: 39).

Initially under the auspices of the East India Company, labour recruitment for the tea industry was mainly the effort of individual plantations or companies (Phukan, 1984). Subsequently, from 1878, the Tea Districts Labour Association (TDLA) coordinated labour recruitment, adopting a systematic indentured labour system that continued until 1926 (Baruah, 2001; Chatterjee, 2001). After the abolition of this system, recruitment of labour from outside Assam continued more subtly, and only stopped in 1960 when 'the position of labour supply in the tea gardens in Assam had reversed from shortage to surplus and unemployment in tea gardens appeared on the scene' (Baruah, 2001: 54).

Many of those recruited to work on tea plantations over the years settled in Assam at the end of their contracted period. Consequently, there are many 'tea-labour' villages in the tea-growing districts of Assam, mostly situated close to tea plantations and relatively isolated from the indigenous Assamese villages. The 1921 census estimated that migrants to the tea plantations and their descendants made up one-sixth of the total population of the province (*c*.1.3 million). The workers on the tea plantations now constitute the oldest of Assam's large modern-day immigrant groups (Baruah, 2001).

However, it should be recognized that tea was not the only commodity to attract investors and immigrants to Assam in the colonial period. In the late 1830s the British military discovered significant oil reserves in Assam and in the following decades coalfields were developed. Assam's forests came under colonial silvicultural management in order to provide timber for India's railways (Stebbing, 1922) and the construction of roads and buildings fuelled further development. Immigrants also came to occupy many of the new middle-class positions available; ones that required new skills, such as knowledge of the English language. In summary, Baruah (2001: 45–6) notes, 'What Assam saw in the late nineteenth century was nothing short of an economic revolution accompanied by massive ecological destruction.'

Following India's independence in 1947, Assam was initially divided into five constituent states. Subsequently, the region was further divided: Nagaland was formed in 1963, Meghalaya in 1970, Mizoram in 1972 and Arunchal Pradesh in 1987. This was a top-down process rather than a response to sustained political mobilization as elsewhere in India. The prime mover in the break-up of the region was a powerful central government under Indira Gandhi's leadership, which decided that by creating new states it would be able to contain, and even pre-empt, insurgencies in the northeast region. This policy was largely a failure. Baruah (2001: 91) argues: 'The Assamese have come to see the break-up of Assam as a mark of Assam's lack of control over its own destiny. In recent years, militant Assamese subnationalism has successfully tapped this sense of injury and powerlessness.'

Moreover, Assam has, and continues to have, the highest rate of in-migration of any state in India (Baruah, 2001: Weiner, 1978). This has heightened tensions and led to violence and murder and also to the existence of large numbers of refugees (BBC News, 2003g,h). Baruah (2001: 14) notes: 'The anxiety on the part of many of the numerically smaller peoples of the northeast becoming minorities in territories that they had historically regarded as their own has been a recurrent theme in the politics of the region.'

Figures on immigration into Assam have become a source of intense political contestation. to the extent that the 1981 census wasn't conducted in Assam at all. According to the 1991 census, however, out of a total population of over 22 million, nearly 13 million speak Assamese and nearly 5 million speak Bengali as their first language. A further million speak Hindi and another million regard the Bodo tribal language as their mother tongue. In terms of religion, 67% of the current population is Hindu, 28% is Muslim and 3% is Christian (Baruah, 2001).

The actual conflict in Assam in the post-independence period started in 1960–1, when the so called 'language riots' took place in Assam – these were violent conflicts between ethnic Assamese and Hindu Bengalis that led to many deaths. The insurgency in Assam began in earnest in 1979 and was at its height in the late 1980s, when kidnappings, ransom demands and murders transformed the idyllic life of tea plantation (garden) managers into an extremely insecure one. In March 1983, more than 3000 people (mostly Muslims of Bengali descent) were killed during election violence (Baruah, 2001).

On 15 August 1985 the Indian government (under Rajiv Gandhi) and the Assam movement leaders agreed to a compromise, the Assam Accord: 'a broad settlement that included . . . significant promises on key economic and developmental concerns that had animated Assamese subnational politics' (Baruah, 2001: 116). The Accord was not easy to implement, however, not least because the Bodo people felt disenfranchised and continued their violent protests. The Bodo movement claims that Assam is in fact illegally occupied by the so-called Assamese and has called for a separate Indian state called Bodoland since 1987. In total it has been estimated that over 10,000 people have died as a result of the ethnic violence in Assam since the 1980s, most notably because of fighting between the United Liberation Front of Asom (Assam) (ULFA) and the Indian military (BBC News, 2004a).

ULFA began as a radical, militant, left-wing fringe group of the Assam Movement in 1979. It viewed the non-implementation of the Assam Accord as another instance of the central government's lack of interest in protecting the interests of the Assamese. Its ultimate goal though is to restore Assam's lost independence and it attempts to appeal to all people currently living in Assam rather than just Assamese people. ULFA views the relationship between the Indian government and Assam as colonial and argues (quite correctly in the author's view) that Assam does not get its fair share of development resources, given that it provides the rest of India with most of its oil and natural gas, as well as tea. Indeed, it has been recognized that, on a number of key measures, poverty in Assam is actually worse than elsewhere in India despite its natural resources (Das, 2001). Furthermore, local people complain that the development resources that do come into Assam are frequently diverted by corrupt bureaucrats (BBC News, 2003f). ULFA states on its web site:

> Assam was never a part of India at any point of time in history. The fact is independent Assam has been occupied by India, and deploying occupation forces there are oppressing our peoples and persecuting them. ULFA itself and all freedom fighters of Assam are neither planning nor conspiring to break up India! We are not conducting any armed operation inside India. Freedom fighters of Assam are only trying to overthrow Indian colonial occupation from Assam.
>
> In [the] economic sphere, India has been engaged in large-scale exploitation. Despite its rich resources, Assam remains one of the most backward states. Therefore, the question of real threat to the national identity of the people of Assam under the colonial occupation and exploitation of India has become the basic problem. As a whole, the problem has become a question of life and death to the people of Assam. (ULFA, 2004)

However, ULFA's arguments are contested by the Indian government. S. Sinha (2002: 13), the Governor of Assam, has argued that ULFA's claims are, in fact, 'totally wrong and factually incorrect' and blames the British for commencing a period of 'neglect and discrimination'.

While the oil and natural gas industries are in the hands of enterprises owned by the government of India, the state's hugely profitable tea industry is largely privately owned by large multinational corporations and managed from corporate offices based in Calcutta and elsewhere worldwide. Because of the lack of local investment in Assam by the tea industry, ULFA has collected large amounts of so-called 'taxes' from the tea industry and persuaded the tea owners to employ local Assam youth, establish high schools and colleges in tea plantations, move the corporate management to Assam, and improve the quality of food, housing and social services provided to tea workers. Recently it was revealed that, in 1986, Tata Tea engaged in negotiations with the ULFA leadership and subsequently built a hospital as part of its contribution to what the company refers to as community development. By 1990 ULFA ran a virtually parallel government in Assam (Baruah, 2001).

The Indian government's response to ULFA has been to launch counter-insurgency operations by the Indian armed forces (Operations Bajrang, 1990–1 and Rhino 1991–3). Additionally, economic rewards and legal immunity have also reduced the ranks of ULFA, and although ULFA continues to have its strongholds and remains a significant force in Assam, the Indian military also remains in Assam – and has been criticized for several human rights abuses (BBC News, 2004b). The situation is now said to be akin to the so-called 'dirty wars' fought in South America and southern Africa. As Baruah (2001: 145) notes: '. . . the overall picture is one of a substantial rise in the number of incidents of political violence, the exacerbation of Assam's ethnic and political conflicts, and a widening chasm between Assamese subnationalism and pan-Indianism.'

Assam remains on the alert; even though the insurgency has been somewhat contained, the political climate in Assam is still unstable with tea plantation managers being 'routinely' murdered (BBC News, 2003a,b,d). The Indian government has vowed to deal firmly with ULFA and it recently deployed the army to guard the tea estates, protect executives and ensure continuing foreign investment (BBC News, 2003c,e). The Indian and Burmese armies have also mounted joint counter-offensives against ULFA's bases in Burma (BBC News, 2004a).

This is the backdrop against which we should examine the politics of tourism development in Assam.

Tourism Development in Assam

The number of tourists visiting Assam is fairly low due to the political instability in the region. Current estimates put foreign arrivals at approximately 500 per year and domestic arrivals at 14,000, but during the height of the conflict in the 1980s numbers of tourists declined to approximately 30 foreign and 7000 domestic visitors (Bhattacharya, 2001).

In terms of tourism resources, Assam is famous for its tea gardens and the rare one-horned rhinoceros. Hitherto, the latter has been utilized in Assam for tourism development more than the former (62% of domestic and 81% of foreign tourists visit Kaziranga whilst in Assam (Bhattacharya, 2001).

Kaziranga National Park has the largest population of Indian rhino and is thus a major tourist attraction. It is renowned as one of the finest and most picturesque wildlife parks in India. The park was officially designated as a national park in 1974 by the Indian government, following the first notification in 1969. Originally it was established as a reserved forest in 1908, a game sanctuary in 1916 and a wildlife sanctuary in 1950. It was designated as a 'Natural' World Heritage Site by the IUCN, UNEP and UNESCO in 1985. There are no villages inside the national park but it is bordered on three sides by human settlements and tea plantations. The interior of the park is accessible mostly by elephant. Due to the lack of government-owned accommodation, most international and domestic tourists stay at the privately owned Wild Grass Resort located adjacent to the national park area. In terms of day-to-day management, as at other Indian national parks, poaching remains a serious problem. Moreover, there are problems of low morale among staff, with lack of funds causing shortages of equipment, uniforms and delayed wages (Hannam, 1999). However, 'only with the end of political turmoil in Assam is the full tourist potential of Kaziranga being explored' (World Heritage Sites, 2004). Along with visits to the park itself the resort owners also provide visits to the tea gardens on an ad hoc basis (interviews, 2003).

Assam has though been recognized as of increasing importance to the Indian government in terms of tourism development, with some 10% of the Ministry of Tourism's budget being allocated to the development of tourism in this region: 'Tourism has been identified as one of the most important segments, which could accelerate developmental activities in this region' (Ministry of Tourism, 2000: 55).

Nevertheless, despite the government of India attaching great importance to the development of tourism in the north eastern region, India's national tourism policies (2000, 2001) have until recently represented the north east, and Assam with it, as a largely undeveloped region with many potential tourism resources, but lacking in key tourism facilities. Earlier government policies described the region thus:

> The rich natural beauty, serenity and exotic flora and fauna of the area are invaluable resources for the development of eco-tourism. The region is endowed with diverse tourist attractions and each State has its

Plate 5.1 Assam Tourism Office, Assam, India

Source: Kevin Hannam

own distinct features. The attractions are scattered over the entire region and are largely located in remote areas within highly fragile environments. These attractions and the people of the region constitute the tourism resources at large. The facilities for stay, food, shopping and entertainment are either non-existent or mostly primitive in nature. (Ministry of Tourism, 2000: 53)

In order to develop the tourism infrastructure further in the north eastern region, the Ministry of Tourism has sought to upgrade state-owned tourist accommodation and refurbish specific tourist attractions. It has also developed a marketing strategy for the north eastern region in order to lure both domestic and international visitors. Furthermore, in order to raise the skills base in the region it has recently established a chapter of the Indian Institute of Tourism and Travel Management (IITM) in Guwahati, the capital of Assam. However, in 1998–9 only about a third of the money allocated in the Ministry of Tourism's tourism plans was actually released for development activity (some 356 million rupees were sanctioned in 1998–9, but only 117 million rupees were actually released). In 1998–9, Assam won the highest amount of tourism development assistance (some 46 million rupees were released, as against 137 million rupees sanctioned), however much of this assistance was spent on the establishment of the IITM in Guwahati (Ministry of Tourism, 2000).

In 1999–2000, central government tourism development assistance to the north eastern region reduced on the whole to approximately half that of 1998–9 (Ministry of Tourism, 2001). More significantly, only about a quarter of the money allocated in the Ministry of Tourism's plans for tourism was actually released for development activity (some 190 million rupees were sanctioned in 1999–2000, but only 53 million rupees were actually released). In 1999–2000, Assam's share of tourism development assistance was also reduced (some 7 million rupees released as against 35 million rupees sanctioned). However, other north eastern states gained greater amounts of tourism development assistance in 1999–2000 – Mizoram, Nagaland and Tripura were each awarded approximately 9 million rupees. Special foreign tourist permits are required to visit Mizoram and Nagaland because of the sensitive political and cultural nature of these areas for the Indian government. Overall the lack of take-up of tourism development assistance is blamed by central government officials on the levels of corruption and violence in the northeast as well as lack of entrepreneurial activity in the region. Conversely, local interests in Assam, meanwhile, blame the lack of development take-up on the difficulties in engaging with corrupt central and regional government bureaucracies (personal interviews, New Delhi, 2003, 2004; Guwahati, 2003).

In 2002, the Indian government reorganized the Ministry of Tourism to include aspects of heritage management, and thus the Ministry of Tourism became the Ministry of Tourism and Culture. Although the central principles of the national tourism policy remained largely unaltered the policy was given a more positive gloss. Interestingly, in its annual report, the Ministry of Tourism and Culture (2002: 132) repeats the aforementioned description of the potential tourism resources of the north eastern region, however, it revised the last line to: 'The facilities for stay, food, shopping and entertainment are improving tremendously', rather than being largely 'non-existent' as represented in previous reports.

Furthermore, in 2002, the Ministry of Tourism and Culture developed a 'special tourism marketing campaign for the North Eastern region' targeted primarily at domestic tourists with the slogan: 'India's North East: paradise unexplored', a place where tourist experiences 'go beyond words' (Ministry of Tourism and Culture, 2002: 136). Part of this new marketing strategy has involved the development of a new website for tourism to the north east region. This website proclaims that:

> They're untamed and unexplored. They're full of lush green valleys, lofty mountains and tumultuous rivers. They're home to an extraordinary range of flora and fauna. They're the states of North East India, whose natural beauty awaits the traveller looking for something different.
>
> Begin your travels in the Himalayan Shangrila of *Sikkim*, where orchids bloom on the hillside. Journey on to the plains of *Assam* – tea country and producer of more than half of India's petroleum. Experience sunrise in *Arunchal Pradesh*, the first part of India to greet the morning sun. Explore the princely traditions of *Tripura*, the second smallest Indian state. Discover the tribal crafts and culture of *Nagaland*. Take home exquisite bamboo and cane souvenirs from *Mizoram*. Enjoy the marionette-like *Manipuri* dance of the Land of the Jewels, Manipur. Relax in the sylvan surroundings of the Abode of the clouds, *Meghalaya*.
>
> Welcome to an India you never knew existed. Welcome to the North East. (http://www.northeastofindia.com, 2004)

Such representations clearly draw a veil over the complex political situation in Assam. Moreover, the amount actually sanctioned for tourism development assistance in the region was further reduced to 114 million rupees in 2001–2, with approximately half this actually being released (62 million rupees). In Assam itself, some 39 million rupees were sanctioned in 2001–2 but only 19 million rupees were released (Ministry of Tourism and Culture, 2002). Thus, significantly, the overall picture over the past few years is of declining tourist development assistance to the north eastern region of India and the state of Assam in particular, against a backdrop of increasing government claims that it is doing more to develop the region's tourism infrastructure.

Conclusion

The development of so-called tea tourism is still in its infancy and visits to the tea gardens of Assam are very much on an ad hoc basis. The Assam State Tourism Development Corporation inaugurated an annual Tea Tourism Festival in December 1995 (Assam Tea, 2004), however it has been unable to attract significant levels of domestic and foreign tourists (Bhattacharya, 2001). In contrast, the Darjeeling International Tea Festival has developed a spectacle of national and international importance (Chatterjee, 2001).

India's contemporary tourism development strategies in Assam can be seen not only as a means to normalize social relations but also as a continuation of internal colonial authority set against a backdrop of continued ethnic violence in the region. As the largest producer of tea in India, Assam has the potential for developing tea tourism but at present the conflicts in the region have mitigated any concerted development in this area. Thus tea tourism should be seen perhaps as a missed opportunity for the development of Assam.

References

Assam Tea (2004) *Assam Travel*. Online document: http://www.northeast indiadiary.com/assam-travel/assam-tea.html (accessed 17 March 2004).

Baruah, S. (2001) *India Against Itself: Assam and the Politics of Nationality*. New Delhi: Oxford University Press.

BBC News (2003a) *Tea manager shot dead in Assam*. 26 May.

BBC News (2003b) *Assam tea manager killed*. 7 July.

BBC News (2003c) *Army to guard Assam tea estate*. 13 October.

BBC News (2003d) *Assam on alert after rebel threat*. 14 November.

BBC News (2003e) *Indian PM firm on Assam violence*. 20 November.

BBC News (2003f) *Q&A: India's violent north-east*. 21 November.

BBC News (2003g) *Two die in Assam ethnic clashes*. 23 November.

BBC News (2003h) *Over 17,000 flee Assam violence*. 26 November.

BBC News (2004a) *Screws tighten on Indian rebels*. 2 January.

BBC News (2004b) *Captured rebel: India tortured me*. 5 January.

Bhattacharya, P. (2001) Tourism. In A. Bhagabati, A. Bor and B. Kar (eds) *Geography of Assam*. New Delhi: Rajesh.

Blaikie, P. and Brookfield, H. (1987) *Land Degradation and Society*. London: Methuen.

Bryant, R. (1992) Political ecology: An emerging research agenda in Third-World studies. *Political Geography* 11 (1), 12–36.

Bryant, R. and Bailey, S. (1997) *Third World Political Ecology*. London: Routledge.

Chatterjee, P. (2001) *A Time for Tea: Women, Labor and Post/Colonial Politics on an Indian Plantation*. Durham, NC: Duke University Press.

Das, H. (2001) Insurgency and development: The Assam experience. In K. Gill and A. Sahni (eds) *Faultlines: Writings on Conflict and Resolution*. New Delhi: Bulwark.

Grove, R. (1995). *Green Imperialism: Colonial Expansion, Tropical Island Edens and the Origins of Environmentalism 1600–1800*. Oxford: Oxford University Press.

Guha, A. (1991) *Medieval and Early Colonial Assam*. Calcutta: Bagchi.

Hannam, K. (1999) Environmental management in India. *Journal of Environmental Planning and Management* 42 (2), 221–33.

Ministry of Tourism. (2000) *Annual Report*. New Delhi: Government of India.

Ministry of Tourism. (2001) *Annual Report*. New Delhi: Government of India.

Ministry of Tourism and Culture. (2002) *Annual Report*. New Delhi: Government of India.

Northeastofindia.com (2004) *Welcome Page*. Online document: http://www.northeastofindia.com/ (accessed 17 March 2004).

Peet, R. and Watts, M. (eds) (1996) *Liberation Ecologies: Environment, Development, Social Movements.* London: Routledge.

Peluso, N and Watts, M. (2001) *Violent Environments.* Ithaca: Cornell University Press.

Phukan, U. (1984). *The Ex-Tea Garden Labour Population in Assam.* New Delhi: DR Publishing.

Sinha, S. (2002) Violence and hope in India's northeast. In K. Gill and A. Sahni (eds) *Faultlines: Writings on Conflict and Resolution.* New Delhi: Bulwark.

Stebbing, E. (1922) *The Forests of India.* London: John Lane.

ULFA (2004) *ULFA Homepage.* Online document: http://www.geocities.com/CapitolHill/Congress/7434/ulfa.htm. (accessed 17 March 2004).

Weiner, M. (1978) *Sons of the Soil: Migration and Ethnic Conflict in India.* Princeton, NJ: Princeton University Press.

World Heritage Sites (2004) *Kaziranga National Park.* Online document: http://www.wcmc.org.uk/protected_areas/data/wh/kazirang.html (accessed 17 March 2004).

Chapter 6

Amidst the Misty Mountains: The Role of Tea Tourism in Sri Lanka's Turbulent Tourist Industry

RABINDRANATH B. GUNASEKARA* AND
JANET HENSHALL MOMSEN

Islands have always captured the imagination and Sri Lanka is no exception. Shaped like a teardrop, it lies just south of the Indian subcontinent and a few degrees north of the equator. Sri Lanka is twice the size of Vancouver Island and is dominated by the central highlands, the main tea-growing region. These highlands, made up of narrow gorges and deep river valleys cut into a plateau, have an average elevation of 5000 feet (1500 m) above sea level, rising at the highest point to 8,281 feet at Pidurutalagala Peak. Sri Lanka is one of the most densely populated countries in the world (294 people per sq km) and yet it has a landscape of great variety – from uncrowded tropical beaches to cool misty mountains covered in tea plantations. In this chapter we shall consider the long history of tourism in Sri Lanka and the role of the tea industry, the world's third largest after India and China, in attracting visitors to the island.

Sri Lanka as a Tourist Attraction

Because of its position in the Indian Ocean at the nexus of the sea-going trade routes between Africa and Asia, historically Sri Lanka attracted many visitors who came to trade and conquer. Chief among these were the

* Rabindranath 'Raba' B. Gunasekara died of a heart attack on 3 August 2003 while doing research for this chapter in Sri Lanka. The paper is based on his preliminary notes and documents he collected while in the field with some additional material and interpretation.

Portuguese, the Dutch and finally the British. Each colonial power left its mark on the landscape, yet didn't entirely destroy the ancient temples and irrigation works of the Sinhalese. It is this combination of Western influences, in an inherently oriental setting, that forms the basis of the modern tourism industry.

The Greeks and Romans called Sri Lanka 'Taprobane', while in ancient India it was known as 'Lanka'. The island plays a prominent role in the great Hindu Indian epic known through South Asia, the *Ramayana*. In this tale, Rama's wife Sita is abducted by the Ravana, the King of Lanka. Ravana takes Sita to his favourite retreat in Lanka, the Asoka Vana. In this magnificent park with beautiful orchards and grottoes and pleasure gardens he hopes to win her affection. Rama sent Hanuman, the divine monkey chief, to find Sita. He rescued her and burned down the city of Lanka. In search of Sita, the epic tells that:

> Hanuman saw the shoreline of warm white sand and scattered stones and water pools, and behind that many tall swaying palms, and plane trees, and forests of aloes. He saw rivers meet the sea, and saw where pearls and cowrie shells and fine corals had been spread to dry. He fled inland, over stacks of gold and silver from the demon mines that lay blazing in the sunlight, and then he saw the City. Beautiful Lanka was built on a level place just below the highest summit of the three-peaked hill Trikuta, as though built on clouds. She had four gates facing in four directions and her strong gold walls were the color of sunshine. (Buck, 1978: 185)

Thus it was the combination of natural and man-made attractions, the weather and the precious metals and gems that were noted – as they are today. Around 1292, Marco Polo landed in Ceylon (Seilan) en route between China and Venice and reported that Sri Lanka is 'better circumstanced than any other island in the world' (Marsden, 1987: 348). The 14th-century Arab traveller Ibn Battuta left descriptions of the island he called 'Serendib'. Ibn Battuta visited Adams Peak in Sri Lanka in 1344 and lived in the Maldives for two years.

By the 19th-century European settlers were arriving and attitudes were changing. From the 1830s to the 1880s, young English and Scottish men went to Ceylon to try to make their fortunes as coffee planters. However, British women did not follow them into the hills until towards the end of this period. For the settlers it was a time of cultural anxiety about racial and gendered identities combined with visions of economic and cultural transformation of nature. The planter William Boyd wrote:

[a] new era is dawning on Ceylon . . . English civilisation will bless and enrich the whole country, causing the wilderness to blossom as a rose, and making Ceylon, as it was in former times, a garden of the world and the granary of India. (Boyd, 1888a: 410)

However the climate, even the relatively cool climate of the hills, was seen as injurious to the nervous system of Europeans, especially to women and children (Millie, 1878).The cholera epidemic of 1845 took a heavy toll with one-fifth of the population of Kandy dead within a few weeks (Boyd, 1888b). Thus it was both the material reality as well as the imaginary geography of the tropics that were perceived as threats to outsiders.

The first plantations were very isolated from each other:

As far as the eye could see the horizon was bounded by this perpetual jungle . . . Frequently as evening approached, enveloped in thick mist, not a sound was heard but the sharp bark of the red elk, the scream of the night hawk, varied by the crashing of elephants in the forests. The birds have no song during the day, insect sound is mute, and the silence can almost be felt. The moaning sound of the wind passing over the forests serves only to increase the feeling of gloom. (Millie, 1878: n.p.)

This isolation was more imagined than real as the plantations were surrounded by local villages and often the planter shared his house with a Sinhalese concubine (Duncan, 2005).

Health conditions in the hills improved and, with the opening of the Suez Canal in 1869, the length of the journey between England and Ceylon was much reduced, allowing white women to join the men on the plantations. This supposedly allowed the moral regeneration of the planter class. It also brought more regular visitors as Ceylon became a stopping point on the journey from Australia to England.

The Tea Industry

Coffee was the plantation crop of the early part of the 19th century but, by the 1870s, a fungal disease had decimated the coffee trees, so planters turned to tea. In 1867 a Scotsman by the name of James Taylor introduced tea to Ceylon. The area planted in tea rose from 10 acres in 1867 to 1000 acres in 1875 and to over 384,000 acres at the turn of the century (Fernando, 2000). Planting material was brought from Assam as early as 1839 and both Assam and Chinese varieties of tea had been introduced by the 1870s. Imported seeds were expensive, however, and soon seedlings were raised locally. Tea planting spread most rapidly in the region of Nuwara Eliya.

Without the coffee disease tea might not have been introduced to Ceylon and, although some planters tried replacing the coffee with cacao, tea soon came to dominate (Fernando, 2000). At the start of the new millenium there are over 221,000 hectares (324,900 acres) under tea cultivation in Sri Lanka, representing about 3.8% of the area of the country (Fernando, 2000: 73). Ceylon teas are classified into three categories, depending broadly on climatic zones (where the agro-ecology affects the chemistry of the tea plant) and on the tea shoots harvested for processing. Tea factories are situated on the tea estates so that a minimum of time is lost between plucking and processing.

Low-grown tea covers over 65,000 hectares (95,550 acres) of the southwest of the island below 600 metres (2000 feet) (Fernando, 2000). These teas were originally planted in areas covered by tropical forest. When brewed they are strong in flavour and dark coloured and now account for half of the total production (Fernando, 2000). This zone is now dominated by smallholder tea production and smallholders now control 53% of all the tea land (Fernando, 2000: 154). Smallholdings have been encouraged by governmental policies of redistributing plantation land. Fernando suggests that the smallholder sector is the most dynamic segment of the private sector in Sri Lanka's tea industry (Fernando, 2004). These growers contribute 60% of the total tea produced and earn around 70% of the income from the nation's tea exports, mainly due to the high prices currently commanded by low-grown tea (Fernando, 2000: 155). Mid-country teas come from the northern part of the central highlands at altitudes between 600 and 1200 metres (2000 to 4000 feet). These teas are full-bodied and are good taken with milk (Fernando, 2000: 73). High-grown teas, manufactured in factories above 1200 metres (4000 feet) make up about 30% of total production. It is said that the tea grown on the highland Nuwara Eliya estates produces the 'champagne' of Ceylon teas, with a flavour best appreciated without milk (Fernando, 2000: 76).

Tea plants used to be planted in straight lines in squares, rectangles or triangles, with spaces to allow for complete coverage when the plants were mature (Fernando, 2000). The modern method adopted on slopes is 'contour planting', where the lines of tea bushes follow the contours of the land. This method reduces soil erosion, especially when combined with drainage and windbreaks, and permits a more economical distribution of plants. Precision farming is used to optimize the application of fertilizer. A tea plant grown on the tropical plains can come into production in about three years, however at higher altitudes it takes longer. Tea plants are pruned at regular intervals to encourage young shoots and are shaped into flat-topped bushes about one metre (39 in) high, convenient for picking the leaves.

Plucking of the tea is done all year round in Sri Lanka. The pluckers are traditionally Tamil women and they select the leaves to be plucked and collect these in baskets carried on their backs. A plucker will aim for a daily target of between 15 and 20 kilos (33 to 44 lbs) of leaf. The sight of the women in their colourful saris working in the brilliant green fields of the tea estates is unforgettable. Tea is processed as soon as possible after being picked and tea factories can be seen on most estates. Early factories depended on water-power and were built next to rivers. Nowadays tea factories are found at all altitudes throughout the tea-growing regions. The factories are usually large, rectangular, multi-storied buildings with rows of windows that are used for both light and ventilation in the 'withering' rooms. They typically sit atop hillocks on the tea-covered slopes of the estates and are open to breezes on all sides. Inside there are usually four or five floors, with an open central atrium from which hot air can be pumped to the upper lofts. This movement of air is essential to 'wither', but not dry, the tea leaves and buds skilfully spread out on burlap over racks. Once adequately withered, the leaves and buds are crushed and allowed to ferment briefly (less than two hours) before being dried in machines, sifted, graded and packed. The entire operation from tea bush to packaged dried tea can be accomplished in under 24 hours. The distinctive architecture of these factories with their many windows is a familiar feature of the landscape.

The Turbulent Growth of Sri Lanka Tourism

In the early 20th century, Western tourists came to Sri Lanka to learn about the work of tea estates and to enjoy the cool climate and mountainous scenery of the tea-growing regions. Clare Rettie writing in the 1920s noted the attractions of the highland tea estates.

> Though tea estates are to be seen, scattered about in many parts of Ceylon, that invaluable plant is at its best up on the hills. A short time spent in Nuwara Eliya, and in the region near that well-known hill station, gives one a very good idea of tea cultivation, and makes a delightful change from the low country. To leave the sultry heat of Colombo in the morning, and in the evening to sit comfortably by a blazing log fire, is to enjoy a piquant contrast. (Rettie, 1929: 66)

She describes daily life on the tea plantations, and the picking and the processing of the tea in great detail. She also tells the visitor what not to do on the plantations in the way of interfering with traditional ways. At the beginning of her book she provides a key to seasonal weather changes for prospective visitors to the island. She suggests that January and February are the best months to visit Sri Lanka as the monsoon rains are over and the weather is 'cool and pleasant . . . and travelling in the wilder parts of the island is comparatively easy, as the roads are then in good condition' (Rettie, 1929: 10). She goes on to say: 'April, May and June are considered by residents to be specially healthy, and there is certainly very little fever then, but to those who are not acclimatized the heat is likely to prove trying, and on that account, those months had better be avoided by visitors'. Clearly this information is aimed at Western visitors for whom a tropical climate, and its associated diseases, would be considered dangerous.

However, large-scale international tourism had to wait for the introduction of regular scheduled air carriers, and from the mid-1960s onwards Sri Lanka experienced a spectacularly rapid growth in tourist arrivals and foreign exchange earned. In 1966 Sri Lanka attracted only 18,969 tourists and earned just US$1.3 million, but just five years later those numbers had more than doubled to 46,247 tourists bringing in US$3.6 million in foreign exchange (Ceylon Tourist Board, 1982: 42). By 1976 the numbers had jumped to 118,971 visitors and US$28.2 million in earnings and in 1982, 407, 230 tourists arrived (Ceylon Tourist Board, 1982). The earnings that year were US$146.6 million, making tourism the fourth largest foreign exchange earner for Sri Lanka (Ceylon Tourist Board, 1982). To augment and modernize this growing and increasingly important sector of the economy a new governing authority, the Ceylon Tourist Board, was set up, and under its jurisdiction came other entities such as the Hotels Corporation and the Ceylon Hoteliers Association. Today the Ceylon Tourist Board has been renamed the Sri Lanka Tourist Board. In 2003 Sri Lanka privatized the business of destination marketing. The new Tourism Marketing Bureau is directed and managed by members of the private sector and has a budget five times the previous tourism marketing budget. This increased budget comes from a 1% tax on total turnover from tourism businesses and an increased tourist departure tax (Ratnapala, 2003: 135).

However, the industry has still not fully recovered to the pre-war level. The peak of tourist arrivals was in 1983 and the communal riots that inflamed the island in that year and led to the outbreak of civil war between the government of Sri Lanka and minority terrorist groups such as the Liberian Tigers of Tamil Ealem (LTTE) brought about a rapid decline in tourism. In 1986, 16 people were killed in an explosion on a plane owned by Air Lanka, then the national air carrier. The Tamil Tigers were suspected but no one claimed responsibility. After a trough in 1987 tourism gradually increased again although it continued to react quickly to terrorist attacks. In 1991 the Tigers were suspected of the suicide killing of the former Indian Prime Minister Rajiv Gandhi, and two years later the Tigers assassinated Sri

Lanka's President Ranasinghe Premadasa. In 1996 hundreds were killed or wounded when a truck driven by a Tamil Tiger suicide bomber exploded in the heart of the financial district of Colombo, and in 1998 another suicide bomber devastated Sri Lanka's holiest Buddhist shrine, the Temple of the Tooth, a major tourist attraction in the city of Kandy (the southernmost city of the nation's triangle of historic sites).

A major crisis that befell the industry was the 24 July 2001 terrorist attack on the Bandaranayake International airport. This attack was particularly important as it targeted the only international airport in Sri Lanka – the only port of entry for the vast majority of tourists – and hence had a very public and immediate impact on tourist arrivals. The violence and ensuing instability turned the island into a destination only the adventurous would consider.

Ironically, prior to the 24 July terrorist attack, the tourist industry as a whole had been enjoying one of its best years since the civil war began. According to statistics from the Ceylon Tourist Board, tourist numbers for June 2001 were 28,323 or 30% higher than in the corresponding month of the previous year (Ceylon Tourist Board, 2001). Sri Lankan authorities have estimated the economic damage of the airport attack to be about US$350 million, but some analysts believe the final figure, including losses in the tourist industry, to be significantly higher. Much more damaging than the physical destruction of the airport and aircraft were the travel warnings issued by the United States and by European governments, particularly those of Great Britain and Germany, affecting the majority of potential tourists. The US State Department lifted its travel warning soon after the 11 September attacks on New York and Washington, but the other countries kept their warnings in place. Some Sri Lankan officials suggested that these travel warnings were politically motivated and were a way of forcing the government to resume the internationally mediated peace talks with the Tamil Tigers rebels. The ceasefire came into effect in 2002 and peace negotiations have been taking place intermittently at various locations in Asia and Europe. However, internal political rivalries in Sri Lanka and disputes over the distribution of aid for victims of the 2004 tsunami led to the virtual collapse of the ceasefire in 2006.

The ceasefire allowed much of the east coast and some north western coastal areas to be opened up once again to tourists. For the previous 20 years tourists had been restricted to the south of the country, including the central cultural triangle. In 2003 the number of tourists visiting Sri Lanka in August, September and October surpassed any previous year. But the industry remains very fragile with over 2000 bookings cancelled in November 2003 because of political instability and a constitutional crisis

(*Lanka Monthly Digest* (*LMD*) November 2003a: 64). Despite this the industry has a target of one million visitors annually, and had reached about half that level in 2003 (Ondaatjie, 2003: 90). However, the tsunami of 26 December 2004 damaged beach resorts in the south and east of the island and resulted in a dramatic decline in tourist arrivals. Ondaatjie suggests that once the one million tourist goal is reached then Sri Lanka should market its tourism industry in separate segments, such as sports, history, beaches and eco-tourism. Sri Lanka has developed a Ten Year Tourism Master Plan and expects to reach the one million tourist level by 2007 (*LMD* November, 2003a: 67). In 2001 gross earnings from tourism were US$213 million and in 2002 US$248 million, and the Tourist Board sees a possibility for tourism to become the top foreign exchange earner in the not too distant future (*LMD* November, 2003). Sri Lanka already has a relatively high average level of bed-nights at 10.5 per visitor, underlining its image as a vacation rather than a stopover destination (de Alwis, 2003: 63). And it is still seen as a place for cheap holidays with tourist daily expenditures being in the range of US$60 to $70 per day (de Alwis, 2003). Sri Lanka is currently mainly a tourist destination for cheap package holidays from Europe, but this will have to change if foreign exchange earnings are to increase significantly. The recent granting of 'Approved Destination' status with China, the world's leading consumer of tea, may help to make Sri Lanka a regional hub, encompassing South India and the Maldives (Ratnapala, 2003). This may also lead to more individual and high-spending tourists and in this development tea tourism has an important role to play.

Tea Tourism

The former Chairman of the Sri Lanka Tourist Board recently declared: 'I must say "Congratulations!" to some of the operators here, for linking tea with Sri Lanka and promoting it. But there is a lot more that can be done'(de Alwis, 2003: 63). He went on to suggest that the tea auction in Colombo (the largest in the world) could be considered as an event suitable for tourists, who would be able to enjoy it if a viewing gallery were to be provided, perhaps combined with a fine tea restaurant and a tea museum (de Alwis, 2003). At the moment, the main tea tourism activities are visits to plantations to watch the plucking and then the processing of the leaves. This is usually followed by a visit to a 'tea shoppe', typically located nearby in a renovated plantation house, where the tourist can drink tea, have a snack and purchase souvenirs (mainly small boxes of tea packed in attractive locally designed and created packaging).

New directions in tea tourism can be seen as part of the promotion of both heritage tourism and eco-tourism. They are aimed at individual or small groups of tourists more interested in learning about the country than in the '3S' tourism (or 'Sun, Sand and Sea/Sex') hitherto marketed to international tourists. For these new tourists price is less of a determinant than the unique experience offered by Sri Lanka and its tea estates. The recent privatization of Regional Plantation Companies (Fernando, 2000: 187), and of tourism marketing in Sri Lanka, is encouraging several new operators to target this market. The most prominent new actor is the Tea Factory Hotel located at Kandapola, near Nuwara Eliya, the old colonial hill station. Nuwara Eliya enjoys spring-like weather throughout the year and is dotted with English-style houses and many gardens. Today, it also is a centre for golf.

History of the Tea Factory

As interest in tea planting grew, the government sold virgin Crown land to pioneer planters in the 1870s. Among the bidders was a Mr W. Flowerdew who became the first proprietary planter of what was to become the Hethersett estate. Mr Flowerdew chose for his plantation the name Hethersett after a village in England, his homeland. In Tamil, the plantation is known as Pupanie, which, when translated into English, means 'Flowers of Frost' – a picturesque way of describing the cold mist that occasionally descends on Hethersett. By 1881 however, Flowerdew had sold the plantation, which then passed through the hands of several different owners, each of whom contributed to its development. The Hethersett tea plantation has played an important role in the development of Sri Lanka's tea industry. The Hethersett factory was the first to command the highest price in the world for silver tip tea from Ceylon. This achievement ensured that the Hethersett trademark would become synonymous with pure Ceylon tea of quality.

In the mid-1930s the top of a hill was flattened to create a plateau for a new factory, which is the hotel today. When it was first built it was regarded as a remarkable work of engineering. The factory was powered by an oil-fired engine with flywheels and pulleys to operate the large fans for withering the tea, and also the rollers and sifters. By 1968, however, the Hethersett factory had passed its heyday and it finally closed in 1973. It stood disused for almost two decades. In 1992, Mr G.C. Wickremasinghe, a director of Aitken Spence & Co. Ltd and a prominent Sri Lankan businessman, on a chance visit to Kandapola, happened to see the silhouette of the old building through the evening mist. He immediately had a vision of transforming the superbly sited factory shell into a unique, luxury 'theme' hotel. Now restored, the Hethersett tea factory is poised to regain its former prominence, this time not for its tea but as a successful and innovative hotel. The hotel has 57 rooms and has retained many of the features of the old factory. The old pine floors were sanded to bring out their natural lustre, and the original brass screws were removed and polished before being put back into the floorboards. The withering lofts became the guest rooms spread over five floors. The central atrium was left open, with the two large withering fans still in place on its walls. These are the very same fans that drew hot air from the dryers and distributed it to the lofts. The lobby, bar and restaurant all lead off this atrium, and the restaurant buffet table is supported by old tea chests, now anchored to the floor. The tea bushes are only a few steps from the hotel door and panoramic views over the rolling hills are visible in all directions. The search for 'authenticity' in tourist attractions has encouraged this elaborate form of preservation and presentation.

Innovation continues at the Tea Factory. In November 2003 the Tea Factory established a new restaurant, at 6800 feet (2073 metres) above sea level, the highest restaurant in the country. This restaurant is in an old railway carriage. Guests are welcomed aboard the 'train' by its 'guard' with a shrill whistle and a cheery 'All aboard!'. Once aboard authenticity is reinforced by locomotive acoustics and movement. The hotel also opened a new spa facility in November 2003 'for the discerning traveler' (*LMD*, November 2003b).

The Tea Factory Hotel is unique in Sri Lanka where the hotel industry is generally old-fashioned and finds it difficult to attract high quality staff (Miththapala, 2003). As such the Tea Factory has attracted a plethora of international awards. In 1996 the architect of the hotel, Nihal Bodhinayake, received a commendation in the South Asia Architecture Awards for his conversion of the old tea factory. In 1998 the Tea Factory Hotel was awarded the title of 'Most Innovative Product' marketed at the Travel and Tourism Fair in Ahamadebad, India. In 2000 the Tea Factory was given an award by the Royal Institute of Chartered Surveyors in London for technical ingenuity in the field of conservation and enhancement of the natural and built environment. Finally the Tea Factory received one of five merit awards from the UNESCO Regional Advisor for Culture in Asia and the Pacific in 2001. This award recognized the impressive conversion of an old factory into a luxury hotel complex, demonstrating a challenging adaptive reuse project. It was seen as contributing to the cultural and historical continuum of the community. Information in this section has been taken from the hotel's web site (http://aitkenspenceholidays.com/teafactory/index.htm)

The Tea Factory is clearly providing a highly visible and well-marketed symbol of tea tourism but it is not the only aspect of this form of tourism available in Sri Lanka. The Tea Factory is owned by one of the three largest travel and tour operators in Sri Lanka and this company is responsible for over half the tourist business in the country. It is vertically integrated, and backward and forward local linkages are minimal. Other tea tourism groups are much smaller but may have a wider impact on local communities.

The Woodlands Network, a women's group in Bandarawela, coined the term 'tea tourism' several years ago. For a long time they were ignored by the tourism industry but have now started a community tea tourism project. This involves the Greenfield tea plantation at Haputale in the southern part of the highland tea region, which has made tea tourism a central part of its diversification project. The estate lies at over 5000 feet (1500 metres) and is included on the International Fairtrade Tea Register. It now grows only organic tea, and the estate is inspected annually by British, Dutch and Australian Organic Growers organizations. It has been found that organic tea has about half the caffeine content of conventionally grown tea. The factory has been rebuilt and tea nurseries established to help replant the estate tea land. The estate has also developed flower gardens, vegetable plots and a visitor centre; and tourist cottages and a restaurant will soon be constructed. The local community has decided to offer cultural performances, indigenous health care (*Ayurveda*) and an introduction to Sri Lankan food. Staff are recruited from the estate's Tamil workers and a training programme has been started. A share of the profits from the sale of tea is directed to the Social Committee, which is responsible for deciding how funds are used for improving facilities on the estate. It is hoped that this new project will increase the self-esteem of the workers and contribute to their self-empowerment (http://www.uvanetwork.lk/). Other community-based tourism projects are being promoted in the same area and include guest houses and other developments. These projects are seen as being 'pro-poor', as they are aimed at returning profits to the local community.

Eco-tourism is also being linked to tea tourism. The Sinharaja World Heritage Site is the last great lowland Gondwanan rainforest in Sri Lanka and contains the richest store of biodiversity in the country (Sri Lanka Tourism Cluster, 2002). Much of the area around the World Heritage Site is covered by abandoned tea plantations, so the plan is to convert the estates to organic tea cultivation. An 'eco-lodge' with 20 rooms, 11 tree houses and 9 chalets at ground level is planned and a Visitor Centre, craft displays, nature trails and a canopy walkway will be developed (Sri Lanka Tourism Cluster, 2002). Guests will be introduced to the history of tea production and food served to visitors will be organic. This project is being organized by the Sri Lanka Tourism Cluster, made up of both private and public groups including the Sri Lanka Tourist Board, Sri Lankan Airlines, the Tourist Hotels Association of Sri Lanka, the Travel Agents Association of Sri Lanka and the Sri Lanka Association of Inbound Tour Operators (Sri Lanka Tourism Cluster, 2002).

Tea tourism has aspects of heritage tourism, eco-tourism, health tourism and rural and farm tourism in Sri Lanka. It can be both high-end and exclusive or community-based and 'pro-poor'. Its leaders include both private and public entities and also community-based groups. One particular aspect associated with it is food tourism. Many areas emphasize organic foods, Sri Lankan cuisine, and use of traditional or *Ayurvedic* healing. In marketing to tourists Sri Lanka is developing a growing interest in specialist teas. Not only green (started in 1981) and black teas, highland and lowland, organic and non-organic, but also flavoured teas. Tea bags, instant tea and ready-to-drink (RTD) teas are also manufactured in Sri Lanka (Fernando, 2000). Exporters can provide customized and specialized services to the upper end of the tea market, as well as consumer products designed for both the premium end of the volume market and the gift and souvenir market. The use of indigenous raw materials and traditional design coupled with the skills and services available in Sri Lanka has led to a rapid growth in value-added tea exports. These specialized products now account for over half of the total tea exports (Fernando, 2000: 180). Thus Sri Lanka's tea producers are well prepared to work with the tourism industry by introducing visitors to the range of teas and the attractive and cheap tea souvenirs available. By bringing the consumer to the market as a tourist, the food supply chain is reduced and foreign exchange earnings are maximized.

Conclusion

Indeed the tea industry has already set a target of increasing exports of tea from the present US$730 million, or 14.3 per cent of total exports, to over US$1 billion (*LMD*, 2003b). It plans to reduce the production of inferior teas. The tea industry also sees that one of the ways of rebuilding the tea industry is by enhancing its links with tourism. Diversification into fruit and vegetable production for tourist consumption, eco-tourism and the development of 20 state-run bungalows to attract tourists to the tea estates will be immediate outcomes of these initiatives (*LMD*, 2003). Thus, as in other tropical plantation economies, tourism and agriculture can cooperate to the benefit of both.

The subtleties of Ceylon tea and its various niche products are not well known outside Sri Lanka. Attracting tourists on tea-oriented tours will change this. Such visits should include a range of activities such as visits to tea estates, tea factories, tea museums and tea tasting (Jolliffe, 2003). The tea exchange in Colombo may provide a unique tea-related experience for tourists. The most high profile symbol of tea tourism in Sri Lanka today is the luxury hotel known as the Tea Factory Hotel, however, this hotel has few real links with the contemporary tea industry that can be appreciated by guests. Smaller-scale efforts in eco-tourism and community-based projects may be more effective in linking tourism and the tea industry and in providing economic benefits to a wider group of local stakeholders. In post-tsunami Sri Lanka, the location of the tea plantations in the 'misty mountains' rather than along the damaged coastal areas, should give a new impetus to tea tourism on the island, as it fills the gap left by the previously most common beach-based 'sun, sea and sand' type of tourism.

References

de Alwis, R. (2003) The business of selling dreams. *LMD*, October: 63.
Boyd, W. (1888a) Autobiography of a periya durai. *Ceylon Literary Register* 3.
Boyd, W. (1888b) Ceylon and its pioneers. *Ceylon Literary Register* 2.
Buck, William (ed.) (1978) *Ramayana. King Rama's Way*. New York: A Mentor Book.
Ceylon Tourist Board (1982) *Annual Statistical Report, 1982*, Colombo: Research and International Affairs Division, Ceylon Tourist Board.
Ceylon Tourist Board (2001) *Monthly Statistical Bulletin on Tourism, June*, Colombo, Sri Lanka.
Duncan, James (2005) Home alone? Masculinity, discipline and erasure in mid-nineteenth century Ceylon. In L. Dowling *et al.* (eds) *Gender and Landscape* (pp. 19–33). London and New York: Routledge.
Fernando, Maxwell (2000) *The Story of Ceylon Tea*. Sri Lanka: Mlesna (Ceylon) Ltd.
Jolliffe, L. (2003) The lure of tea: History, traditions and attractions. In C. Michael Hall, Liz Sharples, Richard Mitchell, Niki Macionis and Brock Cambourne (eds) *Food Tourism Around the World: Development, Management and Markets* (pp. 121–36). San Francisco: Butterworth Heinemann.
LMD (2003a) Tourism. November: 67.
LMD (2003b) A train of thought. November: 134.
Marsden, W. (ed.) (1987) *The Travels of Marco Polo*. New York: Dorsett Press.
Millie, P.D. (1878) *Thirty Years Ago: Or Reminiscences of the Early Days of Coffee Planting in Ceylon* (reprinted from the *Colonial Observer*). Colombo: A.M. and J. Ferguson.
Miththapala, S. (2003) Hospitality's human factor. *LMD*, November: 95.
Ondaatjie, G. (2003) The changing face of Sri Lanka's tourism industry. *LMD*, December: 90.
Ratnapala, Lakshman (2003) Tourism by numbers. *LMD*, November: 134–5.

Rettie, Clare (1929) *Things Seen in Ceylon. The Description of a Beautiful Island and the Novel and Interesting Town and Country Life of its People* (reprinted 2002). London: Seeley, Service & Co. New Delhi and Madras: Asian Educational Services.

Sri Lanka Tourism Cluster (2002) Ecolodge Initiative. Unpublished paper, November, Colombo.

Tea Factory. Online document: http://www.aitkenspenceholidays.com/teafactory/index.htm (accessed 6 March 2004).

Woodlands Network. Online document: http://www.uvanetwork.lk/ (accessed 6 March 2004).

Chapter 7

The New Tea Appreciation Festival: Marketing and Socio-economic Development in Hunan Province, China

RONG HUANG AND DEREK HALL

This chapter examines the nature and regional context of tea festivals developed in the central Chinese province of Hunan from the later 1990s. Diversity and quality of tea production is an important element in the economic development of rural Hunan, and the region's tea culture has a rich history. Responding to the increasing pressures of tourism, annual (springtime) 'new tea appreciation' festivals, lasting up to two weeks, have been developed by a number of hotels and tea rooms, notably in the provincial capital city, Changsha.

Drawing on original primary sources collected from Hunan, and from secondary data, the chapter goes on to critically evaluate the major ways in which the festival can be employed as a vehicle for projecting a gastronomically-related tourism identity for the region and for enhancing the sustainable development of its rural economy.

In conclusion, the potential of and implications for Changsha's 'new tea appreciation' festivals as a model of tourism development and marketing for other tea-growing regions are addressed.

The Regional Context

Located in the south-central part of the Chinese mainland, Hunan has long been known for its natural beauty. The province is surrounded by mountains on the east, west and south, and by the middle reaches of the Yangtze River to the north. 'Hunan' means south of the lake, and is derived from the fact that the province is located south of Dongting Lake, the second largest freshwater body in China. The province's colloquial name 'Xiang' is taken from the river of that name which flows south to north across it (CNTA, 2004b). Many overseas Chinese in particular are attracted by the unequalled beauty found in Hunan's Zhangjiajie national forest park (Deng *et al.*, 2003; Wu et al., 1992) and the Heng mountains. The Wulingyuan Scenic and Historic Interest Area World Heritage Site embraces these (SINO-CS, 2000; UNESCO, 2001). Some 400 km from Changsha, this area was designated a World Heritage Site in 1992; it is a spectacular natural area extending over some 26,400 hectares (with a 12,680 hextare buffer zone) in north western Hunan. It contains over 3000 quartzite sandstone pillars and peaks, separated by ravines and gorges with streams, pools and water-falls, some 40 caves, and 2 large natural bridges. The region is also home to a number of endangered plant and animal species (UNESCO, 2001; WCMC, 2001).

Within the province as a whole, there are 25 national and provincial scenic resorts, 22 nature reserves of provincial or national importance, and a large number of sites of cultural importance. Hunan is also the home province of Mao Zedong, founder of the People's Republic, and his birthplace at Shaoshan, 104 km west of Changsha, has long been an important visitor centre.

With a total area of 211,800 sq km, a recorded history of over 3000 years and a population of 65 million, Hunan is home to 42 nationalities, with the Tujia, Miao, Yso, Dong, Bai, Hui and Zhuang being the most important ethnic groups. This ethnic complexity acts as an attraction for visitors. Arts and crafts are also important: for example, Xiang embroidery represents one of the four major schools of Chinese embroidery. Hunan has long been regarded as 'a land of fish and rice', as well as a major province for the cultivation of tea, oranges and other fruits (see, for example, Tian & Tan, 2002; Wang & Zhong, 2003).

The Tea Context

Tea is grown widely throughout southeastern China, encompassing some 18 provinces. Since ancient times, the best teas have come from mountainous regions. The methods of tea production practised elsewhere in the world derive largely from the 5000-year Chinese experience. But now much Chinese equipment has become antiquated, while growing is often still done on a small scale by local cooperatives. The mechanisms for buying and selling are largely state-run, although this situation has been changing in recent years, and many private-enterprise organizations are now involved in the export of tea. They are becoming more responsive to market forces and are helping to produce teas that are adapted to the needs of the wider world market.

Tea is purchased through direct negotiation between international tea buyers and individual Chinese export companies. These companies purchase directly from cooperatives, then pre-blend into standard tea types ready for sale to the international market. All Chinese tea is processed at state-controlled tea plants, although the two stages of processing are undertaken at separate locations. During the first stage, the raw leaves are turned into green or black tea. At the second stage, the processed leaves are graded by hand. Trade is facilitated by a twice-yearly (April and October) export commodities fair, held in the city of Guangzhou in the southern province of Guangdong.

The three main types of tea are green, *oolong* and black. The chief difference between these is in the extent of the oxidation process. Green tea is processed for the shortest length of time and black the longest. China also produces several other types of tea: scented teas, which incorporate other plants to enhance the flavour and aroma; compressed teas, which are pressed into solid blocks; white teas, which have a silvery appearance; and *puer* tea, which is sold for its medicinal qualities (Twining & Co., 2001b).

The medicinal and health properties of tea are, of course, somewhat contested. Epidemiological studies suggest an inverse association of tea consumption with cardiovascular disease. The antioxidant effects of flavonoids in tea, including preventing oxidative damage to low-density lipoprotein, are among the potential mechanisms that could underlie the antioxidant and anti-carcinogenic protective effects (Kris-Etherton & Keen, 2002; de Mejía, 2003).

However, examinations of the relationship between tea and cardio-vascular disease have produced mixed research results. Peters *et al.* (2001) found substantial differences according to geographical region. With increasing tea consumption, the risk of coronary heart disease in the UK and for stroke in Australia was actually found to increase, whereas the risk decreased in other regions, particularly continental Europe. Drawing on a large sample from Saudi Arabia, Hakim *et al.* (2003) found a potential protective effect of (black) tea consumption in relation to coronary heart disease, while in North America, Sesso *et al.* (2003) found (black) tea consumption to be not strongly associated with a reduced risk of cardiovascular disease.

Further, epidemiological studies have not yielded clear conclusions concerning the protective effects of tea consumption against cancer formation in humans. Yang *et al.* (2002), for example, suggest that tea may be only effective against specific types of cancer caused by certain aetiological factors. A Japanese study (Nagano *et al.*, 2001) concluded that it could not find evidence that regular green tea consumption is related to reduced cancer risks, although an Indian study (Malik *et al.*, 2003) suggested that the polyphenols in green tea had a greater potential chemo-preventive effect on various types of cancers (such as those of the bladder, prostate, oesophagus and stomach) than did black tea.

Separate studies suggest a positive relationship between (green) tea consumption and reduction of risk for breast (Sartippour *et al.*, 2002; Wu *et al.*, 2003) and prostate (Jian *et al.*, 2004) cancer. But for the tea consumption effects on colon (Cerhan *et al.*, 2001; Su & Arab, 2002) and rectal (Cerhan *et al.*, 2001; Il'yasova *et al.*, 2003; Terry & Wolk, 2001; Woolcott *et al.*, 2002) cancer, research results are mixed; for stomach cancer (Hoshiyama *et al.*, 2002, 2004) they appear inconclusive. However, a positive relationship between tea consumption and bone mineral density (Wu *et al.*, 2002; Yang *et al.*, 2002) and percentage body fat (Wu *et al.*, 2003) is suggested, although most studies conclude that further investigation is required. The potential health benefits of tea, although contested, do add another aspect to the potential appeal of tea-related tourism.

Tea in Hunan

Hunan is located within the major tea-production region of China, and experiences a subtropical humid monsoon climate, which is eminently suitable for the growing of high-quality leaves. As a consequence, Hunan has a long history of tea cultivation, mainly producing flower tea, green tea, black tea and yellow tea. Different locations in Hunan Province are famous for different types of tea and their famous brands. For example, one famous Jasmine flower brand is Monkey King Jasmine tea; Taohuayuan tea king is one of the best green teas in China; and Gunshan Yinjian is a typical example of yellow tea. The tea companies, most of which are still state-run, have their own directly managed estates from which they cultivate tea for retailing and export. In suburban and rural areas, some families also have tea bushes for their own consumption.

Although Hunan is a significant tea exporter, there is considerable potential for growth. In 2001, the total area under tea cultivation in Hunan was 77,000 hectares, producing 610,000 tonnes of tea leaves, the seventh largest province output in China. The production of tea from these leaves generated 5.72 billion yuan (US$68 million). Compared to 2000, this represented a revenue increase of 23%. In Hunan a wide range of tea types are grown, including flower tea, green tea and red tea, which are popular in the international market (Lu, 2002). But per capita average consumption of tea in Hunan is not high (Xiao, 2002).

Although tea leaves can be collected in different seasons, those picked in spring, and especially before *Qingmin* and *Guyu* (two of the 24 Chinese solar periods in springtime) are considered particularly fine, and usually command higher prices as a result.

Almost every aspect of the growing and production of traditional teas is closely controlled. During the early era of communism, and especially during the Cultural Revolution (1966–76), tea drinking was regarded as bourgeois and many tea houses (the Chinese name translates literally as 'tea-art house') were closed down. These have now reopened: visitors sit on cushions at low tables to drink fine quality teas, which are brewed in tiny, satsuma-sized teapots, then poured into even smaller cups. The teapot may be infused three or four times.

In the tea house, consumption is about *appreciating* tea for its flavour, aroma and appearance, rather than the quenching of thirst. But this is a social occasion, albeit without formal dress, at which small snacks, such as preserved fruits or melon seeds, accompany the tea (Twining & Co., 2001a). Significantly, the Chinese tea ceremony focuses on the tea itself, rather than the ritual (as is the case in Japan). It is considered to be a means of keeping the mind in balance. The simple yet harmonious ceremony is intended to promote friendship, and the spirit of the tea ceremony is encapsulated in four qualities: clarity, respect, joy and truth (FML Tea Trading Co., 2004). It is these qualities which the new tea leaves appreciation festivals have tried to adopt and incorporate into an otherwise commercial venture.

This chapter briefly examines and evaluates a small sample of such festivals in Hunan Province, through observation and interviews with stakeholders and participants. In the light of this empirical evidence, it further reflects on the contention that tourism has the potential to enhance the brand image and marketing of tea-producing destinations (Jolliffe, 2003).

Tourism in Hunan

As noted above, Hunan is well endowed with cultural and natural resources. Yet although niche product development and marketing is advancing in the province, thus far tea tourism has been barely considered. Indeed, tea festivals are not included in the China National Tourism Administration's directory of the country's 13 major spring festivals (CNTA, 2004a). But tourism in Hunan is a relatively new phenomenon. Only since 1978 has it been developed as a mass industry and received any priority from government (Qu, 1999; Huang, 2004). Following introduction of the 'open-door' national economic reform policy by Deng Xiao-ping in that year, tourism in Hunan developed rapidly to become a significant contributor to the economic development of the province. In 2001, visitor arrivals totalled 51.5 million, of which 500,000 were from overseas; tourism receipts reached 21 billion yuan (US\$ 2.625 billion) (CNTA, 2003). At the same time, the context for tourism development has changed from a pre-eminently centralized, directed, political instrument to a relatively unfettered element of a commercial enterprise culture (Uysal *et al.*, 1986: 113).

In the first ten years of economic reform, foreign revenue was badly needed and the Chinese government made concerted efforts to attract international tourists (Zhang, 1995). By contrast, little attention was paid to the development of domestic tourism. Despite these circumstances, domestic tourism increased rapidly because of the fast growing economy and marked improvement in living standards. In addition, the Chinese nation has an age-old tradition of travel, based on the premise of expanding one's knowledge, raising one's understanding of the world and society, enhancing self-cultivation, making friends and conducting cultural exchanges (Zhang, 1987). Thus, by the mid-1990s a government official was able to acknowledge that 'domestic tourism should now be the foundation of China tourism' (Liu, 1995: 14).

Prior to 1992, foreign investment was only allowed in the hotel sector, but with a more open economic reform policy, restrictions on travel agencies and aviation operators were lifted in that year, since when Hunan's tourism has gradually geared itself to the free market economy environment. At the turn of the century, the province had 186 hotels, 167 travel agencies and 3 airports (HNTA, 1985–98). By this time, Hunan's tourism development growth rate was above the national average, and the province had become one of the country's top ten for tourism development growth (Qu, 1999). Hunan has thus become an important driver in the WTO's forecast that China will become the most visited tourism destination and the fourth ranked tourist-generating country in the world by 2020 (WTO, 1997).

But there is an urgent need for the province to improve research and development, particularly market research and new product development, and this is expressed in the tea-appreciation festivals. For Hunan, this is a significant challenge, partly because of limited financial resources and available expertise (Qu, 1999). During the past 20 years of rapid growth, no large-scale research project has been undertaken or commissioned by the provincial tourist board or any travel business in Hunan on any of the province's major overseas markets: Hong Kong, Taiwan, Macao and other

Southeast Asian countries. This is particularly crucial as Hunan is less accessible to these markets than are China's coastal provinces. Europeans and North Americans are infrequent visitors except as business travellers. This suggests the need for collaboration and coordination with other provinces of Central China to build partnerships in developing both domestic and international specialist tourist markets.

Thus the context for tea tourism development in Hunan Province faces a number of challenges but nonetheless has considerable potential. Growing tourism demand (both domestic and international), abundant natural and labour resources, and a developing infrastructure, all point to opportunities for the development of various niche tourism activities. Further, as an indigenous activity, tea tourism and tea festivals in particular, would appear to be a highly appropriate vehicle for the consolidation of domestic tourism, while enhancing the range of attractions for overseas markets.

Further, emphasis on the claimed health and medicinal benefits of tea consumption, and on linkages with the Hunan rural economy and those employed in the tea-picking and production sectors, can enhance the contribution of tea tourism to the sustainable development of the province as a tea-producing destination. The interrelationships between tourism, tea and the regional economy have the potential to assist: diversification of tourism products and marketing; the creation of added value for agriculture; the raising of quality of food and drink; the improvement of diet and health awareness; the promotion of regional image and identity; and thus the embedding of tourism within the regional economy.

The Nature and Evolution of Tea-Appreciation Festivals

In Changsha, six 4- or 5-star hotels and a number of tea houses (which exist in most towns and cities) now hold a new tea appreciation festival in springtime. Two hotels – the Tongchen and Haitian – were selected for interview with their management since they have the longest experience (from 1996) of organizing and presenting such an event. There appears to be little literature on the role and nature of tea festivals across China as a whole, although every year tea leaf products are presented as part of food and beverage exhibitions in big cities, particularly in the south of the country adjacent to the major tea-producing areas, such as Guangzhou and Shanghai.

Although tea drinking is a part of Chinese daily life, somewhat ironically, removal of ideological constraints on some aspects of tea consumption has been superseded, since the economic reforms started, by the adoption of

Western lifestyles perceived as fashionable. As part of this change, tea drinking lost favour, particularly among young people, while coffee and manufactured, branded soft drinks became popular. However, by the end of the 1990s, people started to emphasize tea drinking again, not least because of its perceived health benefits. The business prospects of tea performance companies – who provide services in tea houses, restaurants and hotels – have improved since that time as the result of customers demanding a higher standard of service in tea houses.

The motivation for holding new tea-appreciation festivals derives from the fact that in China living standards are rising, often rapidly, and many people are now paying greater attention to the attributes of a healthy lifestyle. Tea drinking is perceived as being able to contribute to such a lifestyle (Xiao, 2002), and is re-emerging almost as a fashion accessory for new, relatively young, urban elites. Embracing this fashion trend, a number of hotels now participate in new tea-appreciation festivals to enhance their image and hence attract more (higher-paying) customers.

The tea-leaf sales companies actually involved in the new tea-leaf-appreciation festivals are mainly companies set up by tea farmers or tea-house owners. Although the 'experience' economy (see, for example, Pine & Gilmore, 1998) is only gradually emerging in China, the employment of traditional sales techniques alone is now often insufficient for tea sales companies. Consumers demand both a higher quality of product and also supplementary services and experiences. Tea sales companies have taken advantage of the general trend back to emphasizing traditional Chinese culture and lifestyle after a flirtation with Western popular culture and fashions for almost two decades. As part of this change, they have established partnerships with various hotels to attract potential customers to increase sales.

In Hunan, from the later 1990s, tea drinking became popular again for both the old and the young, and tea 'culture' companies, mainly emphasizing the tea ceremony and its history were reborn. Some higher-grade hotels (mostly 4- or 5-star) began cooperating with these companies to organize 'new tea-appreciation' festivals in their ground floor areas, accessible to the general public. The customers for the festivals are mainly well-paid working-class or middle-class people, mostly from within Hunan.

Festival activities involve the consumption of tea made with newly picked leaves, traditional methods of tea making and drinking, accompanied by traditional Chinese music and musical instrument performances, and tea knowledge competitions. The partners involved in holding and promoting such a festival include a tea-making performance company, which provides tea performance personnel, a tea sales company which provides the new tea leaves, and hotels which provide festival space and overall management.

Survey

In order to inform an evaluation of the new tea-leaf-appreciation festivals in Hunan, a series of semi-structured interviews were conducted during the summer of 2003. The interviewees included five sets of stakeholders:

- representatives from two each of:
  - hotels in Changsha – the Tongchen and Haitian hotels – which host the new tea-appreciation festivals;
  - combined tea production and sales enterprises;
  - tea-leaf sales companies;
- together with
  - one provincial agricultural officer, as the government officer in charge of Hunan tea industry development; and
  - 25 festival customers interviewed during participation in the festivals at the two hotels noted above.

Hotels' perspective

The Tongchen International Hotel, opened in 1998, is the biggest luxury (5-star) hotel in Hunan and is managed by a foreign management company. It is 30 minutes drive from Changsha's Huanghua Airport, and only five minutes away from the city's central railway station. By way of contrast, the Haitian Hotel is owned by Hunan Province armed police and general fire brigade, and is of 4-star standard. It is located in a technology park, Wangchengpo, close to the city bus station and 4 km from the city's government quarter.

Management representatives of the Tongchen and Haitian hotels both reported that they had received positive responses to the festivals from their residential guests who mainly praised the hotels for promoting a healthy Chinese lifestyle (assumed to be implicit in tea consumption). Members of the general public who came into the hotels in a non-residential capacity for the tea-drinking festival were, however, the main customers for this event, rather than the hotel residents themselves. Although all expressed enjoyment with drinking good quality tea, and with Chinese traditional tea-making and drinking performances, some complained that tea drinking was more expensive here than in tea houses.

According to the hotels' managements, every year their new tea-leaf-appreciation festivals attract around a thousand participating customers each. But of these, only about 20% actually purchase the new tea leaves after tasting them. The two hotels reported that they derived profits from the event, but that the festival appeared insufficient as an attraction – perhaps because of geographically limited promotion – to attract extra staying guests.

There appear to be two critical issues for raising added value for the festivals and their hosts. First, much wider and targeted promotion is necessary. Notably, the hotels and tea houses involved in staging the festival appear not to involve travel agencies or to seek a wider collaboration with the tourism industry in support of these events. But second, this needs to be tied to a wider context in which the festival is linked to a range of other local and regional attractions that will encourage guests both to stay, in the first place, and then to stay for longer. Issues of cooperation and networking at a number of levels – within Changsha, within Hunan and between Hunan and neighbouring provinces – need to be explored in some detail. Linkages with the tea industry itself and the promotion of Hunan as a tea-producing destination could focus attention on the nature and conditions of tea picking and the province's tea landscapes with a view to enhancing their contribution to sustainable development.

Further, greater added value could be derived by more closely associating the festival with Hunan cuisine. There are claimed to be more than 4000 Hunanese dishes, a regional gastronomy which belongs to one of eight major culinary schools in China. Hunan cuisine is noted for its sourness, pungency and aroma. Although festival promoters would not want to lessen the role of tea, a supplementary role of wider gastronomy within the festivals would certainly help to add value and perhaps broaden appeal to those not immediately attracted by tea alone.

Tea production and export enterprises' perspective

Representatives from the two, currently state-owned, enterprises that are the main tea companies in Hunan, dealing with tea planting, processing, sales and foreign trade, were interviewed. The Hunan Tea General Corporation of China (HTGCC) has an annual sales volume of 35,000 tons, representing around 70% of tea sales volume in the province. The Corporation has eight business branches, nine self-owned tea-processing plants, two holding companies and a research centre for organic food. It additionally has eight domestic branch offices and four foreign trading branches (HTGCC, 2003). The company produces over 20% of all black tea exported from China. The second company, Hunan Tea Import and Export Corporation, is mainly involved in the export business.

Neither tea company has joined a new tea-appreciation festival because both considered that this type of festival could not help them with large volume sales. They do participate annually in tea-leaf and tea-products exhibitions nationally and internationally in order to promote their companies and to increase their sales. Both reported that their main markets were international rather than domestic, and the HTGCC in particular considered its domestic market to be China as a whole: the province of Hunan was not a focus market.

During the interviews, both companies' representatives reported that their enterprises' management systems were in a transition stage. Both had been state-owned and were now seeking to become stock companies. Therefore, the enterprises' top management teams were undergoing change. This was still the position by mid-2004. Possibly after transition they would have new strategies on promoting sales, which might incorporate participation in tea-appreciation festivals.

Tea-leaf sales companies' perspective

Of the two companies interviewed, one was a tea performance company – Yi Qin Yuan Tea Room – which is a part of the Hunan provincial Yi Qin Yuan Tea Limited Company. It is the first private company in the province to embrace tea production, sales and research. The company has organized several courses for tea culture and tea cooking performance. The second organization interviewed was a typical small private tea house in Changsha.

Although tea sales companies made profits from tea-making and drinking performances, they claimed that these were minimal compared to tea-leaf and tea-product sales, although they were unwilling to provide specific data on these. They pointed to a lack of active promotion, particularly in the media, both before and during the events, as a major shortcoming needing to be rectified.

The provincial agricultural officer's perspective

During the interview with the provincial agricultural officer responsible for the Hunan tea industry, it was indicated that the provincial government has not supported this kind of event. It has only led and organized the main tea companies in Hunan to attend national or international tea products exhibitions. The province has not realized the importance of this kind of event. The government's main emphasis has been on developing international markets for export, so it has not paid much attention to the domestic market, either from the tea consumption or tourism dimensions.

As the officer admitted, in Hunan the tea leaves used both at such festivals and domestically were mostly sourced from other provinces rather than from Hunan itself. Under these circumstances, Hunan tea companies should reappraise their marketing strategies and degree of involvement in such local and regional initiatives.

Customers' perspectives

As indicated in Table 7.1, customers attended the festivals for a range of reasons, although, unsurprisingly, the most important were related to appreciating tea, tradition and a relaxing atmosphere. That almost two-thirds gained knowledge of the festivals by word of mouth indicates the potential that exists for the development of more sustained promotion and marketing efforts. That a further fifth were informed through hotel window promotion posters emphasizes the relatively localized nature of participation and the need to broaden the geographical scope of promotion. With two hours as a median length of time for customers' attendance, there is some potential for adding value during this time to the relatively low spending level of customers, who appear largely to be of an age and occupational position that might suggest the availability of further disposable income.

Evaluation and Conclusions

In this relatively early stage in the evolution of the tea-appreciation festivals, there is clearly a great deal of potential for enhancing the local and regional economy, promoting image and identity, and generating a sense of cultural continuity and integrity in a period of rapid change. But to achieve these goals, a number of organizational enhancements need to be implemented.

First, much wider and informed promotion is necessary. National and international markets need to be evaluated and targeted. Local and regional stakeholders – hotels, tea companies at all levels, tourism agencies, city and provincial authorities – need to be involved in the projecting of a positive and consistent marketing and promotion message and image consonant with Hunan being a 'tea destination'.

Second, such promotion needs to be tied to a wider context in which the festivals are linked to a range of other complementary local and regional attractions – such as nature tourism (e.g. Liu *et al.*, 2003; Nianyong & Zhuge, 2001; Zhu *et al.*, 1996) – that will encourage guests to: (a) stay in the festival

Table 7.1 Summary responses to questions put to festival customers

Question	Summary responses	
Why did you come to this festival?	Appreciation of tea drinking	56%
	Appreciation of tradition	36%
	To relax with friends and/or family	36%
	Good environment for business discussion	24%
	Accompanying tourists 8%	
How did you know about this festival?	By word of mouth	60%
	From the newspaper (20%)	
	Hotel window promotion poster (20%)	
Normally when do you come to the festival, morning, lunch time or evening time?	Most came in the:	
	evening	64%
	afternoon	32%
How long are you staying?	Mostly between one and three hours, with 2 hours cited by 64%	
How much have you spent at this festival?	Usually between 100 and 500 yuan	
How do you evaluate this festival?	A wide range of comments: Positively: good quality tea, interesting performances Negatively: needed better information and promotion, organization could be tighter, noisy at lunchtime, background music was not always traditional Chinese	
Age of interviewees	All between 23 and 50 years of age:	
	20 to 29	28%
	30 to 39	52%
	40 to 49	16%
	50+ :	4%
Gender of interviewees	Female	48%
	Male	52%

hotels and other local accommodation; (b) extend their stay, both temporally and geographically; and (c) return for further visits.

Third, tea tourism can assist the province's sustainable development by emphasizing stronger linkages with the regional tea economy and through promoting tea-production landscapes as attractions and to enhance the conditions of those involved in tea-growing and picking activities.

Fourth, greater added value can be derived by more closely associating the festivals with Hunan cuisine and the projection of regional identity through gastronomy. This in its turn can build on the claimed health ar medicinal properties of tea consumption to emphasize a healthy lifestyl through both drinking tea and eating healthy, fresh local and regional produce with a guaranteed quality.

Issues of cooperation and networking at a number of levels – within Changsha, within Hunan, and between Hunan and neighbouring provinces – clearly need to be explored much more vigorously. Local partnerships among festival, tea-industry and tourism-industry stakeholders are essential for strong promotion and identity projection, while interprovincial collaboration between China's tea-growing regions can help attract national and international tourists (and especially overseas Chinese) otherwise attracted to the country's coastal regions.

By better enhancing the linkages between tea festivals, their comple-mentary services and attractions, and the regional rural economy, the embeddedness of tourism, healthy lifestyles and tea imagery can add both sustainable economic value and identity value to Hunan Province as a tea-tourism destination.

It is, perhaps, premature to consider Changsha's new tea-appreciation festivals as a model of tourism development and marketing for other tea-growing regions. Shortcomings in promotion, in recognition of the potential of added value and in collaboration need to be overcome, requiring substantial action. Much greater investment in market research is required by the stakeholders. Nonetheless, these festivals clearly hold the potential for enhancing urban and regional economies, for sustaining a growing niche tourism industry in Hunan, for encouraging collaboration and partnership, and for projecting a regional image based upon positive attributes of a healthy lifestyle. which can be placed alongside other regional attractions such as spectacular natural environments, cultural distinctiveness and ethnic heterogeneity. Thus tea, and tea-appreciation festivals, need to be viewed as two of a range of interlinked local and regional resources employed for the sustainable economic, social and environmental enhancement of Hunan through the careful and balanced development of domestic and international tourism.

References

Cerhan, J.R., Putnam, S.D., Bianchi, G.D., Parker, A.S., Lynch, C.F. and Cantor, K.P. (2001) Tea consumption and risk of cancer of the colon and rectum. *Nutrition and Cancer* 41 (1/2), 33–40.
CNTA (China National Tourism Administration) (2003) *Fact & Figure. Hunan Summary*. Online document: http://www.cnta.gov.cn (in Chinese).

NTA (2004a) *Festivals of Season: Spring*. Online document: http://www.cnta.gov.cn/lyen/festival/season/spring.htm.

CNTA (2004b) *Hunan*. Online document: http://www.cnta.gov.cn/lyen/shen/hunan/index.htm.

Deng, J., Qiang, S., Walker, G.J. and Zhang, Y. (2003) Assessment on and perception of visitors' environmental impacts of nature tourism: A case study of Zhangjiajie national forest park, China. *Journal of Sustainable Tourism* 11 (6), 529–48.

FML Tea Trading Co. (2004) *The Spirit of Tea Ceremony*. Xiamen: FML Tea Trading Co. Online document: http://www.fmltea.com/Teainfo/spirit-cerlemony.htm [sic].

Hakim, I.A., Alsaif, M.A., Alduwaihy, M., Al-Rubeaan, K., Al-Nuaim, A.R. and Al-Attas, O.S. (2003) Tea consumption and the prevalence of coronary heart disease in Saudi adults: Results from a Saudi national study. *Preventive Medicine* 36 (1), 64–70.

HNTA (Hunan Tourism Administration) (1985–98) *Hunan Tourism Statistics*. Changsha: Hunan Tourism Administration.

Hoshiyama, Y., Kawaguchi, T., Miura, Y., Mizoue, T., Tokui, N., Yatsuya, H., Sakata, K., Kondo, T., Kikuchi, S., Toyoshima, H., Hayakawa, N., Tamakoshi, A., Ohno, Y. and Yoshimura, T. (2002) A prospective study of stomach cancer death in relation to green tea consumption in Japan. *British Journal of Cancer* 87 (3), 309–13.

Hoshiyama, Y., Kawaguchi, T., Miura, Y., Mizoue, T., Tokui, N., Yatsuya, H., Sakata, K., Kondo, T., Kikuchi, S., Toyoshima, H., Hayakawa, N., Tamakoshi, A., Ohno, Y. and Yoshimura, T. (2004) A nested case-control study of stomach cancer death in relation to green tea consumption in Japan. *British Journal of Cancer* 90 (1), 135–8.

HTGCC (Hunan Tea General Corporation of China) (2003) *Company Profile*. Changsha: Hunan Tea General Corporation of China.

Huang, R. (2004) Provincial government roles in Chinese tourism development: The case of Hunan. In D. Hall (ed.) *Tourism and Transition: Governance, Transformation and Development* (pp. 169–83). Wallingford: CABI Publishing.

Il'yasova, D., Arab, L., Martinchik, A., Sdvizhkov, A., Urbanovich, L. and Weisgerber, U. (2003) Black tea consumption and risk of rectal cancer in Moscow population. *Annals of Epidemiology* 13 (6), 405–11.

Jian, L., Xie, L-P., Lee, A.H. and Binns, C.W. (2004) Protective effect of green tea against prostate cancer: a case-control study in Southeast China. *International Journal of Cancer* 108 (1), 130–5.

Jolliffe, L. (2003) The lure of tea: History, traditions and attractions. In: C.M. Hall, L. Sharples, R. Mitchell, N. Macionis and B. Cambourne (eds) *Food Tourism Around the World: Development, Management and Markets* (pp. 121–36). Oxford: Butterworth-Heinemann.

Kris-Etherton, P.M. and Keen, C.L. (2002) Evidence that the antioxidant flavonoids in tea and cocoa are beneficial for cardiovascular health. *Current Opinion in Lipidology* 13 (1), 41–9.

Liu, C.X. (1995) Tourism administration goes macro. *Travel China*, 30 April, 14.

Liu, K.-W, Zhang, D.L. and Wang, X.-M. (2003) Hunan (China) flora with rich ornamental plants. *Acta Horticulturae* 620, 403–9.

Lu, C-Y. (2002) WTO's influence on China tea industry development. *China Tea* 24 (5), 35–8.

Malik, A., Azam, S., Hadi, N. and Hadi, S.M. (2003) DNA degradation by water extract of green tea in the presence of copper ions: Implications for anticancer properties. *Phytotherapy Research* 17 (4), 358–63.

de Mejía, E.G. (2003) El efecto quimioprotector del té y sus compuestos. *Archivos Latinoamericanos de Nutrición* 53 (2), 111–18.

Nagano, J., Kono, S., Preston, D.L. and Mabuchi, K. (2001) A prospective study of green tea consumptiom and cancer incidence, Hiroshima and Nagasaki (Japan). *Cancer Causes and Control* 12 (6), 501–8.

Nianyong, H. and Zhuge, R. (2001) Ecotourism in China's nature reserves: opportunities and challenges. *Journal of Sustainable Tourism* 9 (3), 228–42.

Peters, U., Poole, C. and Arab, L. (2001) Does tea affect cardiovascular disease? A meta-analysis. *American Journal of Epidemiology* 154 (6), 495–503.

Pine, B.J. and Gilmore, J.H. (1998) Welcome to the experience economy. *Harvard Business Review*, July–August, 97–105.

Qu, F. (1999) *Hunan Tourism Industry.* Changsha: Hunan Geography Press.

Sartippour, M.R., Heber, D., Zhang, L.P., Beatty, P., Elshoff, D., Elashoff, R., Go, V.L. and Brooks, M.N. (2002) Inhibition of fibroblast growth factors by green tea. *International Journal of Oncology* 21 (3), 487–91.

Sesso, H.D., Paffenbarger, R.S., Oguma, Y. and Lee, I.M. (2003) Lack of association between tea and cardiovascular disease in college alumni. *International Journal of Epidemiology* 32 (4), 527–33.

SINO-CS (Scottish Information Network Online for Chinese Studies) (2000) *World Heritage Sites in China. The Wulingyan Scenic Area.* Edinburgh: SINO-CS. Online document: http://www.sino-cs.ac.uk/html/Heritage/h_wly.htm.

Su, L.J. and Arab, L. (2002) Tea consumption and the reduced risk of colon cancer – results from a national prospective cohort study. *Public Health Nutrition* 5 (3), 419–25.

Terry, P. and Wolk, A. (2001) Tea consumption and the risk of colorectal cancer in Sweden. *Nutrition and Cancer* 39 (2), 176–9.

Tian, Q.-S. and Tan, S.-X. (2002) Experiment summary of early high production of Navel orange grown in the mountainous region of Hunan Province. *South China Fruits* 31 (6), 11–12.

Twining, R. and Co. (2001a) *China: Culture.* London: R. Twining and Co. Online document: http://www.twinings.com/en_int/world_of_tea/china_cult.html.

Twining, R. and Co. (2001b) *China: Production.* London: R. Twining and Co. Online document: http://www.twinings.com/en_int/world_of_tea/china_prod.asp.

UNESCO (2001) *Wulingyan Scenic and Historic Interest Area.* Paris: UNESCO. Online document: http://whc.unesco.org/sites/640.htm.

Uysal, M., Wei, L. and Reid, L.M. (1986) Development of international tourism in PR China. *Tourism Management* 7, 113–19.

Wang, Z. and Zhong, C. (2003) Kiwifruit research and commercial development in Hunan Province, China. *Acta Horticulturae* 610, 69–71.

WCMC (World Conservation Monitoring Centre) (2001) *World Heritage Sites: Protected Areas Programme.* Cambridge: WCMC. Online document: http://www.wcmc.org.uk/protected_areas/data/wh/wulingyu.html.

Woolcott, C.G., King, W.D. and Marrett, L.D. (2002) Coffee and tea consumption and cancers of the bladder, colon and rectum. *European Journal of Cancer Prevention* 11 (2), 137–45.

WTO (World Tourism Organization) (1997) *2020 Vision*. Madrid: WTO.

Wu, A.H., Yu, M.C., Tseng, C.C., Hankin, J. and Pike, M.C. (2003) Green tea and risk of breast cancer in Asian Americans. *International Journal of Cancer* 106 (4), 574–9.

Wu, C., Deng, J. and Li, S. (1992) Economic evaluation of outdoor recreation benefits in Zhangjiajie national forest park. *Scientia Silvae Sinicae* 28 (5), 423–30.

Wu, C.-H., Yang, Y.-C., Yao, W.-J., Lu, F.-H., Wu, J.-S. and Chang, C.-J. (2002) Epidemiological evidence of increased mineral density in habitual tea drinkers. *Archives of Internal Medicine* 162 (9), 1001–6.

Wu, C.-H., Lu, F.-H., Chang, C.-S., Chang, T.-C., Wang, R.-H. and Chang, C.-J. (2003) Relationship among habitual tea consumption, percent body fat, and body fat distribution. *Obesity Research* 11 (9), 1088–95 .

Xiao, J.-X. (2002) Hunan Province 2001 tea industry records. *China Tea* 24 (3), 24–5.

Yang, C.S. and Landau, J.M. (2002) Effects of tea consumption on nutrition and health. *Journal of Nutrition* 132 (12), 2409–12.

Yang, X.C.S., Maliakal, P. and Meng, X.F. (2002) Inhibition of carcinogenesis by tea. *Annual Review of Pharmacology and Toxicology* 42 (1), 25–54.

Zhang, G.R. (1987) Tourism education in PR China. *Tourism Management* 8 (3), 263–6.

Zhang, G.R. (1995) China's tourism since 1978: policies, experiences and lessons learned. In: A. Lew and L.Yu (eds) *Tourism in China: Geographic, Political, and Economic Perspectives* (pp. 3–17). Boulder, CO: Westview Press.

Zhu, J., He, Y. and Ji, W. (1996) China's nature reserves: issues and analysis. *Chinese Biodiversity* 4 (3), 175–82.

Chapter 8

Tea Culture and Tourism in Fujian Province, China: Towards a Partnership for Sustainable Development

HONGGEN XIAO

Culture is normally understood as everything that is learned, shared and transmitted among groups of human beings from generation to generation (Mennell *et al.*, 1992). By extension, 'tea culture' is a shorthand term for the ensemble of perceptions and attitudes, traditions and new practices, and appreciations and tastes that people hold or bring to the tradition and art of tea. It is therefore not surprising that a study of tea culture in relation to tourism (or tourism in relation to tea) is often associated with research that aims at explaining how tourism (or tourists as a social group) came to facilitate the development of different attitudes, practices and tastes for the art of tea.

The relationship between tea and tourism is not new. In China, due to its long and colourful history, variety, and diverse geographical locations of production, Chinese tea has been promoted internationally as one of the top eight culturally loaded souvenirs or goods for tourists (CNTA, 2004a). Many of the dimensions in the art or culture of tea have been associated with and exploited for tourism. These encompass the growing and processing of tea leaves (as in agri-tourism development that includes tea), the brewing of fine teas for a maximum extraction of flavour and aroma (as in tea ceremonies, demonstrations and festivals for tourists), the cultivation of a taste for all kinds of delightful ceramics and other tea accessories (as in the touristic purchase of tea-related souvenirs, gifts and goods), the collecting of old poems, songs and stories about tea for the enrichment of an attraction or destination, and even leisurely enjoyment, with the extraordinary brewing of *kung-fu* tea in pleasant surroundings for a short retreat from the stresses and strains of modern life.

Compared to Taoist recluses, Buddhist monks, literati (men of letters or scholar-officials in old China), and craftsmen and traders, tourists form a relatively more recent social group that has been playing a role in adding flavours to the story of tea. In a nostalgic account of the departed splendours of an ancient tea culture that lingers more often in books, tourism was seen as a potential force to revive such ancient traditions, as Blofeld noted in the case of Hangzhou:

> Already the tradition of drinking Dragon-Well Tea made with clear water from Tiger-Run Spring has returned. Among the countless visitors to Hangchow's West Lake, many climb to the spring to enjoy this memorable pleasure. (Blofeld, 1985: xii)

China is one of the earliest countries to produce tea. Among its many tea provinces, Fujian (on the southeast coast) is the home of red and *oolong* tea (partially fermented tea) such as *Da-Hong-Pao* (Great Red Robe) in Wuyishan Area and *Tie-Guan-Yin* (Iron Goddess of Mercy) in An'xi County. Over the years, tea-related resources in Fujian Province have been considerably exploited to embrace tourism, forming a partnership for a mutually sustainable development. The provincial master plan for tourism development has included 'tea culture' as one of Fujian's major cultural tourism products (FJTA, 2001: 82–5). The purpose of this chapter is to examine the development of tea and tourism (or tea-related tourism) in Fujian Province. First, this is done through a description of tea-related routes, sites and souvenirs/goods that are currently promoted to the tourist markets in this province. Two destinations are further documented where tea is regarded and promoted as a major attraction – the case of Wuyishan City and the case of An'xi County in Fujian Province. The chapter concludes with a discussion of the future scenarios that will incorporate tea into tourism development in southeast China's coastal province.

Research Data

Web-based information coupled with other secondary sources constitute the major perspective of data collection for this research, as cyberspace resources such as gophers and worldwide webs are now thought of as 'powerful and indispensable tools for social scientists' (Babbie, 1999: 421). As a governmental agency and destination marketing organization at the provincial level, Fujian Tourism Administration (FJTA) is hierarchically situated in between China National Tourism Agency (CNTA) and municipal bureaus in the vertical or top-down structure of tourism administration in China. Currently under FJTA there are nine municipal tourism bureaus representing the nine municipal administrative regions in this province. Hierarchically, FJTA and these municipal bureaus form the power network for decision- or policy-making with regard to tourism development in Fujian. The official website of FJTA (www.fjta.com) was used as a major source of information for this study, as it provides rich and retrievable information related to various aspects of tourism in the province, encompassing: statistics and research; policies and regulations; organizations and associations; travel agencies and tour operators; accommodation and restaurants; routes, sites and destinations; and crafts, goods and local specialities. Similar to its hierarchical top-down structure, FJTA's web site is resourcefully linked to CNTA's web site (www.cnta.com) at the top as a member province and to the nine municipal sites within the province. Due to the structure, organization and nature of these sites, the information about tea-related tourism retrieved from these sources is taken as highly reliable in that it reflects the actual state of tea-tourism development in Fujian, and is valid for the interpretation of their partnership.

Other sources such as the *Master Plan for Tourism Development in Fujian Province* (FJTA, 2001) and local government web sites or documents were also used in the discussion, especially for the two tea-tourism case studies. The dual role of the researcher as both an insider and an outsider adds to the reliability and validity of this unobtrusive research with regard to tourism development in Fujian.

Tea-related Tourism in Fujian

Fujian Province, located on the southeast coast of Mainland China, facing Taiwan across the Strait and bordering Zhejiang, Jiangxi and Guangdong Provinces (see Figure 8.1), has an area of 121,400 sq km and a population of 32.82 million people (1999 census). It has nine municipal regions under the provincial administration: Fuzhou, Ningde, Nanping, Putian, Quanzhou, Longyan, Sanming, Xiamen and Zhangzhou (alphabetically), all of which have experienced considerable tourism development.

Tourism is one of the major industries in this province. According to the latest figures released in the *Yearbook of China Tourism Statistics* (CNTA, 2003), Fujian was ranked as one of the top four provinces in terms of international tourism receipts (with US$1100 million for 2002) and one

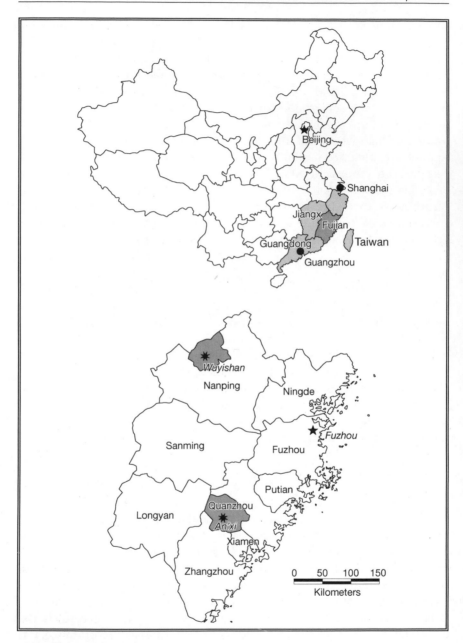

Figure 8.1 Location map and tea tourism destinations in Fujian Province, China

of the top six in terms of inbound tourist arrivals (1.82 million arrivals for 2002). The statistics for domestic tourism (CNTA, 2001) also showed that Fujian was ranked well above average in the year 2000 in terms of domestic tourism expenditure (per capita) and the rate of domestic travel for its urban and rural residents. The province stood in tenth place in China by the number of star-rated tourist hotels (213 properties) and twelfth by the number of travel agencies/tour operators (338 in total, with 36 operating international business and 302 handling domestic markets), offering total tourism employment for 380 thousand people (CNTA, 2001). By the year 2000, annual total revenue from tourism in this province was reportedly RMB 30,500 million yuan (or approximately US$3813 million), covering some 7.8% of the provincial GDP for that year. Of this growth, tea, however small in the overall picture, has a unique place in Fujian's tourism through its offering of a variety of experiences and attractions.

Tourists as Sightseers: Tea-related Routes or Sites

Four out of the nine municipal administrative regions have already incorporated tea as tourist sites or attractions in the design and promotion of major tourist routes (Table 8.1). According to the current postings on the websites of FJTA and the municipal tourism bureaus, these tea-related routes or sites primarily offer tour participants sightseeing experiences related to tea production, tea arts/ceremonies and tea cultural events. With the exception of a couple of packages/routes which focus exclusively on tea or tea culture as tourist attractions, most of these tours have also incorporated other products or attractions for sightseeing. Agri-tourism or rural tourism is often an alternative tourist experience that will include sightseeing trips to tea gardens. Another type of sightseeing takes the form of tea arts or ceremonies, where tourists form the major audiences for such shows. These ceremonies often take place halfway through the trip on an itinerary day as a tea break (usually with some promotional intentions), or are placed prior to or after the regular meals to enhance the profile of a destination with its locally grown (or prepared) tea. A third form of tea-related sightseeing takes place in tea museums and tea festivals. In July 2004, for example, Tianfu Tea Museum (located in Zhangzhou Municipal Administrative Region of Fujian Province) was designated by China National Tourism Administration (CNTA) (2004b) as one of the first 203 agri-tourism model spots in China. Tea festivals and ceremonies that are also of appeal to tourists will be discussed later under a separate heading.

Table 8.1 Tea-related tourist routes or sites in Fujian

Municipal regions	Tea-related routes or sites
Fuzhou	N/A
Longyan	*Zhang-Ping-Zhi-Lu* (A tour to Zhangping County): a one-day package that includes sightseeing in mountainous tea gardens.
Nanping	*Wuyi-Cha-Wen-Hua-You* (Wuyi tea culture tour): a one-day package with visits to tea gardens and viewing of tea arts exclusively in Wuyi Mountain World Heritage Sites.
Ningde	N/A
Putian	N/A
Quanzhou	*Shan-Lin-Tian-Yuan-Feng-Guang-You* (mountain and rural sightseeing tour): a one-day package featuring tea gardens, leaf picking, and tea songs in addition to other idyllic views.
	Gong-Nong-Ye-Guan-Guang-You (industrial/agricultural sightseeing tour): a two-day package with one day featuring exclusively on tea arts, tea gardens, tea processing and tea ceramics.
	An'xi-Cha-Du-Wen-Hua-You (An'xi tea culture tour): a one-day package exclusively on tea culture or arts in An'xi county. Activities include: visit tea growing gardens, learn and sing tea songs, watch tea dance, enjoy/sample tea ceremonies.
Sanming	N/A
Xiamen	N/A
Zhangzhou	*Hua-Guo-Zhi-Xiang-Pin-Shang-You* (home of fruits sampling tour): a two-day package that includes visiting tea museums and tasting fine tea.

Note: This list is adapted from the section termed *'Jing-Pin-Xian-Lu'* (key tourist routes) posted at www.fjta.com (2004) and its links to the websites of municipal tourism bureaus (retrieved on 2 July 2004)

Tourists as Purchasers: Tea-related Souvenirs or Goods

Based on the promotions of local specialties for visitors by FJTA and the municipal tourism bureaus, the majority of the municipal regions (six out of nine) have targeted tea and/or tea-related porcelain as one of the major tourist souvenirs (Table 8. 2). In Fujian, tourists can purchase a great variety of such tea products, ranging from the partially fermented *oolong* tea (for example, *Da-Hong-Pao*, Great Red Robe, *Tie-Guan-Yin*, Iron Goddess of Mercy, *Fo-Shou*, Buddha's Hand, and *Shui-Xian*, Water Fairy), to unfermented white tea, and red (or black) flower teas such as jasmine. Speciality shops for the exclusive sale of tea products can be spotted in major tea destinations such as Wuyishan City and An'xi County. In these boutiques, tourists will be invited for or treated to free sampling of finely brewed teas after a nice demonstration of tea arts or tea ceremonies. Tea production has become highly diverse in terms of producers – a co-existence of state-ownership, local private businesses and joint venture productions. To date, several more prominent brands have emerged in the tourist markets.

With the popularity of tea as tourist souvenirs, the production and sale of ceramics or tea utensils such as teacups and teapots have also flourished. In Fujian, this is best represented by the porcelain produced in Dehua County of Quanzhou Municipal Administrative Region. The local bureau

Table 8.2 Tea-related tourist souvenirs and/or goods in Fujian

Municipal regions	Tea-related souvenirs or goods
Fuzhou	*Jasmine tea* (from Fuzhou City)
Longyan	*Wan-Ying tea*, an all-purpose tea mixed with Chinese herbs and medicines for better health (from Yongding County)
Nanping	*Wuyi cliff tea* (from Wuyishan City) *Osmanthus flower tea* (from Pucheng County)
Ningde	*Great white tea* (from Fu'an County)
Putian	N/A
Quanzhou	*Oolong tea* (from An'xi County) *Porcelain and tea ceramics* (from Dehua County)
Sanming	*Lei-Cha*, or the ground tea (from Jiangle County) *Lian-Xin tea*, or lotus seed sprout tea (from Jianning County)
Xiamen	N/A
Zhangzhou	N/A

Note: This list is adapted from the sections termed '*Dang-Di-Te-Chan/Lu-You-Ji-Nian-Pin*' (local specialties/tourist souvenirs) posted at www.fjta.com (2004) and its links to the websites of municipal tourism bureaus (retrieved on 2 July 2004).

has promoted porcelain production itself as a tourist participatory activity, coupled with souvenir purchase of various styles and sizes.

Tourists as Samplers: Tea Ceremonies or Festivals

The most 'staged' aspect of tea culture for tourism can be seen from the tea ceremonies and/or festivals held in major tea destinations. For example, Wuyi Cliff Tea Festival was held in 1990, 1992, 1993, 1995, 1998 and 2003. According to the municipal host, such shows are primarily for the purposes of promoting tea products and enhancing tea culture for economic revitalization (Wuyishan City Government, 2004). Similarly, in An'xi County, the *'Cha-Wang-Sai'* (or Tea Master's Contest) is not only held locally, but, since 1996, the county government has also started to hold such events in major gateway cities such as Guangzhou, Shanghai, Beijing and Hong Kong. Much like its competitor or partner in Wuyi World Heritage, these contests were also held for both promotional and economic purposes. In one of the 1996 contests held in Hong Kong, for example, an auction price for 100 g of *Tie-Guan-Yin* tea was an incredible HK$110,000 (approximately US$13,750).

Visitors to such ceremonies and/or festivals are most frequently attracted by tea-related performances, ranging from tea poetry recitation, tea stories and legends, tea songs and dances, to the sophisticated demonstration of *'cha-yi'*, which is the highlight of tea arts known as *'kung-fu* tea'. *Kung-fu* tea is a traditional form of tea drinking, originating from the southern part of Fujian Province where *oolong* tea is grown, and which is passed down from generation to generation. In China, the word *kung-fu* applies not just to martial arts, but to every activity that requires time and effort to achieve mastery, ranging from Taoist physical training such as Taiji, to the meticulous form of brewing fine teas, which was scarcely altered for a thousand years. In Fujian Province, the highest grades of teas such as *Da-Hong-Pao* and *Tie-Guan-Yin* are usually set aside as *kung-fu* tea, which involves a variety of skills, coupled with the use of different kinds of teapots and accessories for its blending and brewing. In history, it was recorded that there were talented blenders who made a living by preparing special blends to suit the tastes of individual families in their neighbourhoods. Though blends of this sort are no longer available today, the high quality *oolong* teas produced in Fujian Province are still brewed in this intricate *kung-fu* manner, which produces a very bitter taste (many times stronger than an ordinary brew), with the resulting tea being often sipped from a tiny cup.

What is more appealing for tourists is the art of preparing tea. Although many of them do not really enjoy it for the first time, they are usually willing to try it upon invitation. Based on the observation of this researcher while touring in Wuyi World Heritage Site in 2000, such 'neophylic inclinations' (Cohen & Avieli, 2004: 7) for seeking strangeness and novelty were more often found in domestic sightseers than in international tourists. While the Chinese tourists could wholeheartedly appreciate the arts and enjoy the bitter taste of such *kung-fu* teas, many foreign visitors were reluctant to take part in such sampling, even though the sophisticated processes may look inviting. As an echo to their arguments on ethnic restaurants (Cohen & Avieli, 2004), it would be also interesting to ask, by extension, whether and to what extent Chinese teas or ethnic Chinese stores and tea houses in North America and Europe have adequately prepared outbound tourists for their visits to the many tea destinations in China.

Tourists as Participants: Tea-related Agri-tourism Programmes

In Fujian, tea-related tourist destinations are more likely to be located in rural mountainous areas where they have usually originated from agri-tourism programmes. The practical needs to sell tea products and to enhance the awareness of the place have led to the embracing of tourists as a targeted group. Apart from being sightseers, purchasers and samplers, tourists have also actually participated in tea tourism programmes. In An'xi County, for example, visitors joining the tea culture tour are provided with some hands-on experience of tea processing, depending on the season of their visits. In Wuyi tea gardens, activities such as leaf picking, stir-frying and roasting are also open to tourists at particular times or dates.

Another fun activity for tourists to participate in at the tea gardens comes from the poetry and songs associated with teas. In China, tea and poetry or songs have always gone together. There are poems and songs commemorating tea gardens, rocky springs and mountain scenes, or relating the joys and sorrows of the tea pickers. Others describe the delight of drinking tea or the warmth of tea lovers' feelings. These have substantively added to the fun and interest for domestic tour participants, while, for the foreign tourists who have occasionally joined such programmes, the meanings of such songs and poems are hard to translate, as 'so much is said in so few words' (according to one tour guide observed by this researcher while travelling in Wuyishan Area).

Tea Tourist Destinations in Fujian

Wuyishan City

Wuyishan City is located in the north of Fujian Province (see Figure 8.1), with an area of 2803 sq km and a population of 215,300 people (1999 census). Tourism is booming as a major source of economic revenue for the local municipal government. The area was first designated as one of the key scenic spots by China's central government in 1982. By 1999, Wuyi Mountain was designated by UNESCO as a world cultural and natural heritage site. With the further expansion of tourism, a resort district within walking distance from the scenic area was developed in the early 1990s, housing businesses and operations primarily for the needs of the tourists and out-of-town visitors – such as dining, accommodation, entertainment, shopping, and other travel-related services (for example, tour-packaging and ticketing). Up till now, there have been more than 20 medium- to large-scale hotels (including a five-star property) and countless small guest houses operating in order to accommodate the large numbers of incoming tourists (currently some two million domestic and international arrivals every year). By the late 1990s, Wuyishan Airport was connected to the major gateway cities of China such as Beijing, Shanghai and Hong Kong.

In such a context of rapid tourism development, the locally produced tea was also exploited to add to the attraction of this destination. In fact, historically, Wuyishan has been known as a key production site of tea in Fujian Province. It's particularly famous for its cliff tea or *oolong* tea, which accounts for about 80% of its annual production (in addition to some 10% of red tea and green tea respectively). Wuyishan is widely regarded as the home of a variety of tea products such as *Da-Hong-Pao* (Great Red Robe), *Fo-Shou* (Buddha's Hand), *Shui-Xian* (Water Fairy), *Da-Bai* (Great White), *Mao-Xie* (Hairy Crab), *Xiao-Zhong* (Small Leaf, also known in English as 'souchong'), *Tie-Luo-Han* (Iron Arhat), *Qing-Xiang* (Clear Fragrance) and others. To date, Wuyishan City has tea gardens of about 15,811 acres, scattered mostly around the world heritage site, with a gross tea production of approximately 5000 tons and revenue of 100 million Chinese Yuan (or approximately US$12.5 million) per year.

This tea heritage was historically established. Since 1302 (Yuan Dynasty in Chinese history), Wuyishan Area has been known as 'the emperor's tea garden', producing and processing tea primarily as gifts to the emperor's palace in Beijing. Since 1607 (Ming Dynasty in Chinese history), tea produced in this area has been sold to foreign countries, primarily to Europe, where 'bohea' (a close sound of its origin – Wuyi) was then used as a synonym for Chinese tea in general, as was reflected in Lord Byron's

(1788–1824) *Don Juan*. In 2003, the city was named by the State Council's Ministry of Culture as 'the home of Chinese tea culture and art'. MacCannell (1976) suggested that naming is part of the sacralization process for a sight or place to attract visitors. The official designation of the city as 'the home of Chinese tea culture and art' was quickly seen as a marker that was of touristic value. In fact, the tea culture in Wuyishan appeals to many of the touristic senses (Adler, 1989), encompassing the aural (e.g. poems, songs, stories, legends and mythological tales related to tea production and drinking), the visual (e.g. the sightseeing of gardens, festivals and tea arts) and the sense of taste and smell (e.g. the sampling of tea ceremonies and the sipping of *kung-fu* teas).

Festivals have been used as an effective promotional tool for the blending of tea and tourism for sustainable development. In Wuyishan City, at the time of writing, the Cliff Tea Festival had been held six times since 1990, with November 2003 seeing it as the first 'Tea Culture and Art Festival', the largest in scope and longest in duration. In this festival, Wuyi tea culture and arts were fully exploited and 'staged' for the development of both its tea and tourism. The festival was hosted by the local government (Wuyishan City Government) as well as trade and research associations (e.g. China International Tea Culture Research Association, China Tea Association, Fujian Tea Association and the Administration Committee of Wuyi Scenic Areas and Resort Districts), with a stated purpose of 'enhancing Chinese tea culture, promoting Wuyi tea products, and facilitating development of both tea and tourism' (Wuyi Travel, 2003). With the presence of a vice-governor of Fujian Province and the support of mayor and deputy mayors of Wuyishan City in the planning committee, the festival has received strong governmental input. The event primarily focused on two aspects: (1) tea business transactions and negotiations; and (2) tea culture/art exhibitions and performance. While the former is also related to tourism to a certain extent (e.g. business travel), the latter was almost exclusively designed for tourists and out-of-town visitors. A huge temporary stage was established in the resort district, providing the venue for a series of 'staged' events, featuring *kung-fu* tea art ceremonies and tea song contests. Other themed attractions or package tours were also provided for the tourists, including visiting the tea boutique street and tea rituals, visiting tea product exhibitions, watching various performances, and sampling a variety of finely brewed teas or eating what they called 'tea-banquets' (i.e. snacks or other foods uniquely prepared to go with tea). With effective and repeated media coverage both provincially and nationally, such festivals and events have quite successfully attracted tourists to the area as well as persuading them to prolong their stay while there.

Despite such aggressive promotions, this theme-driven tourism is still in its infancy. As mentioned earlier, there are currently tea-related tourist routes in the Wuyishan Area developed and promoted specifically for sightseeing packages, and Wuyi Cliff tea can be seen in most boutiques and souvenir shops catering for the tourists. Nevertheless, despite these attempts, further efforts should be made with regard to the expectations and needs of this culturally driven segment, so that future product development can be better focused to provide a satisfactory experience through this alternative form of cultural tourism. At its current stage, the major difficulties and/or problems impeding its further growth come primarily from two aspects.

(1) From the demand side, it is difficult in practical terms (if not entirely impossible) to differentiate the tea-culture tourists from the ordinary visitors or sightseers coming to the area. Due to such vulnerability, the current product development for tea-culture tourism is virtually following an undifferentiated strategy to provide 'something for all'. One tourism professor in Fuzhou (the capital city of the province), who is also involved in the planning and development of tourism in Fujian, regretfully commented on the current development of tea-culture tourism in Wuyishan Area as 'a waste of high quality resources resulting from simple and rough exploitations, and a lack of depth for those potential tourists who are truly keen on Wuyi tea culture' (personal communication, 2001). To some extent, this is reflected in the tourists' and tour operators' perceptions of such tea-culture tourism packages. Based on one observation of this researcher, some serious sightseers were uncomfortable with the obviously made-up ceremonies or shows that they had come across. Upon an inquiry with regard to the extent of repeat business, one tour operator in China Travel Service (Fujian) who was involved in the sale of tea-tourism packages for several years replied that there were hardly any individuals or groups returning for a repeat visit, which is contrary to what is generally assumed about such special interest segments. For tea-culture tourism to be sustained in this area, further market or segmentation research would be desirable to give guidlines for more focused product development.

(2) From the supply side, tea-culture tourism in Wuyishan Area would have greater benefits from a truly differentiated strategy of development. To follow up the former discussion, for example, there could be different packaging and programming for domestic tourists versus international ones, for visitors whose primary motivation is related to tea culture versus those who put this special interest in a subordinate or secondary position. Even with such differentiations, there might still exist a problem of culture transferability (or translatability) in the exploitation of tea-culture tourism.

As can be seen from a former description of tea songs and poems that much with few words, this could be particularly true for foreign visitc who have a greater cultural distance than the overseas Chinese, compatriot. or domestic visitors. Given the fact that Wuyishan City has currently received an annual average of two million incoming visitors, with its world heritage site dominating as a sightseeing destination, it would also be strategically wise to leave this alternative form of cultural tourism as a niche product.

An'xi County

Unlike the previous example, this tea-tourism destination is located in the southern part of the province under the administration of Quanzhou Municipality (see Figure 8.1). An'xi County has a population of 1,050,000 (1999 census) and a geographical area of approximately 3000 sq km. Unlike Wuyishan City, in which tea is a secondary attraction adding to the world heritage site in its broader product development strategy, tea in this county constitutes a major part of people's life. Reportedly, 80% of the people in this county are making a living related to tea, and 30% of the population are directly involved in the growing, production, processing and sale of tea products. An'xi is known as the home of *oolong* tea, which accounts for about one-quarter of all *oolong* tea production in China every year. Its annual export earning is reportedly around US$20 million. Tea gardens in An'xi, which can be seen in almost each of its 24 towns and 433 administrative villages, are much more scattered and extensive in scope, totalling an area of 41,175 acres. In An'xi County, tea is a primary attraction for its tourism development.

Many tea gardens and/or tea-production sites in An'xi have been exploited and used for sightseeing and agri-tourist visits. The major ones include, for example, *Da-Ping-Sheng-Tai-Guan-Guang-Cha-Yuan* (agri-tourism tea gardens in Da-Ping), *Xi-Ping-Tie-Guan-Yin-Fa-Yuan-Di* (the origin gardens of *Tie-Guan-Yin* tea in Xi-Ping), *Ying-Xian-Pu-Sheng-Tai-Guan-Guang-Cha-Yuan* (agri-tourism tea gardens in Ying-Xian-Pu) and *An'xi Tea Factory* in Guan-Qiao. A variety of *oolong* tea products such as *Tie-Guan-Yin* (Iron Goddess of Mercy), *Fo-Shou* (Buddha's Hand), *Da-Ye-Wu-Long* (Big Leaf Oolong) and *Mao-Xie* (Hairy Crab) have become popular souvenirs for tourists.

Similar to its competitor in north, An'xi was designated in 1995 as 'Zhong Guo Wulong Cha Zhi Xiang' (the Home of Oolong Tea in China) by China's Ministry of Agriculture and China Agriculture Association. This authentication or naming has resulted in a series of subsequent structions and promotions of '*Zhong Guo Cha Du*' (the tea capital of ina). One tangible result of this is the construction of a wholesale market exclusively for tea products. With a planned construction of 132 acres in three construction stages, this establishment is by far the largest tea wholesale market in China. Based on field observation, the first two stages of construction were completed and opened for use in December 2000, with a construction area of 100,000 sq m housing more than 700 indoor shops, boutiques and stands, including facilities such as a huge tea shopping hall, a fine product exhibition hall, a multifunctional tea-culture activity centre, and a tiny but attractive tea-culture museum. With the opening of this tea wholesale market, An'xi has now become one of the designated tea markets for China's Ministry of Agriculture and one of the top seven largest tea markets in the whole country, providing a business or sales venue for more than 2000 local tea farmers on a daily basis. The tea-related business and tourism have successfully blended through tea culture in this so-called tea capital of China.

Festivals were also effectively used to promote tea-culture tourism in this area. In December 2000, for example, an event called 'Tea Culture Tourism Festival in the Tea Capital (An'xi), China' was jointly hosted by Quanzhou Municipal Government, Fujian Tourism Administration and An'xi County Government. The festival featured programmes that showcased tea ritual performances, tea masters' contests, *kung-fu* tea ceremonies, China and International tea arts, tea-product exhibitions, and a one-day tea-culture seminar for researchers and academics. As part of the activities during this three-day festival, sightseeing trips to the famous tea gardens in this county were also arranged for those interested in getting some hands-on experience.

With regard to the future development of tea tourism in this destination, the problems in Wuyishan City have also been found to be partly true here. For example, to avoid the current 'something-for-everybody' syndrome, product development for tea tourism should be better supported by market research that differentiates (or at least attempts to differentiate) the domestic from the international segments, and tourists with primary motives for tea from visitors coming primarily for other purposes. Statistics showed that the county received a total of 1.38 million incoming visitors in the year 2002, but, from this general figure, it would be virtually impossible to tell or predict the magnitude of the tea segment. Similarly, it could remain problematic for foreign visitors to fully appreciate the rituals, performances and ceremonies and hence have a good experience because of the complexities of some of the aural and visual aspects of staging tea culture events.

Nevertheless, tea tourism in this destination has unique characteristics that are different from the former. Unlike Wuyishan City, tea culture in this county is a primary attraction that the local tourism bureaus have been promoting. Thus, there is the potential to develop tea culture as a core product and to have other tourist sights or attractions adding to this special interest experience. Due to the magnitude of the wholesale market, another difference from the previous example is that there is potentially a much larger number of business travellers, who come to An'xi for the purposes of buying and selling teas and negotiating business transactions. Based on observation, such tea-related business travel has the potential to become a more important segment in this destination, an aspect which unfortunately has received hardly any research attention.

The Tea-Tourism Partnership for Future Development: Some Afterthoughts

With the increasing sophistication in destination marketing and the subsequent penetration in product development, any resources that are of potential interest to the tourists, regardless whether cultural or physical, would be likely to be exploited for this ever-expanding experience economy (Pine, 2004; Oh *et al.*, 2004). Tea-related tourism provides just one example, establishing links to various forms of tourist experiences such as rural/ agricultural tourism, ethnic/ cultural tourism and even gastronomy/ culinary experiences. Viewed in such a context, the tea-tourism partnership in Fujian Province, China has good potential for further development

As can be seen from the future development projects posted in June 2003 by the provincial tourism administration for the whole province (FJTA, 2003), most of the nine administrative regions in Fujian have incorporated some aspects of tea or tea culture in the planning of future tourism development projects (see Table 8.3)

It should be pointed out that what is seen in Table 8.3 is only a partial reflection of the actual development scenarios with regard to tea-related tourism in this province. In practice, it might well be true that some tea-related projects or programmes in different counties or regions were not reported to the provincial tourism administration and were subsequently not included in the bureau's posting, such as the case recently documented by Jolliffe and Zhuang (2004) describing a vibrant growth in tea-related tourism in Fuding County of Fujian Province. Nevertheless, with favourable policies from the government and enthusiasm from locals and investors for further growth, it can be predicted that greater efforts will be made to target this niche market and also to further explore this alternative form of

Table 8.3 Future tourism development projects that have incorporated tea and/or tea culture in Fujian Province

Municipal regions (with total number of projects)	Future tourism development projects that have incorporated tea or tea culture
Fuzhou (23)	*Lian-Jiang-Chang-Long-Sheng-Tai-Xiu-Xian-Guan-Guang-Yuan* (Agritourism garden for leisure and sightseeing in Chang-Long, Lian Jiang County), including two tea gardens. Planned investment: US$3.66 million. Location: Lian Jiang County.
Longyan (15)	*Yong-Ding-Jian-Tan Spa Tourism District*, including ceremonial tea houses. Planned investment: US$3.65 million. Location: Yong Ding County.
Nanping (29)	*Ethnic Tourism Development Project in Xia-Mei, Wuyishan City*, including a ceremonial/sampling tea house. Planned investment: US$1.2 million. Location: Wuyishan City.
Putian (12)	*Gui-Shan Scenery District in Putian*, including tea gardens. Planned investment: US$15 million. Location: Putian City.
Quanzhou (20)	*An'xi-Long-Men Forest Park*, including rural sightseeing of tea gardens. Planned investment: US$ 7 million. Location: An'xi County.
Sanming (30)	*Zhu-Xi Park*, including an ancient style tea house for ceremonies. Planned investment: US$ 1.07 million. Location: You Xi County. *Jian-Ning-Yuan-Yang Lake District*, including tea houses. Planned investment: US$0.74 million. Location: Jian Ning County. *Jiang-Le-Yu-Hua-Dong Scenery District*, including a tea house for Lei-Cha (the ground tea). Planned investment: US$2.8 milion. Location: Jiang Le County.
Zhangzhou (43)	*Zhang-Zhou-Re-Dai-Zhi-Wu-Da-Guan-Yuan* (Tropical botanical garden in Zhang Zhou), including tea gardens and music tea house. Planned investment: US$1 million. Location: Zhang Zhou. *Xin-Heng-Hui-Cha-Ye-Cheng* (Xin Heng Hui tea plaza in Nan Jing). Planned investment: US$3.75 million. Location: Nan Jing County. *Ping-He-Ling-Tong-Lu-You-Feng-Jing-Qu* (Ling Tong scenery and tourism district in Ping He), including a tea garden. Planned investment: US$1.5 million. Location: Ping He County.

Note: This table was adapted from the list of 209 future tourism development projects in Fujian Province, posted at www.fjta.com/zhaoshang/ (2004). The original list (current as of June 2003) provided information on project names/titles, project description, progress and construction stages, planned investment, modes of ownership, major investors/partners, project managers, and contact details (Retrieved on July 2, 2004).

special interest tourism to satisfy the quest for cultural, rural and culina experiences.

In summary, this chapter has presented a comprehensive overview of the current development of tea-related tourism in Fujian Province. Only empirical research and in-depth case studies focusing on issues touched upon in the previous discussion can provide more practical insights to further understand tea-culture tourists to this province, develop more effective marketing strategies for its tea destinations, and achieve a better supply–demand match in its product development. Specifically, apart from the aforementioned issues, the field will benefit from future research designed with the following purposes in mind:

- to examine tea and tourism (or tea-related tourism) in Fujian Province from the demand perspective: for example, the use of survey research to empirically describe those tourists whose primary interests or motivations are related to tea;
- to estimate the magnitude or size of the tea-tourism segment as well as its impacts on (or contribution to) Fujian's tourism in general;
- to investigate the potential relationship between tea lovers (consumers and purchasers) and tea-culture tourists;
- to conduct in-depth case studies of the established tea-tourism destinations to inform practitioners and decision-makers; and, to use this to complement the above tourism-oriented perspective;
- to look at the tea-tourism partnership from the tea-business or tea-trade perspective, in order to consider the situation from a different viewpoint.

References

Adler, J. (1989) Origins of sightseeing. *Annals of Tourism Research* 18, 7–29.

Babbie, E. (1999) *The Basics of Social Research*. Belmont, CA: Wadsworth Publishing.

Blofeld, J. (1985) *The Chinese Art of Tea*. Boston, MA: Shambhala Publications.

Cohen, E. and Avieli, N. (2004) Food in tourism: Attraction and impediments. *Annals of Tourism Research* 31 (4), the publisher's pdf page proof.

CNTA (China National Tourism Administration) (2001) *The Yearbook of China Tourism Statistics*.Beijing: China Tourism Publishing House.

CNTA (2004a) Online document: http://www.cnta.com (accessed 13 July 2004).

CNTA (2004b) The first list of designated model spots for agri-tourism and industrial tourism in China. Online document: http://www.cnta.com/gonggao/2004/glylv.htm (accessed 11 August 2004).

CNTA (2003) *The Yearbook of China Tourism Statistics*. Beijing: China Tourism Publishing House.

FJTA (Fujian Tourism Administration) (2001) *Master Plan for Tourism Development in Fujian Province*. Fuzhou, Fujian Province: Fujian Tourism Administration.

.'A (2003) *2003 Nian Fujian Sheng Luyou Zhaoshang Xiangmu Huizong Biao* (A list of tourism development projects in Fujian Province in 2003). Online document: http://www.fjta.com/zhaoshang/ (accessed 2 July 2004).

FJTA (2004) Online document: http://www.fjta.com (accessed 2 July 2004).

Jolliffe, L. and Zhuang, P. (2004) Blending tea and tourism for sustainable development in Fujian, China. In R.N. Moisey, M. Joppe, K.L. Andereck and N.G. McGehee (eds) *Measuring the Tourism Experience: When Experience Rules, What is the Metric of Success?* Travel and Tourism Research Association (TTRA) 35th Annual Conference Proceeding, 20–3 June, Montreal.

MacCannell, D. (1976) *The Tourist: A New Theory of the Leisure Class*. New York: Schocken.

Mennell, S., Murcott, A. and Otterloo, V. (1992) *The Sociology of Food: Eating, Diet and Culture*. London: Sage Publications.

Oh, H., Fiore, A.M. and Jeong, M. (2004) Conceptualizing and measuring the four realms of tourism experience. In R.N. Moisey, M. Joppe, K.L. Andereck and N.G. McGehee (eds) *Measuring the Tourism Experience: When Experience Rules, What is the Metric of Success?* Travel and Tourism Research Association (TTRA) 35th Annual Conference Proceeding, 20–3 June, Montreal.

Pine, J. (2004) *The Experience Economy* (a keynote presentation). In Travel and Tourism Research Association (TTRA) 35th Annual Conference Proceeding, 20–3 June, Montreal.

Wuyishan City Government (2004) Online document: http://www.wuyishan.gov.cn/public/wyxs/chaye1/wyycj.htm (accessed 2 July 2004).

Wuyi Travel (2003) An action plan for the First Wuyi Tea Culture/Art Festival and Sixth Wuyi Cliff Tea Festival. Online document: http://www.wuyitravel.com/shownews1 (accessed 16 August 2004).

Chapter 9
Tourism Development and the Tea Gardens of Fuding, China

LEE JOLLIFFE AND PEIFEN ZHUANG

The province of Fujian in China is a major source of tea production. In the rural tea-growing area near the city of Fuding interest is emerging in the development of tourism in conjunction with tea gardens. This chapter takes a case study approach in examining the context for the development of tea-related tourism at this location. It is based on visits to the area, on a survey of those involved in the tea and tourism industries there, and profiles both a local tea company operation and an emerging pilot project in tea tourism. The authors continue to be involved on a consultative basis with the tea gardens. As part of this work a proposal for a pilot tea-tourism project has emerged; it calls for the construction of a 'tea interpretation centre' adjacent to the tea gardens and for an adjoining tea house to be built and operated by the local Women's Federation with the aim of reducing poverty and increasing the employment of women.

Tea in Fujian

Tea has been grown in Fujian for centuries, although it is recognized that, in the long history of tea production in China, Fujian is a relative newcomer (see Chapters 2 and 8). The mountainous and hilly terrain and moderate climate provide a suitable environment for growing tea. Today Fujian leads the province in tea production (*People's Daily*, 2002). Teas produced in the province include green, *oolong*, black and white teas. As Pettigrew (1999: 22) indicates: 'White teas are very rare and are seldom found outside China where they are produced in the mountain areas of Fujian.' In addition compressed tea, *puer* tea and flavoured tea are produced.

Pettigrew (1999) indicates that there have always been difficulties in learning the details of Chinese tea production. This has been in part because China was closed to Western visitors for many years, and also because the Chinese have seemed to be protective about disclosing information regarding tea production. For many years it was therefore difficult to gain admittance to tea gardens in China. Goodwin (2003) reflects this position with regard to his travels to Fujian to learn about tea. However, in recent years China has opened up and it is now possible for outsiders to visit Chinese tea gardens and to learn about tea production, as is evidenced by the research undertaken for this chapter. This new business climate provides an opportunity for the development of tea-related tourism products, experiences and projects in Fujian and in other areas of China.

Tea and Development

The World Commission on Environment and Development (1987 quoted in WTO 1998) has defined sustainable development as: 'development that meets the needs of the present without compromising the ability of future generations to meet their own needs' (WTO, 1998). For this development to take place, planning is necessary, so that a responsible form of tourism develops – one which achieves a balance between the economic benefits and the social and environmental costs of tourism. Ideally, sustainable tourism should be designed to benefit local communities, generating and retaining income in these locales.

In the case of tea and tourism a number of different types of sustainable development initiatives can occur. For example, programmes interpreting tea (e.g. tea arts or tea tours) can contribute to diversifying the revenues of tea gardens and factories and also local communities. The packaging of tea as souvenirs offers a locally produced product, which can be available to tourists through local shops, directly benefiting the local economy. The architecture associated with tea gardens can be transformed into facilities for tourism, such as tea houses, welcome centres for tourists and accommodation, all forms of local development that create employment and contribute to local economies.

In Sri Lanka, Tourism Concern has worked with one of the tea gardens on a sustainable tourism project, and it is this project that first coined the term 'tea tourism' a number of years ago (Tourism Concern, 2001). Projects such as this one provide a model for other initiatives in tea-growing areas. In Jiangxi Province (Wuyan County), Chinese local authorities have encouraged the development of ecological tea tourism, aiming to enrich peasants' lives (*People's Daily*, 2002).

Tea and Tourism at Fuding

Tea is an inherent part of Chinese society and culture. The idea of tea and tourism is therefore a natural extension of the culture and can be seen as a distinctly Chinese form of cultural tourism. There are signs of interest in tea-related tourism development in China, as cited above in the case of Jiangxi Province. In cases of tea-related tourism development there can be positive local employment impacts for women. It seems there would be potential for this type of development in the Fuding area of Fujian Province, where sustainable development and gender equality in employment within tea gardens has been encouraged by a Canadian International Development Agency (CIDA) project based at the Fujian Agriculture and Forestry University (Tea Gardens Project, 2001).

Tea is produced in a number of areas of Fujian, including the Wuyi Mountains and Ansi. In addition in the Fuding area, tea is produced in the mountain valleys of the Taimu mountain range and processed and packaged in nearby Fuding City. Special teas produced here include 'Fuding white tea' and 'Fuding big sprout'. The Fuding Foreign Trade Corporation identifies the city as one of the main centres for white tea production and export in China. While the Corporation assists tea companies with the development and marketing of their tea, the companies producing tea are also now able to undertake their own marketing.

The tea gardens profiled here lie in the shadows of the Taimu mountain range, some 45 km from Fuding City. State authorities have in recent years encouraged the upgrading of outdated tourism facilities at Taimu Mountain, a popular touring destination. They have also worked at improving access, by building and improving roads into the area.

In 1988 the State Council of China approved the listing of the 92 km sightseeing area as 'The Taimu Mountain State Key Scenic Spot'. A number of agencies are concerned with tourism in the area, including the Administrative Bureau of Taimushan Scenery District, which is responsible for managing visits. Located on the boundary between Fujian and Zhejiang Provinces, the area includes mountains, streams and waterfalls, caves, grasslands, seashore, islands, lakes and cultural spots in addition to the adjacent tea gardens. A resort hotel is located at the foot of the mountain (Fuding Taimu Dianoxin Hotel), adjacent to a park and local souvenir shops.

Area tourism development has been weak, as noted in 2002 (Fujian Tourist Authority, Tourism Trade Administrative Committee of Fuding City and Taimushan Tourism Economic Development Zone): 'In the past because of the fatal limitation of traffic condition to her, though Taimu

Mount is beautiful, her [synthetic] developing level is too low, especially her comprehensive receiving capacity within the spot is too weak so that her tourism development is relatively backward.' This statement appears to acknowledge the lag in the tourism development of the area and recognize the need for a responsible approach to future development.

In China lack of transportation in rural areas has been identified as one of the barriers to tourism development (Mak, 2003). With the recent construction of the Tong San highway, giving access into the Fuding area from Fuzhou, and the new 'tourist' road being constructed adjacent to the Taimu Mountains, this area is now more accessible for tourism. During field research it was reported that tourism increased after the Tong San highway was built. A survey of domestic tourism undertaken by the Fujian Tourism Authority has shown that due to the establishment of the highway during the National Day holiday of 1–8 October 2002 there was an increase in the level of visits by 11.4% over the previous year.

The majority of visitors to the Fuding area and the Taimu Mountains came from the nearby Zhejang Province and the city of Fuzhou. It was reported that most visitors were with family, relatives or friends while less than 10% were on organized tours. However, some visitors noted problems associated with increased visits in terms of rubbish on the mountain paths and in the caves, a lack of directional signage, slow food service and unacceptable levels of food sanitation. Others researching tea tourism in China noted quality issues in the delivery of service elements during visits to tea-related sites (Zoe, 2004). While it is understood that the general level of service quality in China is improving, these are issues that need to be tackled to ensure visitor satisfaction.

The Survey

After visiting the tea gardens the researchers decided that in order to determine the state of tourism in relation to the tea gardens a limited survey should be undertaken. Twelve respondents were selected to represent the local tea, travel and accommodation industry. This included two local tourist guides employed by Fuding Ocean Tourist Agent, a local hotel clerk, two officials from the related local tourism department (Administration Committee of Taimu Mountain), two officials from the statistics department (Fuding Statistic Bureau), the owner/manager of the Tianhu Tea Company, a sales clerk from the Tianhu Tea Company, one official from the local agricultural department (Fuding Ocean and Fishery Bureau) and two shop owners near Taimu Mountain who sell the Tianhu Company tea as souvenirs.

Survey respondents reported offering products and services for tourists that included accommodation and food, souvenirs, tourism information and tour services. In addition several reported being responsible for the planning of tourism in the area. Respondents who were asked if improvements or expansions were needed to the tourism infrastructure within the next five years, agreed with the need to improve a number of area features (Table 9.1).

Survey participants reported that current visitors are primarily domestic tourists, and estimated an even split between day visitors (excursionists) and overnight visitors (tourists). The primary motivation for visiting the area is seen as leisure (by 83% of respondents). Half of the respondents indicated that tourists visit the area for holidays. Visits by international tourists was not identified as having any significance for the area: this is obviously an area for potential development, as Fujian ranks fifth in China in terms of international tourism arrivals (Strizzi, 2001).

In terms of the gender and age groups of visitors the majority were described as: men and women, predominately in the 18- to 25- and 26- to 35-year-old age range. A small proportion (25%) reported the majority of visitors as families. This corresponds with the Fujian Tourist Authority survey in which the majority of visitors were in family groups. This indicated a dominance of family-orientated leisure pursuits.

A majority of survey respondents (96%) indicated that the area is on the major tour routes. However, only a few respondents (11%) reported that the tours had a tea-experience component. Since just over half of the respondents represented the travel trade and government tourism entities this should be a reliable finding. The majority (or 83%) of those surveyed were not aware of any plans for managing the visitor numbers in the area: only one survey respondent (employed by a local tourism development agency) reported being aware of a regional plan for managing visitor numbers. In view of the increasing level of visits reported by the local

Table 9.1 Tourism resources needing improvement or expansions

Resource	Respondents agreeing with need
Taimu Mountain Scenic Area	75
New Tourist Route	67
Cuisine	25
Scenery	25

Source: Jolliffe & Zhuang (2004)

tourism authority the planning of tourism is obviously an area that needs attention.

Survey respondents identified a number of methods used in promoting the area that revealed an emphasis on media (83%) and travel agencies (93%). In addition the use of published guidebooks and government brochures was reported by over half of those surveyed (60%). Respondents also reported using a variety of methods to promote their own products or services, however under half the respondents reported using the Internet and a variety of other methods (including media advertising, travel agencies, word of mouth, and promotional campaigns or seasonal promotions).

Respondents were asked about components that had potential in making tea an important tourism product in the area (Table 9.2). The method perceived as having the *least* potential was that of community involvement in tea tourism, a tactic that has been employed elsewhere in developing tourism in relation to tea gardens. Organized tours with a tea history component were seen as having the *most* potential, reflecting the group tour and travel trade presence in the area.

In addition respondents commented on ideas for future tourism development (Table 9.3). It is of note that a number of these comments recognized the potential for the complementary development of the tea industry and tourism; and for the emergence of the Taimu Mountain scenic area as a tea-tourism destination. Suggestions for improvements in these comments included the need for promotion and for attention to service quality, the provision of additional tea-related facilities including a tea house, tourist tea gardens and facilities showcasing 'tea arts'. The comments also demonstrate the emergence of an awareness of the potential for developing tea-related tourism in the area.

Table 9.2 Components with potential for making tea an important area tourism product

Component	Most potential (%)
Organized tours – tea history and local products focus	83
More production of tea as souvenirs for tourists	50
Programs on tea history, products, appreciation	42
A tea house built near the tea gardens	33
Use Internet to attract visitors interested in tea.	17
Community involvement in tea tourism	8

Source: Jolliffe and Zhuang (2004)

Table 9.3 Comments on future tourism development in the area

The government should enhance the investment in and improve the promotion of Taimu Mountain to develop the smokeless industry.
Famous mountains produce famous tea and Taimu Mountain produces quality green tea. Famous mountains and quality tea are complementary. It is important to promote tea and tourism domestically and internationally to enhance brand name recognition.
Develop a prosperous tourism city based on Taimu Mountain and make tourism industry the leading industry in 10 to 20 years.
Improve the promotion of Taimu Mountain.
Improve the overall scenic spot system, including parking lots, standardize charges, improve quality of personnel in the service sector.
Add tea history, tourist tea gardens, tea house, and tea art performance to form the integrated Taimu tourism.

Source: Jolliffe and Zhuang (2004)

The Tea Company

The Tianhu Limited Tea Company is one of a number of tea companies based in the Fuding City area. The other companies include the Pinpinxiang Tea Factory, the Fuding Taimu Famous Tea Company and the Fuding Yuda Tea Factory. Tianhu's Luxueya Tea brand is packaged in a number of types and sizes, and is available for purchase by visitors to Fuding city and the nearby Taimu Mountains. The packaging design incorporates the Taimu Mountains as a backdrop, encouraging its purchase as a souvenir of the area. The tea is certified organic and this certification provides another attribute for marketing the tea. In addition to selling through the small souvenir shops adjacent to the Taimu Mountains the firm also sells through its own tea boutiques located in a number of cities in China. This includes staff at company boutiques who are trained in 'tea arts' and, as is the case in other tea shops in China, it is possible to sample a number of types of tea before making a decision on a purchase.

The company has recently built a factory in Fuding City and is constructing an adjacent 'tea arts' building. Twenty staff are employed year round and about 300–400 seasonal workers are contracted for picking, processing and packaging the tea. The tea company owner, Mr Lin, is interested in further developing the market for his tea by providing a tea house or restaurant adjacent to his tea gardens, in the shadows of the Taimu

ɔle 9.4 Tianhu Tea Company facts

Tea types produced:	Green, flower, white, oolong, black (red), yellow, compressed and others
Tea brands:	Luxeya
Tea gardens size:	100 hectares
Tea boutiques:	Fuding, Fuzcho, Beijing, Shanghai, Jinan (Shandong Province), Luoyang (Henan Province), Zhengzhou (Henan Province), Baotou (Inner Mongolia), Xi'an (Shanxi Province), Changchun (Jilin Province)
Established:	Circa 2000
Factory expansions:	2002 and 2003
Fuding tea arts building:	Opening 2004
Ownership:	Private

Source: Jolliffe and Zhuang (2004)

Mountains. The recent construction of a new road into this area has encouraged this thinking.

There is an absence of food services and related amenities (i.e. public restrooms, shops) in the immediate vicinity of the tea gardens, although some basic food is available at the top of the nearby mountain from a small canteen adjacent to a temple construction site and also on request from a nearby small Buddhist monastery. A short drive away from the tea gardens there is also a resort hotel that provides some services, including a number of souvenir shops. The survey results noted some issues with service quality provision in this area.

However, the tea company owner Mr Lin has a vision for developing tea-related tourism along with his tea industry, which he has described as follows: 'Famous mountains produce famous tea and Taimu Mountain produces quality green tea. Famous mountains and quality tea are complementary' (interview, Zhuang, 2004). With the majority of seasonal workers (pickers) being women any increase in the tea business will create an economic benefit for them. In addition, the development of related services for tourists at the tea gardens site might also serve to increase their employment. This company profile illustrates the diversification of medium enterprises that holds potential for the sustainable development of China's tourism industry.

Plate 9.1 Showroom at Tiannutea Company Factory, Fuding, China

Source: Peifen Zhuang

Branding of the Luxeya Tea

The Tianu Company tea is sold under the Luxeya tea name. The tea is certified organic and this certification provides another attribute for marketing the tea. The tea is attractively packaged and pictures of the Taimu Mountains and the tea gardens are incorporated into the marketing design. The romance of the Taimu Mountain area is also reflected in the story of Tianhu tea. A legend recounting the origins of tea in the mountain is recanted for promotional purposes, adding to the romance surrounding product marketing. Luxeya is also marketed as the ancestor of Baihao Yinzhen, one of the top ten brands of tea in China (Tianhu Tea Company, 2004).

The Luxeya tea has much to offer for tea-related tourism. It offers a healthy product that has positive attributes, including health benefits, cultural attributes and souvenir packaging. In addition the Tianhu Tea Company is well positioned to develop and market an experiential tea tourism component as part of its business. This is because it controls all aspects of the production and marketing of the tea, from cultivation in the tea gardens, to processing, to the sale in its boutiques and the interpretation of tea arts. The openness of the management to development in this area, as well as an awareness of the potential role of tourism in their business, will contribute to the emergence of tea-related tourism in Fuding.

The Pilot Project

Work reported on above (Jolliffe & Zhuang, 2003) identified the need for both food and tea services in the area adjacent to the tea gardens, and also the desirability of some kind of interpretation of the tea gardens (this might include information on the picking and processing of the different kinds of tea that this location is known for). As a result, in part, of these investigations into tourism in the tea gardens of Fuding, a pilot project 'The Tianhu Fairy Tea Interpretive Centre and Tea House' has been proposed. The project objective is to plan and construct a tea house adjacent to the Tianhu Tea Company tea gardens near Fuding, China in partnership with a local tea company owner; it will be operated by a local women's cooperative. The goals of this project will be to increase women's employment and alleviate poverty while contributing to the sustainable development of tourism in the area. This would be a partnership involving Women's Centres in China, two universities (one in China and one in Canada) and a local tea company (Tianhu Tea Company). This partnership is possible because of the work that the local university (Fujian Agriculture and Forestry University) has done with the tea-garden owner in the context of an organic tea garden project. It is also possible because the tea-garden owner is willing to build a tea house adjacent to his tea gardens and to turn it over to a local women's cooperative to operate.

Conclusion

Domestic tourism in the Taimu Mountains scenic area is at an early stage of development. International tourism has yet to be developed to any extent. With improved transportation access the area has experienced a significant increase in numbers of visits. There is awareness that improvements are needed in the Taimu Mountain scenic area related to the products offered (scenery, cuisine). The opportunity for the development of tea-related tourism is seen as being with organized tours. Other areas of opportunity are the increased packaging of tea as souvenirs for tourists and development of programmes related to tea history and appreciation. In the Taimu Mountain scenic area survey results indicate a lack of interest in community-based tea tourism. However, this response could be due to the lack of awareness by those surveyed of the potential of 'community tourism' and also of the participation of the travel trade which is more corporate in approach.

In Fuding those involved with the local tea and tourism industries demonstrate some awareness of the potential that tea holds in contributing to the tourism development of their area. Survey results and background information indicate some of the challenges inherent in the implementation of tea tourism, including: a lack of awareness of the need for development; a lack of product development and marketing; an apparent reliance on the travel trade and government to develop products; an absence of the infrastructure required for tourism (food service, washrooms, programmes, interpretation); and service quality issues.

The tea company case study is important in that the owner is open to the idea of tea tourism. For example, 'the owner is thinking of how he can develop his business to take advantage of tea tourism' (Zhuang, 2004). Tea tourism may provide an additional revenue stream for tea garden owners and has the potential to augment revenues from tea production and to contribute to the image and branding of the tea company and its products and Mr. Lin is forward thinking in this respect. A local women's group is also open to the possibilities of tea tourism, as illustrated by the pilot project for the development of a tea house operated by the women adjacent to the tea gardens. The case of the Tianhu Tea Company therefore demonstrates both an entrepreneurial approach and a social consciousness on the part of the tea gardens owner towards the diversification of his tea company into offering services and products for tourism for the benefit of the local community. The owner has an insight into the potential of combining tea and tourism for development, in his words: 'Add tea history, tourist tea gardens, tea house, and tea art performance to form the integrated Taimu [Mountain] tourism' (interview, Zhuang, 2004).

Fujian Province has a rich and abundant tea history and culture providing opportunities for the development of tea-related tourism. In Fujian tourism is rapidly developing along with the opening up of China, the introduction of a capitalist market economy and the encouragement of leisure pursuits by government policies. This case has provided a background to this development in Fujian and a glimpse of how the key stakeholders in the local tea and tourism industries for one tea-producing location, Fuding, are proposing to merge tea and tourism for the development of their location. The proposed sustainable tourism project to construct a tea interpretation centre and tea house, if accomplished, may provide a model for the development of similar projects in some of the many other tea-growing areas of China.

References

Fujian Tourist Authority. (2002) Fuding Visitor Survey. Online document: www.fdj.net/shownews (in Chinese) (accessed 1 March 2004).

Goodwin, Jason (2003) *The Gunpowder Gardens: Travels through India and China in Search of Tea* (reprint of 1991 edition). London: Penguin Books

Jolliffe, L. and Zhuang, P. (2004) Blending tea and tourism for sustainable development in Fujian, China. Presentation at Travel and Tourism Research Association International Conference, Montreal, Quebec, June 2004.

Lew, A and Guangrui, Z. (2003) Introduction: China's tourism boom. In A. Lew, L. Yu, J. Ap, J. and Z. Guangnui (eds) *Tourism in China* (pp. 3–11). New York: Haworth Hospitality Press.

Mak, B. (2003) China's tourism transportation: Air, land and water. In A. Lew, L. Yu, J. Ap and Z. Guangnui (eds) *Tourism in China* (pp. 165–94). New York: Haworth Hospitality Press.

People's Daily (2000) China tea culture tourism festival opens. Online document: http://english.peopledaily.com, 19 December.

People's Daily (2002) China's special teas promise rosy future, Online document: http://english.peopledaily.com, 19 September.

People's Daily (2002) Ecological tea tourism. Online document: http://english.peopledaily.com, 10 April.

Pettigrew, Jane (1999) *Tea and Infusions*. London: Carleton.

Strizzi, N. (2001) *An Overview of China's Inbound and Outbound Tourism Markets*. Research Report 2001–5. Ottawa: Canadian Tourism Commission.

Tea Garden Project (2001) *Tea Garden Project Proposal*. Fujian Agricultural and Forestry University, University of New Brunswick Saint John and New Brunswick Community College, Grand Falls.

Tianhu Tea Company (2004) *The Story of Luxeya*. Fuding, China.

Tourism Concern (2001) Developing 'tea tourism' in Sri Lanka, Fair Trade in Tourism Bulletin 1. Online document: www.torismconcern.org.uk.

WTO (World Tourism Organization) (1998) *Guide for Local Authorities on Developing Sustainable Tourism*. Madrid: WTO.

Zhuang, P. (2004) Interviews and field notes. Fuding, China.

Zoe, P. (2004) Tea and tourism in China: An analysis on packaged tea tours offered in Hangzhou, Zhejiang Province, China. Unpublished paper, University of New Brunswick Saint John.

Chapter 10
Tourism and Tea in Kenya: Opportunity for Development?

JACQUELYNE MUHATI AND LEE JOLLIFFE

Kenya's tourism industry originally based on wildlife and beach tourism, more recently has been developing nature and ecological tourism to the point where, with these more environmentally friendly tourisms included, the combined tourism industry is one of the largest earners of foreign exchange industries for the country, along with the agriculture industry. However, it has been recognized that there is a need to diversify the country's tourism product, moving away from wildlife- and beach-based tourism towards forms of cultural tourism (Ondimu, 2002). With tea production being a major industry in the country one of the forms of new tourism could potentially be tea-related tourism. The cultivation of tea was introduced to Kenya in 1903 (Pratt, 1982), planting on a commercial scale began in 1925 (Harler, 1956) and by the late 1990s the country was one of the world's largest exporters of tea (UNESCO, 1997).

This chapter examines the connections between Kenya's two pre-eminent industries of tourism and tea. The methodology for this investigation includes:

- a comparison of the earnings of the tourism and tea industries;
- a review of eco-tourism trends as a context for examining tea-related tourism using Porter's Five Forces Analysis (Kotler, 1999) and a strengths, weaknesses, opportunities and threats (SWOT) analysis of the potential for tea tourism;
- examples of tea-related tourism experiences derived from primary contact with tourism operators and a secondary review of other sources.

From this analysis potential for the future development of tea tourism, defined as 'tourism that is motivated by an interest in the history, traditions and consumption of the beverage, tea' (Jolliffe, 2003b) is assessed.

Tourism in Kenya

Kenya has undoubtedly proved to be one of the most diverse destinations in Africa. Few countries are able to offer visitors the variety and combination of touristic features that Kenya does (Sindiga, 1996; Dieke, 1991; KWS, 1997; KTB, 1997). Several authors agree that Kenya's tourism developed on the basis of wildlife conservation (Sindiga, 1996; Dieke, 1991; KWS, 1997; KTB, 1997; Lavery, 1996), however beach tourism, eco-tourism, cultural tourism, sports tourism and research tourism all form part of the portfolio. There has been considerable growth in tourism traffic and earnings since gaining independence in 1963. and as tourist arrivals increased so did the related earnings. The importance of tourism to the country is clear, as a decade ago it overtook coffee as the leading foreign exchange earner (KTB, 1997) – a trend that continued, as shown in Figure 10.1 (with the exception of 1997/8).

The Kenya Tourist Board (KTB), a state corporation, is responsible for the destination marketing of Kenya on behalf of both the public and private sectors in tourism. Because the KTB is a government agency, the private sector's views are made known to the Ministry for Tourism through the KTB's representatives. The Ministry of Tourism has an overall responsibility for policy guidelines, funding and development of the tourism industry. It also plays an advisory role to the KTB and the private sector regarding standardization of the tourist product, which is done through parastatals, and bodies set up within the ministry (KTB, 2001).

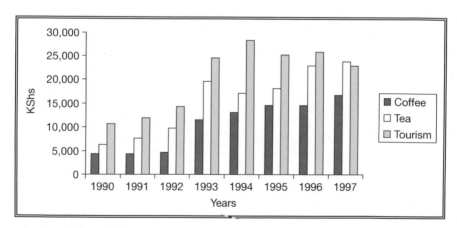

Figure 10.1 Earnings from coffee, tea and tourism 1990–7 (KShs billion)

Source: Figures from Mwangi (1997)

Following years of unregulated mass market tourism, Kenyan tou operators and discerning visitors are looking for an alternative. Arguably this has come in the form of eco-tourism. The previous mass tourism has both cheapened the product and harmed the environment, and the industry is now in the process of moving away from that and establishing products that are more environmentally friendly and community-orientated.

Nature-based tourism is increasingly gaining importance as an important addition to the Kenyan product mix. Nature-based tourism may include culture tourism, village tourism and rural tourism, offering activities mainly based in the outdoors and in natural and unspoiled surroundings. This type of tourism activity has been fuelled mainly by the growth in concern for the environment and a greater awareness of ecological fragility. Increased interest in participating in 'what locals do' is another trend facilitating the growth of nature-based tourism. Typically nature-seeking tourists are aged in their forties and originate from Western Europe, North America and Japan.

An analysis of Kenya tourism using Porter's Five Forces Analysis (Kotler, 1999) provides a background for examining the potential for developing tea tourism in the country. The following principles form the cornerstone of this analysis:

- competitive rivalry
- power of the customer
- power of the supplier
- threats of new entrants, and
- substitute products.

In terms of competitive rivalry there are many countries now offering the same products as Kenya, including Thailand, Dominican Republic and Tanzania, among others. These are direct competitors, though indirect competitors may also include European countries that offer beach holidays, such as Spain.

In the area of the power of the customer in the tourism industry repeat business is not a commonality but rather an exception. Visitors are always looking for new and different products, and their expectations are always changing. Therefore nothing can remain the same over a long period. Even the most successful products have to be improved, modified and adapted by suppliers to keep up with market changes.

Since repeat business is not common, some destinations try to develop unique products in order to address the threat of new entrants. This aspect of the industry makes it very easy for new entrants to appear. Every year there will be a new place considered popular and trendy.

In the case of the European market, which is the main origin of tourists, short-break markets may be considered substitute products. Consumers would need to be convinced to choose long-haul destinations over cheaper short-break holidays. There is need to research what makes people choose short-breaks. Other substitute products may range from replica tourist attractions from abroad, e.g. zoos, or other places that collect African wildlife and offer theme visits portraying African jungles.

The Kenyan Tourism Product

The tourism industry is one of the most competitive in the world, because of the frequency with which several destinations will offer similar activities. Kenya competes directly with wildlife destinations such as Tanzania, South Africa, Zimbabwe, Namibia and Botswana, however it has the advantage of being in the lead position, as well as having an outstanding reputation as the ultimate destination in Africa. It can be described as a mature destination and features widely in many European operators' portfolios. Despite the fact that it is still seen as the most obvious choice for a safari holiday, for the mass market as well as some niche sectors, Kenya is certainly not as fashionable today, largely because its image has been damaged by bad media publicity. However it is clear that Kenyan tourism has not died, and that there is still some affection for Kenya, with it being judged slightly differently when compared with other African countries. Kenya's combination of tropical beaches and wildlife safaris is the most known product, competing fiercely with the Caribbean and other African countries.

Kenya's market profile analysis highlights the tourism product with various features ranging from wildlife, general sightseeing (the Great Rift Valley), adventure tourism (Mount Kenya), religious events, eco-tourism, agri-tourism and cultural festivals, amongst others. These make it possible for Kenya to target various segments of the market from the high-spending specialist groups to the adventure pursuits youth market. While some of these features are not unique to Kenya, they present an opportunity for repositioning the product portfolio, which could lead to better rewards. It is on this basis that Kenya should continue to strengthen its business in long-haul and domestic markets. Maximizing the strengths and minimizing the weaknesses are crucial tasks if the country is to meet and exceed its targets for visitor numbers and foreign exchange earnings. The challenges and opportunities of the Kenyan tourism product in relation to potential tea tourism development are assessed later in the chapter.

The Kenyan tourism product can be hard to define as it encapsulates more than one component of a holiday. The safari holiday can be classified as being in its maturity stage, having been around for many years – though this does not necessarily guarantee it will continue to grow in popularity. Business travel on the other hand is a product that has moved to a leading position in the growth market: it is generating large sums and can be termed a cash cow. Adventure tourism and agri-tourism are new products being introduced as a new package and can therefore be referred to as rising stars.

A product portfolio analysis indicates that competition for the Kenyan market comes in the form of the market source and product type. Therefore, fierce competition for the different aspects of its product portfolio exists. Tea may arguably be the next untapped tourism attraction for Kenya, as it has a rich tea history. Tea is the second most popular drink worldwide and a few tour operations have already been developed around this in some tea-growing parts of Kenya, e.g. Kericho. A number of tour operators in Kenya offer also agricultural tours. Tourists are given the opportunity to visit production areas, seeing the various production stages and even sampling the final product.

Tea in Kenya

Kenya lies on the equator and its 583,000 sq km can be divided into four zones (Lonely Planet, 2004). This includes the coastal belt with its white beaches, coral reefs and hot year-round weather; the Rift Valley and Central Highlands (home to Lakes Nakuru and Bogoria and Mount Kenya); western Kenya with its pristine rainforest and green tea plantations fading away to semi-desert in the south; and the north and east, with areas of vast semi-arid bush land where rain is sparse. Tea requires a hot, wet climate for its growth and production, and both the Central Highlands and western Kenya have these conditions (Figure 10.2). Kenya has a particular advantage for tea production in that tea can be picked for most of the year (Pratt, 1982). Tea estates were first set up after the First World War using tea bushes imported from China and India. In the late 1950s, with the failure of coffee production, many plantations were converted to tea production. These plantations were able to produce a tea that responded to the world's need for a tea that could be brewed instantly (Bramah, 2004). This small leaf tea is described as particularly full-bodied, producing a good colour. 'It is the colour and richness of the teas that makes them ideal for tea bags, which depend on eye appeal' (Evans & Hilton, 1998: 23).

Tea may be cultivated in small tea holdings or in larger tea plantations. Kenya is noted as being unique in that the majority of its tea (66%) is

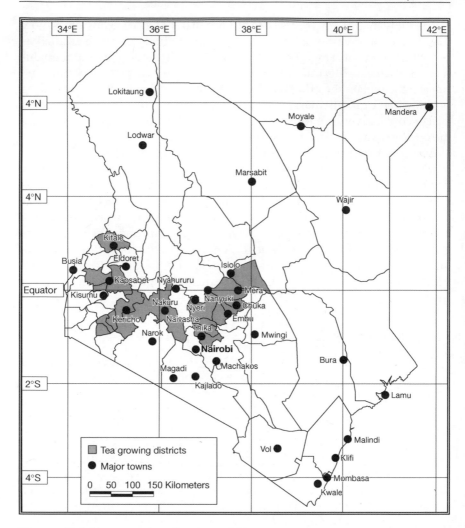

Figure 10.2 Tea growing districts of Kenya

Source: Reproduced with the permission of the Kenya Tea Development Agency

produced by smallholders (Lonely Planet, 2004). In Kenya tea grown by smallholders is collected and processed in the factories owned by the government agency, the Kenya Tea Development Agency (KTDA). However, a few large companies, such as Brooke Bond, George Williamson, Eastern Produce and African Highland, grow tea on their own plantations, process it in their own factories, and do their own marketing. Tea is plucked (picked) by hand and then processed by machine. The majority of tea produced in the country is processed not by traditional orthodox methods that produce a full leaf tea but by the CTC (crush, cut and curl) method rendering a granulated form of tea 'described as a quick infusion tea or fast-brew' (Bramah, 2004). The tea in Kenya is picked by male workers whereas in most other tea-producing regions of the world the pickers or pluckers are mainly female workers.

A number of government agencies and related organizations are involved in the tea industry in the country (Figure 10.3), including the Kenya Tea Development Authority (the KTDA was replaced in 2000 by the Kenya Tea Development Agency) and the Association of Tea Growers, responsible for developing and marketing Kenyan teas around the world. These organizations promote standards and certification for the industry in

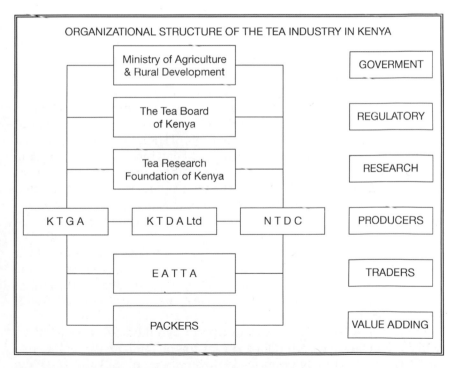

Figure 10.3 Structure of tea industry in Kenya

Source: The Tea Board of Kenya

general. The Tea Board of Kenya, established in 1950 under an act of parliament, licenses tea growers, tea manufacturers and tea exports. The board also carries out research on tea through its technical division, the Kenya Tea Research Foundation. Other agencies involved in the tea industry include the Kenya Tea Development Authority, the Kenya Tea Growers Association, Nyayo Tea Zone Development Corporation and the East Africa Tea Trade Association, which manages the tea auctions at Mombasa.

Kenya currently competes with Sri Lanka for the position of leading tea exporter in the world. By the year 2005, it is projected that Kenya will account for 20–3% of world exports if current growth rates are sustained (Burnet, 2000). It currently earns the country 34 billion Kenyan shillings per annum. Small-scale production accounts for 65% of the area and about 62% of production. Notably, among all of Kenya's other export crops, only tea has maintained this upward trend in production and export earnings. The United Kingdom remains the single most important destination for Kenyan tea, accounting for about 44% of total exports. However, the Kenyan tea industry must also contend with other external challenges posed by overseas buyers. Tea, like other developing country export industries, is increasingly being forced to adopt ethical practices that embrace socially, environmentally and financially responsible business.

Importers, particularly those from the UK, have increasingly been demanding that the tea supply chain comply with employee social and welfare standards. UK tea companies buy tea from around the world, although most comes from Kenya (about 50% of UK tea imports) with other significant suppliers being Sri Lanka, India, Malawi and Indonesia. In many of these countries smallholders either dominate or are a significant element of production. Tea production for the KTDA has largely been concentrated in the Eastern, Central, Rift Valley, Nyanza and Western provinces, in which there are 28 tea-growing districts. There are approximately 350,000 tea smallholders licensed with the KTDA. They own their own land and have tea licences permitting them to grow and pluck the green leaf and deliver it to buying stations run by KTDA, which acts as a managing agent to the smallholder tea sector. This scheme has been acknowledged as the largest and most successful major peasant-based tea scheme in the world (Lamb & Mueller, 1982).

The KTDA sells the majority of its tea through the weekly tea auctions held in Mombasa. It reports selling 75% by this method, 7% through Kenya Tea Packers, 15% through direct sales (overseas and local) and 4% at the factory door (KTDA, 2004). Although Kenyan tea remains unexploited as a tourism product package, tea-related tourism has the potential to increase this latter amount, as more tea might be purchased as souvenirs by tourists visiting some or all of the 51 factories managed by the authority. This is only one of a number of potential linkages that can be identified between the tea and tourism industries (Table 10.1).

Table 10.1 Linkages within the tea and tourism industries

Tourism characteristics	*Tea market characteristics*	*Implications for agri-tourism*
High foreign exchange earner	High foreign exchange earner	Both sectors are major foreign exchange earners and therefore combining the main features to form a tourism product presents high foreign exchange earning opportunities
Eco-tourism projected growth	Projected growth in the tea market	There is projected growth in both markets, indicating a long-term potential for the economy
Smallholder domination at community level	Smallholder domination	Smallholders dominate both sectors, providing the opportunity to improve livelihoods at community level and hence promote sustainable development.
Growth of sustainable development importance	Emerging ethical issues in sustainability	Corporate social responsibility within these sectors may also provide a further opportunity in sustainable development.
High potential for financial returns and therefore economic restructuring	High potential for financial returns and therefore economic restructuring	Both sectors provide backward linkages that are the backbone of the economy.
UK remains an important destination for Kenyan tourism	UK remains the single most important destination for Kenya tea accounting for about 44% of total exports	There is an added advantage to cross-market both products to the main market, which also has a historic link and can therefore be considered safe.

Tea-related Tourism Products

The nature and scale of tea production in Kenya provides opportunities for the development of tea-related tourism. In addition the seasonal nature of tourism demand (Sindiga, 1996) means that there is capacity to develop tea tourism products for the 'shoulder' seasons. The dominance of tea gardens and estates in particular parts of the country forms a distinct feature of the landscape that will be attractive to tourists seeking this kind of environment. The preponderance of smallholdings growing tea provides an opportunity for tours to small farms so that visitors can be introduced to the growing of tea on a small scale; and the large tea factories should also provide prospects for tours. Teatime and afternoon tea are also traditions in Kenya that can be experienced at hotels and other food service outlets, reflecting the country's past as a British colony.

Several products have thus been identified as being available for tea-related tourism. The Kericho Tea Hotel (Case study 1) provides lodging and serves afternoon teas in the middle of a tea estate. The hotel arranges for visits to tea factories and for guided walks through the tea gardens. This situation provides an excellent model for integrating a number of tea-related experiences at one site. At Kericho and at other locations visits to tea farms (Case study 2) provide a cultural experience for visitors and offer a product component that can be added to existing packaged tourism products such as safaris. At Mombasa (Case study 3), while no dedicated tea-tourism product currently exists, there is potential for using the port's tea history to develop tourism.

Case study 1: Kericho Tea Hotel

The town of Kericho was named after the English tea planter John Kerich. It is located at a 6000 feet altitude in the Kenya Highlands, surrounded by hectares of tea plantations, and is the tea-growing centre of western Kenya. Tea is a major source of employment in the area as the tea needs to be picked every 17 days and the same picker picks each patch (Lonely Planet, 2004). The Kericho Tea Hotel was built by Brooke Bond Limited in 1955 and initially used as a club for employees. Today the hotel offers lodging and it arranges visits to nearby tea estates and factories as well as guided walks through the tea gardens for its guests. It is also possible to take afternoon tea at the hotel. As one visitor to the hotel recounted:

> There is much more than tea-taking at this resort that you might be forced to change your itinerary and spend a longer time than you planned. This is exactly what happened to me. As I sat enjoying my

favourite beverage at the airy and beautiful lawn garden, the captivating scenery yonder was too enticing for me to spend a little more time here – the tea plantations stretched endlessly like a rich green carpet as far into the horizon as the eye can see. As I marveled at this scenery, the waiter arrived with yet another enticing attraction that I couldn't resist – a list of activities available at the hotel, one of them being a nature walk [through the tea gardens] which he assured me would be full of fun and discoveries. Irresistible! (Yellow Pages Kenya, 2004)

The hotel reported averaging several tour groups monthly with bookings handled centrally through the Kenya Tourist Board branch in Utalii house; it is possible that it could achieve greater success with this packaged product if more resources were available for sales and marketing. It is also reported that the hotel was renovating its guest rooms: this improvement may contribute to the development of packaged tours that could include experiences in the surrounding tea gardens (Mutai, 2000).

Case study 2: Visits to tea farms

In the tea-growing area of Limuru amid the Ngong Hills, 30 km northwest of Nairobi, there are vast tea plantations. Here, there are organized visits to small tea holdings such as Mitchel's Kiambethu Tea Farm (Lonely Planet, 2004). Some safaris include visits to tea farms such as this one. In the Kenyan Highlands visits to the tea estates at Kericho are also arranged through the Kericho Tea Hotel. The hotel has on average about two tour groups per month for whom they organize trips to the tea factories and other areas of interest around Kericho, for example trekking into the forest. The group may consist of five to ten people.

Case study 3: Mombasa

In the port city of Mombasa, a tea auction is held every Monday. At these auctions the tea sold is not only from Kenya but also from a number of other countries in Africa. In 2003 Kenya maintained its lead in sales of tea at this auction: 'The country sold 110,526 tonnes of tea between January and June and was expected to sell more in the second half of the year' (*Daily Nation*, 2003). This history of tea in Mombasa could be used for touristic purposes, interpreting the port city as a 'tea port', which could be of interest for tea tours, as this activity could be combined with visits to tea farms and tea sites in other parts of Kenya.

Tour Operator Survey

A number of Kenya tour operators were asked for information about visits to tea farms and tea factories. The firms surveyed were all members of the Kenya Association of Tour Operators. Enquiries were sent to 19 operators and there were responses from 11 (a response rate of 58%). All operators indicated that they would be able to arrange visits to tea farms either near Nairobi (e.g. Limuru) and several indicated that tours to outlying areas (e.g. Kericho) could also be arranged. Some of the companies offered brief custom tours (a few days), while others proposed a traditional safari itinerary, with tea experiences interspersed. A sampling of the product offered by the respondents who provided some detail indicates that this product is at an early stage of development (Table 10.2).

Judging by the comments made by tour operators (e.g. 'We have had agricultural tourism but it has been restricted to areas around Nairobi where there [are] tea and coffee estates this has been on a very minimal scale') tea tourism has only been offered on a small scale to date. Both Limuru (near Nairobi) and Kericho were destinations for tea visits mentioned by a number of the operators. The Kiambethu Tea Estate is a destination mentioned by several of the operators. Its popularity may in part be because it is near Limuru, and hence in close proximity to Nairobi. One response

Table 10.2 Tea tour products offered by Kenya tour operators

Custom tours offered to tea gardens and tea factories, not in major tourism areas but in the vicinity of national parks.
A two-day package from Narobi to Kericho to visit the tea gardens and stay at the Kericho Tea Hotel with a guided tour of the surrounding tea farm and visit to a nearby tea factory. Includes the services of an English-speaking guide/driver.
Opportunities to visit tea farms and tea factories as part of tourism packages including, visits to a tea farm on the outskirts of Nairobi – The Kiambethu Tea Farm, and several tea farms and tea factories in Kericho area.
An 11-day, 10-night tea safari. Tea experiences include: Lunch and afternoon tea on Kiambethu Tea Estate with a lecture on local history of the area and production of tea and take part in a guided walk of the nearby forest and the tea plantations (Day 2).   Lunch at the (Kericho)Tea Hotel followed by a visit to one of the tea plantations where a guided tour of the tea-processing factory will be given. It may also be possible to join a local family for 'Chai' (tea). Dinner and overnight at the Tea Hotel (Day 4).

included a detailed description of a visit to this tea farm, about 30 km from Nairobi:

> Kiambethu Tea Estate located in the outskirts of Nairobi about 30 km at an altitude of 7000 feet above sea level with lush acres of tea plantations that seem to vanish in the horizon. Here two English families Mitchell & McDonnell in the early 1900s built this Estate. These families are said to be the first to have ventured into the tea business. You will have a lecture on the history of the area and also about the production of tea. In the afternoon take a walk through the tea plantations and forests which display the conditions needed for the growth of tea. The lecture on growth of tea is a good learning experience. For instance, you will see tea pickers on the farm plucking the top two leaves and bud from each plantation. (Alefran Tours and Safaris Ltd)

Another operator observed that, while the tea visits were not to major tourism areas, the tea areas have a natural beauty and attractive landscape. And yet another operator indicated that a tea tour, if offered, could hopefully be part of a new line of agricultural tourism. There is clearly some recognition of the potential for developing tea-related tours and a willingness to offer this product, if only on a custom tour basis.

Developing Tea Tourism in Kenya

With major areas of Kenya under tea cultivation there is potential for the development of more tourism related to tea. The opportunity to visit tea gardens and learn about tea cultivation and production, possibly visit a tea auction, sample teas and purchase tea-related souvenirs could appeal to the growing segment of cultural tourists looking for new experiences. While there are opportunities for developing tourism related to tea in Kenya there are also challenges and obstacles to be overcome. A strengths, weaknesses, opportunities and threats analysis provides a framework for assessment (Table 10.3).

Strengths

The nature of Kenya's tea production, with both small-scale holdings and large tea estates and factories provides opportunities for a variety of 'tea experiences' for tourists who visit tea farms, tea gardens, tea estates and tea factories. There is also the opportunity to visit and experience one of Africa's tea auctions at Mombasa. That tea drinking is a part of Kenyan

Table 10.3 SWOT analysis – tea and tourism in Kenya

Strengths	Opportunities
• Kenya has established itself as amongst the most popular destinations in Africa • Reputation of relative political stability • Well established transport and accommodation infrastructure • Wide range of products, all year climate • English is a widely spoken language • Established name among tour operators • Tea gardens form a historic part of the landscape with many small holdings • Africa's main tea auction at Mombasa • Tea drinking traditions • Strong tea and tourism industry groups	• One of the few destinations to combine various features in one package holiday • Potential for other products e.g. agritourism (Tea, coffee and flowers) • Can spread tourism geographically • Ability to self promote in other African countries as it is seen as a model • Potential for interpretive visits and tours to tea farms, auctions • Developing culinary and gastronomic aspects of tea • Opportunities for tourism and tea partnerships, e.g. community projects
Weaknesses	Threats
• No clear tourism policy to identify where the industry is heading • Deteriorating infrastructure • Level of tourism development support low • Mass market tag • Entry visa requirement • Perceived as 'old product' • Large mechanized factories producing tea • Lack of interpretation of tea cultivation, production and traditions for visitors	• Similar countries with same products • Terrorism threat • Negative travel advisories from the west • Lack of a clear management structure • Over-reliance on the selected major markets • Perceived corruption in government • Short tea history in relation to other tea destinations (i.e. China, Japan, India) • Labour unrest in the tea industry • Little tradition of tea-related tourism

society means that tea services can be experienced at different levels, from the *chai* (black tea with milk) or *chai masala* (black tea with milk and spices) served at local cafés to afternoon tea at luxury hotels and beach resorts. The fact that the tea and tourism industries are both highly organized should provide a structure for potential partnerships in the development of tea-related tourism.

Weaknesses

A number of constraints for development are also evident. These include the large and mechanized scale of the industry as well as the characteristics of employment and labour relations within it, which may not provide a suitable backdrop for developing tea-tourism experiences.

The highly mechanized, large-scale nature of the majority of the tea industry may make it unsuitable for traditional forms of cultural tourism where tourists seek authenticity and want hands-on experiences' but nonetheless could make this aspect of the tea industry of interest as a form of agri-tourism.

Additionally, there is some labour unrest in the tea industry: for example, actions by the unregistered Kenya Union of Small-Scale Tea-Owners (KUSSTO) might prevent the development of tea tourism in relation to smaller holdings; or actions by the Kenya Plantation and Agriculture Workers Union (KPAWU), who oppose the introduction of machine picking and related potential job loss, might hinder the development of tea tourism in relation to the larger estates (*Eastern Standard*, 2004). There is little tradition of tourism in relation to tea gardens, other than a few opportunities for independent and group travellers to tour tea estates and visit their factories.

Opportunities

One potential for development lies with the former Nyago Tea Zone now called the Kenya Tea and Forests Conservation Zone (Riungu, 2004). The mandate of this authority includes both forest and environmental conservation and the development of community projects. There is a potential here for the emergence of community-based tourism projects in relation to the tea gardens located in this buffer zone. Both the Zone organization itself and the relevant tourism authorities might be interested in this type of development because of its potential for forward and backward linkages with the local economy and also its potential for generating profits that might be turned back to conservation efforts. This also ties in with government tourism policy directive to develop the tourism sector in tandem with other economic sectors.

There is also potential for the gender diversification of local employment though tea-related tourism. With most of the tea 'pluckers' traditionally being male it may be possible to increase the employment of females through the provision of tea-related services for tourists. In addition, those producing tea through smallholdings may be able to diversify their incomes through the involvement in small-scale tourism initiatives related to tea.

Another possibility is the development of tea-related visits in conjunction with the tea auctions at Mombasa. The auctions have a rich and colourful history and it is possible that the interpretation of this history could be incorporated as a cultural element to complement other cultural resources in the city. The tea auction is only held on Mondays and arranged visits would be of interest to 'extreme' tea tourists who would like to experience a tea auction. These tourists have been identified as being willing to go anywhere for tea experiences and making vacation decisions based on availability of tea facilities and potential tea experiences (Jolliffe, 2003a).

Tea tourism may not be able to be developed as a stand-alone tourism activity but might be able to complement the existing nature tourism and eco-tourism focus. Tea services are an accepted part of food service and hostelry services so there is potential to develop these into products for tourists, e.g. 'afternoon tea' tours. In some areas there is potential for developing community-based sustainable tourism development initiatives related to small-scale tea holdings. Developing tea tourism could contribute to diversifying the tourism product, which in the past has mainly consisted of beach, wildlife and urban attractions (Sindiga, 1996). There is also opportunity that tea tourism may be used to increase tourism demand overall, thus extending the tourism season in some situations.

Threats

Issues related to the safety and security of travelling in Kenya may pose a threat for the development of tea-related tourism in the country. In addition, in a competitive international tourism marketplace Kenya is a country with little tea history in relation to other tea destinations (e.g. China, Japan and India). The labour unrest within the tea industry may also result in limited access to tea farms and factories for tourists thus limiting the potential development of tours for tea tourism. That there is little tradition or culture of tea-related tourism may also pose a threat to the further development of this niche area of tourism, partly because of a lack of interpretation of the workings of the tea industry.

Conclusion

Tourism and tea both have considerable importance to the economy of Kenya. The country has proved itself to be a diverse tourism destination yet one in which both tour operators and visitors are looking for alternatives to the traditional mass-market offerings. Tea-related tourism may offer such an opportunity as part of eco-tourism, cultural tourism or agri-tourism. Tea tourism may also afford an opportunity for Kenya to offer a product different from that of its direct and indirect competitors. Since little tea-related tourism seems to currently exist in Kenya there is also the opportunity to offer tea experiences as a new form of tourism for new markets. Considering all the possibilities, tea-related tourism could provide the Kenyan tourism industry with an opportunity to reposition their overall product in the marketplace. There are also considerable opportunities for the cross-marketing of tea and tourism, particularly with the tea-loving UK market, which is a prime consumer of both Kenyan tea and tourism experiences.

The nature of the tea industry in Kenya, consisting of both a large number of smallholders and a small number of large-scale tea factories, provides both opportunities and constraints for tea tourism. Most of the tea in Kenya is produced using modern, non-traditional methods, and is sold for blending and use in tea bags. Small tea farms are conducive to small-scale cultural tourism whereas large factory production units may not be. With the high number of tea farms reported to exist in the country there is much opportunity for visits and interpretations of tea growing and plucking. In a country where diversification of employment and family income is needed, tea tourism may provide valuable opportunities for tea-farm families to supplement their income. In some rural communities, community tourism projects may be developed in relation to tea holdings, particularly by the Kenya Tea and Forests Conservation Zone, an organization with a mandate to develop such projects. With the larger scale tea estates and factories there may also be the potential to develop industry visits and create an interpretive element, for example Brook Bond might be able to do this in conjunction with its tea estates and factory at Kericho.

Therefore, from this limited review, while little tea tourism has been developed to date there appear to be sufficient resources, both in terms of the tea gardens and factories and also other sites related to tea, to afford opportunities for the tea and tourism industries to work together to develop tourism related to tea. Both the industries are highly structured and this organization may provide partnership opportunities for developing tea-related tourism products and experiences. Tea experiences could complement other major tourism products, such as safari tourism and beach tourism, and contribute to developing the agri-tourism product in relation to tea, an endeavour that could encompass, for example, walking tours, horse riding, photography and educational visits to tea farms. As tourism in Kenya strategically moves away from (safari) parks and beaches this tea-related tourism could be ideally situated as a new niche area of cultural and educational tourism.

References

Akama, S.J. (1997) Tourism development in Kenya. Problems and policy alternatives. *Progress in Tourism and Hospitality Research* 3, 95–105.

Bramah, Edward (2004) Personal correspondence. London: Bramah Tea and Coffee Museum.

Burnet, D. (2000) Twin project in Kenya. Unpublished document.

Daily Nation (2003) (Nairobi), 9 July.

Dieke, U.C.P. (1991) Policies for tourism development in Kenya. *Annals of Tourism Research* 18, 269–91.

Dieke, U.C.P. (2001) Marketing the tourism product in Africa. *Advancing Knowledge Development in African Business International Conference, Washington, DC, April 2001.* (pp. 275–82) International Academy of African Business Development.

Eastern Standard (2004) Tea machine plans opposed. *English Standard* (Nairobi) – 10 February.

Evans, Sarah Jane and Hilton, Giles (1998) *The Book of Coffee and Tea.* London: Whittard.

Harler, C.R. (1956) *The Culture and Marketing of Tea.* London: Oxford University Press.

Jolliffe, Lee (2003a) Something's brewing: Tea and tourism in Canada. Presented at the Travel and Tourism Research Canada Conference, October 2003.

Jolliffe, Lee (2003b) The lure of tea: history, traditions and attractions. In M. Hall, L. Sharples, R. Mitchell, N. Macionis and B. Cambourne. *Food Tourism Around the World: Development, Management and Markets* (pp. 121–36). London: Butterworth-Heineman.

Kenyan Government (1998) Kenya economic survey, 1998. Nairobi: Central Bureau of Statistics, Ministry of Planning and National Development.

KTB (Kenyan Tourist Board) (1997) Development Plan 1994–1997. Nairobi: KTB.

KTB (2001) Marketing plan 2003–2007. Nairobi: KTB.

KTDA (Kenya Tea Development Agency) (2004) Online document: http://www.ktdateas.com (accessed 24 August 2004).

KWS (Kenya Wildlife Service) (1996) Fact file. Nairobi: KWS.

KWS (1997) Fact file. Nairobi: KWS.

KWS (1998) Fact file. Nairobi: KWS.

Kericho Tea Hotel (2004) Online doucment: http://www.yellowpageskenya.com/travel/kerichoteahotel.asp (accessed 19 July).

Kotler P. (1999) *Marketing Management.* New Jersey: Prentice Hall.

Lavery, P. (1996) *Travel and Tourism* (3rd edn). Huntingdon: Elm Publications.

Lamb, L. and Muller, L. (1982) *Control, Accountability, and Incentives in a Successful Development Institution: The Kenya Tea Authority.* World Bank Staff Working Papers, No. 50. Washington, DC: The World Bank.

Lonely Planet (2004) *Kenya.* London: Lonely Planet Publications.

Mutai, B. (2000) Implications and implementation of electronic commerce technology. Unpublished MA thesis.

Mwangi, J. (1997) Tourism statistics: Computer applications to statistic management. Unpublished document.

Ondimu, Kennedy I. (2002) Cultural tourism in Kenya. *Annals of Tourism Research* 29 (4), 1036–47.

Pratt, James Norwood (1982) *The Tea Lovers Treasury.* San Ramon, CA: 101 Productions.

Riungu, Catherine (2004) Why tea zones easily defied the 'Nyayo' tag. *Daily Nation.* Nairobi, 17 February.

Sindiga, Isaac (1996) Domestic tourism in Kenya. *Annals of Tourism Research* 23 (1), 19–31.

UNESCO Courier (1997) Kenya becomes world's leading tea exporter. 50 (12), 43–52.

World Travel and Tourism Council (2000) Various reports. Online documents: www.wttc.org.

WTO (World Tourism Organization) (2000) Various reports. Online documents: www.wto.org.

Yellow Pages Kenya (2004) Kericho Tea Hotel: Seductively appealing. Online document: http://www.yellowpageskenya.com/travel/kerichoteahotel.asp (accessed 14 September 2004).

Part 4: Transforming Tea: From Tea Experiences to Tea Destinations

Chapter 11

China's Tea and Horse Trade Route and its Potential for Tourism

HILARY DU CROS

Tea can be presented as an experience, for example participating in tea-drinking ceremonies or viewing associated tea ware in museums. It can also be presented as a process with temporal and spatial dimensions resulting in the consumption of valued goods. Tea has always been a product in great demand. It is one of the first internationally traded goods (along with coffee and tobacco), partly due to the addictive nature of caffeine. Specifically, tea is linked to a process where it is grown, processed, branded and traded both locally and over great distances. Historical, ethnographical, archaeological and architectural evidence of this process in pre-industrial times is still accessible through an examination of the 'Tea and Horse Trade Route' in southwest China. This chapter will look at the nature of this heritage asset briefly with regard to its history and cultural significance, discuss its tourism potential, and identify opportunities and constraints for its sustainable development as a tea-tourism route for both domestic and international tourism markets.

The Heritage Asset

The Tea and Horse Trade Route in southwest China links the provinces of Sichuan and Yunnan with Tibet (see Plate 11.1). 'Border Tea' (as it is more commonly known in Mandarin) is consumed by over 20 million people in western China. Tea originated in China and has been traded outside its borders for over a thousand years. Early sites of tea growing include Xishuangbanna in Yunnan, and Mt Mengding in Sichuan. The Tea Research Institute in Menghai believes the original site of tea production is in southern Yunnan but further research into this important aspect is still ongoing. The much-prized imperial tribute tea – *Puer* – is grown in the

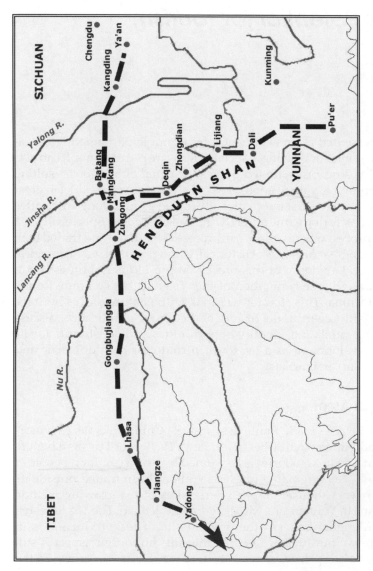

Plate 11.1 Tea and Horse Trade Route (from *www.silkroadfoundation.org*). This is a simplified version of the route which is more like a network (see Tu and Kuang, 1995: 9 for a full map).

Xishuangbanna region and around the Simao County in southern Yunnan (see Plate 11.2).

Tea was first brought to Tibet from China in AD 641 and was traded for horses as well as being transported using horses. Numerous villages and towns along the route played a role in trade (see Plates 11.3, 11.4). For instance, Dayan Ancient Town, Lijiang, was once an important tea trade and processing centre (now a world heritage site). Smaller villages produced other goods that were also traded up and down the route. Nearly 50,000 horses carried tea to Tibet at its busiest in the 1700s. However, the tea trade diminished after 1951, when Tibet began producing its own tea (du Cros, 2001a). Nonetheless, new markets have opened overseas for *Puer* tea, which appears to be sent increasingly by modern transport modes in either its raw or processed form to specialist tea sellers in North America and Europe (see, for instance, Numitea, 2004). This increasing overseas interest in the tea is likely to be a cause for celebration for those in China and Hong

Plate 11.2 Puer Tea Performance, Yunnan, China

Source: Hilary du Cros

Kong advocating the preservation and presentation of the tea trade as a living culture as well as its associated tangible heritage.

The Tea and Horse Trade Route could be classified as a linear cultural landscape that includes nodes, linkages and features that demonstrate it is a culturally significant transport and communication network. These elements include remaining and authentic sections of the original road, inns, tea plantations (including historic tea gardens, trees and growing fields), factories, houses, markets (or retail areas associated with tea or the trade route's other goods and features, for example, salt and silk), horse stables and stud farms. Note should also be made of intangible heritage associated with the trade route, such as the knowledge of the different ways of processing and drinking *Puer* tea and its importance in celebrating the Autumn Moon Festival.

At present one of the main issues for the Tea and Horse Trade Route as a heritage route is that the government is more likely to invest money in conserving heritage assets of international or national significance. It believes these assets are likely to be more appealing to tourists and their conservation and development for tourism will provide economic benefits

Plate 11.3 Churning Tea, Yunnan, China

Source: Hilary du Cros

to the underdeveloped southwest of China. The precedent for this belief is the success of the world heritage inscribed sites, such as that of the Dayan ancient town in Lijiang, which is now also currently a highly popular domestic heritage tourism attraction. Although Lijiang was important to the process of trading tea this is not the reason why it was inscribed on the world heritage list, nor why tourists flock to it today (see Plate 11.4).

However, before the trade route can be nominated as a world heritage linear cultural landscape or even an asset of high national significance, it still requires extensive documentation of its remaining elements and greater attention to their protection under existing planning and historic relic legislation. In addition to this it will need a carefully and rigorously researched claim about its founding role in the history of growing and processing tea in China. Accurate and detailed documentation linking it to the relevant areas of the main tea- and horse-trading towns needs to be undertaken by rigorously researching and identifying the tangible cultural assets within those cities, towns and other stops that still retain authentic examples of elements associated with the route.

Plate 11.4 Lijang Village, Yunnan, China
Source: Hilary du Cros

Such stops along the route include: places in Xishuangbanna, Simao, Puer, Mohei, Kongque Ping, Jinghong, Weishan, Eryuan, Jianchuan, Dali, Shaxi Valley, Xizhou, Zhoucheng (horse markets), Lijiang, Tiger Leaping Gorge, Shigu Town, Zhongdian, Deqing and into Tibet; and the upper route, including Mojiang, Wuliang Mt, Yuanjiang, E'shan and Kunming (see Tu & Kuang, 1995; He, 1999; Simao Tourism Office, n.d.). Finally information is needed on the stretches where the horse caravan may still be used to transport goods, and further documentation of oral histories of tea growers/processors, caravan leaders, horse drivers, traders and tea ritual tradition bearers. As this region modernizes, much of this information is in danger of being lost and needs to be recorded not only for the purposes of better presenting the asset's value to tourists, but also for posterity.

Previous Efforts to Document and Conserve the Asset

Although there have been no systematic efforts in this area regarding the trade route equal to that for the Silk Road, a number of conservation projects have been carried out on its features (individually or in groups). The broadest attempt to document the trade route's features was carried out by Hong Kong photographers in collaboration with local counterparts in Yunnan and Sichuan. The work received mainly non-government support from the China International Tea Culture Society, the *Women's Voice of Yunnan* magazine, and the expenses were paid for by Agfa Film Company and the Yuxi Cigarette Factory (a rare example of corporate/state commercial sponsorship – though unfortunate part related to cigarettes). The photographers documented aspects of living culture and tangible remains for part of the network that was most easily accessible, leaving some branches untested. Information on the network was provided to the team during a national conference on tea culture in 1994 in Kunming (Tu & Kuang, 1995).

The ancient tea and market towns of Lijiang, Weishan and Dali are national listed historic towns where local authorities have undertaken conservation and urban planning measures towards their ongoing preservation. Of these, Lijiang's Dayan Ancient Town has probably received the most attention, following a severe earthquake in 1996. The authorities were offered foreign aid by the World Bank to assist in the rebuilding and repairs of its traditional style buildings in a way that would also remove the infill of modern buildings and boost the integrity of its traditional vernacular street-scape. The Ancient Town was then able to be defined by clear boundaries and designated under the historic town criteria, which would then pass 'the authenticity test' (see b.(i) in Section 3.10.1 of the World

Heritage Convention) for historic towns. It then had to show evidence that it had set various management and legislative measures in place to satisfy section b.(ii) of the World Heritage Convention nomination process. Laws were used at the national, provincial and local levels to protect the city's historic properties, sites and landscapes. Some of these laws were already in place prior to the nomination of the site and some followed as a result. In addition to the protection and guidelines provided by these laws, there are a county master plan, a site protection plan and an infrastructure plan. At present China finds it easier to integrate such measures for specific heritage assets of high heritage significance in urban areas, but is less able to conserve or regulate development in relation to group listings, particularly where they cross many administrative districts. The Great Wall is another linear cultural landscape that has suffered from ad hoc conservation and policy implementation, partly because of its scale (see du Cros *et al.*, 2005).

In 2001 the World Monument Fund (WMF) listed the Sideng Market in the Shaxi Valley (located between Dali and Lijiang – see Plate 11.1) on their 100 most endangered World Monuments list (WMF, 2004). It has been identified as the last intact 'caravanserai-like' stopover in China. Even so, this asset saw the last of the caravans in the 1950s when they were replaced by an alternative route and modern transport methods. Previously it was completely dependent on the trade route and aside from some limited agricultural production the area has stagnated in the intervening period. With the lack of pressure to redevelop and its relatively remote location, much remains of the trade route stop. Key features include the market and village buildings, associated shrines, the oral histories of the route and local non-Han ethnic cultures (mainly the Bai and Yi). The Yunnan Provincial Ministry of Culture (which is ever in search of more world heritage nominations) is funding studies with the hope that more cultural sites will be inscribed on the world heritage list (Feiner *et al.*, 2002).

The WMF listing enabled funding to be raised overseas for a rehabilitation project to illustrate how 'rural communes and their society and economy can be developed in a sustainable way by taking advantage of specific local potential and assets' (Feiner *et al.*, 2002). It particularly targeted the economic benefits of tourism by allowing for some sensitive development, while trying to safeguard the cultural values of the asset and the ecological qualities of its setting. To this end, a number of recommendations were made to enhance the character of the historic Sideng village, which will hopefully prevent tourism infrastructure and domestic visits from adversely impacting upon it as its popularity grows. Less important in this planning was how the core message of this cultural landscape will be relayed and what impression visitors will have of the village's role in the Tea and Horse Trade Route. Even so, it provides an important start to works that could potentially add another layer of meaning to the visitor's understanding of the tea-trading process in southwest China.

Heritage Routes as Tourism Routes in China

Typical tourism product development strategies can include: building new attractions; bundling together attractions (encouraging the clustering of attractions); the creation of tourism precincts; the use of special events; and creation of linear routes or itineraries. Linear routes are an opportunity for attractions to work together cooperatively. Such a strategy is also seen as a low-cost tourism development option by some destinations (McKercher & du Cros, 2002).

In China, the Silk Road is an example of a heritage route that is being packaged successfully as a linear tourism product. The Silk Road has been well promoted and conservation works on its key archaeological sites have been ongoing since the 1980s. The Getty Conservation Institute and other overseas partners have been working with local heritage officials on archaeological conservation projects associated with some of the key grotto sites since 1990. This work has assisted in preparing the sites to withstand tourism (Getty Conservation Institute, 2004).

The Tea and Horse Trade Route has sometimes been described as a type of 'southern Silk Road', as silk was transported along it from the south of Yunnan (Feiner *et al.*, 2002), but it is not and never has been actually part of *the* Silk Road (Bonavia *et al.*, 1998).The trade of tea and horses was always foremost, and therein lies the Tea and Horse Trade Route's own unique identity. While most of the attractions of the Silk Road are archaeological sites and finds, the Tea and Horse Trade Route has more recent architectural features that have a greater degree of preservation, and can also be linked directly to customs and memories of the local people living along it. Hence there is a wider range of options available for interpreting and marketing its core message to tourists. Even so, the Tea and Horse Trade Route's market appeal for the mass tourism market domestically and internationally may be *decreased* by its relationship to the Silk Road. A clever and comprehensive development of the route's value as the key to experiencing tea culture and trade in China could aid in avoiding negative market associations of it being 'almost the Silk Road' or the 'poor man's Silk Road with ethnic dancing'.

Even so, the Tea and Horse Trade Route is listed as an important asset on the official Yunnan Tourism web site (YPTA, 2004) and small adventure tourism operators are trying to incorporate it into cultural tours of main attractions (Edward Adventure Tours, 2004). This could be expanded if appropriate conservation measures, visitor facilities and interpretation materials are provided at more locations.

An assessment of the Tea and Horse Trade Route's potential as tourism route has been made, which briefly outlines key market appeal and robusticity issues. This assessment uses an upgraded version of the du Cros tourism assessment model developed over the last three years by analysing Hong Kong and mainland Chinese heritage assets (du Cros, 2000; 2001a; 2001b and 2002; McKercher *et al.*, 2003; du Cros & Ho, 2004). It should be seen as a rough guide to what one might expect if a holistic approach was taken to marketing and conserving the Tea and Horse Trade Route's features: an approach similar to that taken for the Silk Road, but with emphasis on its role in southwest Chinese trade in more recent times.

Market Appeal

Tea culture is of great interest to tea specialists, especially those in Hong Kong, Japan, Korea and the rest of China. At present, tea culture or the presence of the Tea and Horse Trade Route is barely touched upon by tourism promotions, which, at the time of writing, focus on exoticism of ethnic peoples, animals and vegetation. Any investigation of current brochures and websites from the region will show this, particularly the official provincial tourism sites. However, the Tea and Horse Trade Route's tourism potential was noted in the recent master plan for Yunnan Province sponsored by the World Tourism Organization (World Tourism Organization *et al.*, 2001), but not strongly enough, as nothing has yet been implemented. Although traffic along the Tea and Horse Trade Route has dwindled in recent years, it still offers a rich opportunity for tourists to learn more about historic tea production and trade in China through its tangible and intangible heritage. For instance, there is some market appeal for tour packages that follow the old Tea and Horse Trade Route from Xishuangbanna in the south of Yunnan, stopping at tea farms, archaeological sites, villages and towns (including Dali and Lijiang) on their way north into Tibet. Shorter packages that take less time are also possible for some stretches of the Trade Route, particularly the segment between Dali and Lijiang (see Plate 11.1). The potential of the Trade Route to yield these and other products has assisted its assessment as having a high ranking for market appeal in this brief assessment of its tourism potential (see Figure 11.1).

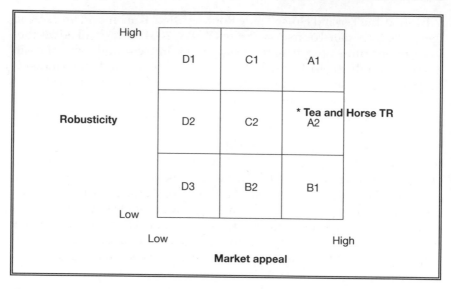

Figure 11.1 Placement in the market appeal/robusticity mix

After assessment of the Trade Route's potential market appeal using the model, several aspects really stand out. The smaller or more isolated features are most suitable for international tourists, compared with the domestic market, as little has been done to alter their appearance. Some of the towns (Dali and Simao) have tried to commodify tea culture for domestic tourists in ways that would not appeal to international and specialist tea tourists. A different type of experience is required for each market in this area for a feeling of engagement to occur. Accordingly, the former needs more work in some areas before the Tea and Horse Trade Route can reach its full potential.

Accessibility is an important part of assessing a potential product's market appeal. It involves observations of access *to* features, landmarks and other attractions, ease of access *for* visitors from central tourist areas, and also psychological factors regarding access. This is a heritage asset that could be consumed as part of any tourism package in southwestern China and is currently being developed as an add-on or complementary experience for those that visit the main attractions of Lijiang and Dali. However, to access more of the Trade Route in order to fully experience tea culture, more places, offering a diverse range of experiences, need to be visited. Physically, this could be achieved by a mixture of air and coach transport. Both Jinghong (in Xihuangbana, south Yunnan) and Kunming (Yunnan's capital city) have international airports, which are linked to other Asian countries; local airports exist at Lijiang, Zhongdian, Chengde (Sichuan) and Simao. Roads between the main centres are being upgraded to national highway standard to facilitate tourist travel and economic development generally. The psychological factors of visiting the features outside the main gateways may deter some visitors, particularly as tourism facilities are likely to be basic.

Accordingly, current facilities and interpretation for visitors is minimal outside town centres. This will become a major problem if the tea culture and the Tea and Horse Trade Route are heavily promoted without appropriate infrastructure to deal with the increased level of visits that this would encourage. One amusing comment (that is probably also true) given to the author was that tea-specialist tourists require frequent access to toilet facilities on road trips after the constant sampling of tea, hence the facilities had better be available and to an international standard to satisfy this market. Given current attitudes to providing such facilities in rural areas in China, it is likely that attractions there, such as tea-growing farms, would not only have to provide their own facilities but would also need to lobby local authorities to provide rest stops and signage along the main highways. Current facilities barely service the needs of domestic sightseeing tourism.

Robusticity

The visitor and cultural heritage management issues differ from that of the Silk Road as there is likely to be emphasis on retaining and revitalizing the living culture associated with the route. Also, the cultural significance of this asset as a whole has never been formally assessed as there has been no complete inventory of its extent and no detailed examination of its relationship to the cultural and historical development of south-west China. An approximate assessment of its significance is that, nationally, it is a rare type of asset. With the rapid change and destabilization of the urban settlements of most of eastern China, areas such as the Yunnan, Sichuan and eastern Tibet triangle are developing at a slower rate, hence the survival and partial functioning of this network and its culture. Unlike the Silk Road to the west, it has maintained its role as a trade network beyond the advent of maritime trade routes; and hence it has some living culture that overlaps with modern times. Sometimes it is closely associated with tangible features such as the Sideng marketplace in Shaxi Valley and Dayan Ancient Town, Lijiang (a world heritage site). As such, the impacts of tourism on this living culture need to be carefully monitored.

More needs to be done towards capacity-building at a village level to assist in safeguarding and presenting some of the more remote features, particularly if a tea-tourism route is developed outside the historic towns of Dali, Lijiang and Weishan. This goal requires more of a holistic approach that will take into account local cultural and ecological factors in how it incorporates external aid and expertise. It is promising that philanthropic organizations, such as WMF, are already showing an interest and are using a sustainable tourism development framework. Even so, two of the main obstacles to the sustainable development of the Tea and Horse Trade Route for tourism are its sheer scale and that it is very difficult to get administrative action at a local level that can support such policies. Hence, it is accorded a moderate rank for robusticity (see Figure 11.1).

Conclusion

Overall, the tourism potential of the Tea and Horse Trade Route as a heritage tourism route can be assessed as moderately high. It is a heritage asset with a high market appeal and moderate robusticity. The theme of tea growing, processing and trading will be critical to the successful marketing of the Tea and Horse Trade Route, if it is to retain its own identity and become a complementary attraction to world heritage sites in the region and the Silk Road further north.

The risk with some of the current domestic tourism promotions is that this special identity could be easily ignored or degraded and a great opportunity would be lost. Its development as a tea-tourism route, which takes in more than the current historic towns, would be worth pursuing for a specialist audience internationally and as a great educational resource locally. Ideally, it needs an overarching authority or task force to generate policy for the whole Trade Route and oversee its implementation at the local level, possibly established within Yunnan Provincial Tourism Association or the China National Tourism Administration with links to cultural heritage agencies. Specialist heritage expertise and support will be also required to assist in its implementation at the local level before quality niche tea tourism products will be available.

References

Bonavia, J., Lindesay, W. and Qi, W. (1998) *The Silk Road*. Hong Kong: Odyssey.
du Cros, H. (2000) Planning for sustainable cultural tourism in Hong Kong SAR. Unpublished report to Lord Wilson Heritage Trust.

du Cros, H. (2001a) Socio-cultural assessment component, Yunnan provincial tourism master plan. Report to the World Tourism Organization, China National Tourism Administration and the Yunnan Provincial Tourism Administration.

du Cros, H. (2001b) A new model to assist planning for sustainable Cultural Heritage Tourism. *International Journal of Tourism Research* 3(2): 165–70.

du Cros, H. (2002) The tourism potential of heritage routes: A case study from Yunnan, China. Conference Paper for 'Tourism and Hospitality on the Edge', 12th CAUTHE Conference, Fremantle, Australia.

du Cros, H. and Ho, P. (2004) Wun Yiu archaeological site tourism feasibility study site assessment report. Unpublished report to the Hong Kong Antiquities and Monuments Office, Hong Kong.

du Cros, H., Bauer, T., Lo, C. and Song, R. (2005) Cultural heritage assets in China as sustainable tourism products: Case studies of the Hutongs and the Huanghua section of the Great Wall. *Journal of Sustainable Tourism* 13 (2): 171–94.

Edward Adventure Tours (2004) Tours of Yunnan/The ethnic peoples of Yunnan. Online document: http://www.edward-adventures.com.

Feiner, P., Shiwen, M. and Schmid, W.A. (2002) sustainable rural development based on cultural heritage. The case of the Shaxi Valley rehabilitation project. *DISP* 151: 79–86.

Getty Conservation Institute. (2004) Online document: http://www.getty.edu/conservation/field_projects/sitecon/.

He, C. (1999) *Scenic Regions of Yunnan. A Cultural, Historical and Geographical Overview*. Kunming:Yunnan Press.

McKercher, B. and du Cros, H. (2002) *Cultural Tourism. The Partnership between Tourism and Cultural Heritage Management*. Binghamton, NY: The Haworth Press.

McKercher, B., Bauer, T., du Cros, H.and Ho, P. (2003) Cultural tourism assessment, northern new territories tourism development plan. Report to Hong Kong Tourism Commission.

Simao Tourism Office (n.d.) Notes on the Tea Horse Trade Route.

Numitea (2004) Product information on Yunan tea. Online document: www.numitea.com.

Tu, N.H. and Kuang, W.D. (eds) (1995) *In Search of the Ancient Tea Caravan Route*. Hong Kong: Hong Kong China Tourism Press.

World Monument Fund (2004) 100 most endangered sites. Online doucment: http://www.wmf.org/.

World Tourism Organization, China National Tourism Administration and the Yannan Provincial Tourism Administration (2001) Yunnan Provincial Tourism Master Plan. Report to the World Tourism Organization, China National Tourism Administration and the Yunnan Provincial Tourism Administration, China.

Yunnan Provincial Tourism Administration (2004) Online document: http://www.yunnantourism.net/index.asp

Chapter 12

Hangzhou: China's Green Tea City

KEITH DEWAR AND WEN MEI LI

'A fine tea has always been mentioned in the same breath with beautiful women'

(Su Dongpo, AD 960–1127)

宋代詩人蘇東坡詩云 "從來佳茗似佳人"

For the monks and scholars of China, tea was a precious and noble drink. Tea tasting was an intellectual pursuit, a means of cultivating moral character and creating a feeling of well-being.

Whether for scholars or monks or for the common people, Hangzhou has for centuries been synonymous with tea, its history and legend. There is little doubt that the city draws much of its appeal and image from its connection with the culture and development of the green tea industry. Tourists have come for more than a thousand years to see this beautiful city and to drink the yellow green Longjing (Dragon Well, 龍井茶) tea. This chapter provides an overview of the present state of tourism in the city and the place of tea and tea culture as an attraction both now and well into the 21st century.

Hangzhou, a Cultural and Natural Heritage City

Its place at the heart of the fertile Yangtze River delta made Hangzhou a rich and prosperous city, and historically a city of great beauty with its many gardens and canals. It is now one of the wealthiest areas in China (Xinhua News Agency, 2001).

Current trends

The fast changing face of China offers exciting challenges to the tourism industry, but it also makes it difficult to predict the future of the industry.

It is clear that the quality of services and programmes is improving and becoming more sophisticated. Yet, this fast changing world could also cause major problems for an industry still in its infancy. Crowding, lack of authenticity, environmental issues, and strains on the social structure of communities are just some of the issues that will have to be faced in the coming decade. Hangzhou will face all these challenges and is working strategically to see that tourism is a positive force for both guests and hosts.

International tourism to Hangzhou

The international arrivals for Hangzhou are increasing at a rate considerably beyond those predicted by the Tourism Bureau (Figure 12.1). Foreign visitors accounted for 482,100 of the total 861,200 international arrivals in 2003. The remainder was from Hong Kong 151,500, Macao 8,000 and Taiwan 219,600. It should be noted that there was a temporary drop in numbers in 2003 of 18.5% as a result of SARS; and the Iraq war impacted on the tourism industry around the world. China was particularly hard hit by SARS as it was the centre of the outbreak. In spite of the visitor numbers from Western countries being smaller, the increase was an average 11%. The largest market share is still dominated by East Asian countries with 41% of the share. Vistor numbers from Hong Kong and Taiwan were

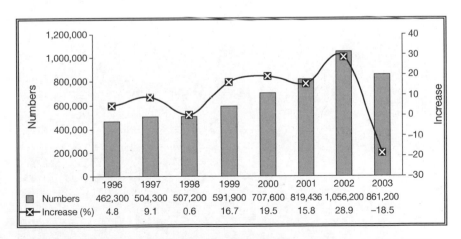

	1996	1997	1998	1999	2000	2001	2002	2003
Numbers	462,300	504,300	507,200	591,900	707,600	819,436	1,056,200	861,200
Increase (%)	4.8	9.1	0.6	16.7	19.5	15.8	28.9	−18.5

Figure 12.1 International* arrivals to Hangzhou, all modes, 1996–2003

Note: *Figures including Taiwan, Hong Kong and Macao

Sources: Hangzhou Tourism Bureau (2001, 2002); Hangzhou Tourism Commission (2003, 2004)

18% and 26% of the market respectively (Hangzhou Tourism Commission, 2004). Increases in visitor numbers continue as the Hangzhou Tourism Commission continues major marketing efforts in the West to ensure the city gets its fair share of visitors and the accompanying foreign exchange.

The Hangzhou Tourism Bureau (2001), projected the city would receive 904,100 international arrivals by the year 2005. This target was already reached by 2002 with over one million foreign visitors. This would suggest that the 1.26 million by 2010 and 1.72 million by the year 2015 predictions will also be surpassed. In fact by the end of 2002, approximately 27 million people were visiting the city including one million overseas visitors (Hangzhou Tourism Commission, 2004).

By 2002 tourism was generating 29 billion Yuan (US$3.5 billion) accounting for 15.8% of the city's total GDP (Long & Qin, 2003). These figures are considerably higher than estimated and also much higher than the 5% forecast by the World Tourism Organization (WTO) for the East Asia region generally. If these geometric trends continue there will be

Plate 12.1 China Tea Museum, Hangzhou, China

Source: Wen Mei Li

considerable strain on the existing destination resources particularly the popular heritage attractions.

The foreign exchange earnings from Hangzhou tourism were ranked as the sixth among Chinese cities in 2003 with US$422 million (Hangzhou Tourism Commission, 2004). The average expenditure of international visitors and the amount of time spent in the city are also increasing. The economic success of Hangzhou is partly its position close to Shanghai, one the China's major gateways. Its proximity to Shanghai and other major cultural and natural heritage destinations make it an attractive stop on a now well-established tour route in the Yangtze River Delta area. The tourism development in the lower Yangtze region is seen as crucial to the rejuvenation of the nation's tourism, said Zhang Jianzhong, director of the policy office of the State Tourism Bureau (Wang, 2003). Wang further indicates that in 2002 over six million overseas tourists visited the Yangtze River Delta, with an economic impact of US$4 billion accounting for 20% of the foreign exchange of the whole region.

Packaged tours in the area usually include Shanghai, Souzhou, Hangzhou, Wuxi, and the intervening country offering small towns, rural landscapes and cultural tourism stops such as the two famous water towns of Zhou Zhuang (Zhou Village) and Wu Zhen (Wu Town). Most international visitors still come on organized tours but fully independent travellers (FITs) are growing in numbers and find the inexpensive two hour train ride from Shanghai attractive.

Domestic tourism to Hangzhou

Hangzhou's domestic tourism has also grown as dramatically as the international sector (Figure 12.2). In 2003 the city received 27.76 million domestic tourists (Hangzhou Tourism Commission, 2004). It should be noted that this figure includes day trips with no overnight stay. These excursionists account for approximately 21.8% of the city's total domestic tourist market in 2000 (Hangzhou Tourism Bureau, 2001). Even deducting these excursionists from the total, the figure of 18 million domestic tourists in 2001 is still very impressive when compared to other international tourism cities, for example, London, England. London's figure for international visitor arrivals for 2002 was 12.53 million (Visit Britain *et al.*, n.d.).

The popularity of Hangzhou during the three public holiday weeks continues to increase rapidly. The data show that 2.9 million visits made in one week of National Day in 2003 accounted for 10.4% of the total domestic tourists of 27.76 million in 2003. Domestic tourism is well organized and

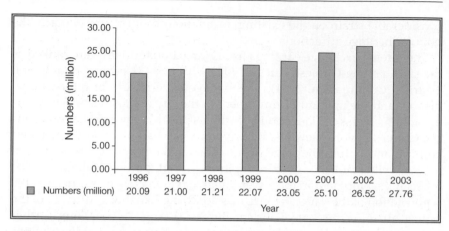

Figure 12.2 Domestic visitors to Hangzhou* 1996–2003

Sources: Hangzhou Tourism Bureau (2001, 2002); Hangzhou Tourism
Commission (2003, 2004)

flourishing in Hangzhou. The key activities are sightseeing (50.5%),
followed by holiday 18.7%, business 11.9% and visiting friends and relatives
(VFR) 6.2% (Hangzhou Tourism Bureau, 2001).

Some problems have been recognized as well. These relate largely to
everyone taking their holidays in the three public holiday weeks. However,
the government is moving towards letting individuals and individual
companies set their own vacation times. This would reduce overcrowding
and help the cash flow of many businesses, spreading income over a longer
period. Hangzhou will have to meet this change with different approaches
to domestic marketing.

The location of Hangzhou, its famous park of Xi Hu, its tea culture, as well
as its standing as an ancient silk manufacturing centre, give the city an
excellent domestic and international brand image. Without much marketing
effort, the city attracts an exceptional number of visitors. If the marketing
of unique products, particularly tea and other heritage features, continues
to improve, the numbers of visitors will most likely continue to increase
steeply for some time. Whether this would be good or bad in the long term
awaits further study and the judgement of history.

Tea as Attraction

If the city's heart is Xi Hu Park, its blood is tea. Speak to any cab driver,
any shop owner or any elderly citizen exercising in the park, and the subject

Plate 12.2 Drying Tea at Meijiawu Village near Hagzhou, China

Source: P.B. Zou

of tea, green tea specifically, will be part of the conversation. The history of tea has been well documented elsewhere in this book and need not be repeated in detail here. The true origins not withstanding, any local Hangzhou tea aficionado will tell you it all started in their city. It is also the place where the Chinese and the more elaborate and ritualized Japanese tea ceremony began.

According to Lu Yu's classic work, Longjing tea was first planted at the famous temples of Tianzhu and Lingying during the Northern Song Dynasty (AD 960–1127). The tea was not given the name Longjing tea until the Southern Song Dynasty (AD 1127–79) (Hangzhou Xihu Longjing Tea Company Ltd, n.d.). The City's Lion Peak Mountain is the focus of the early history of Longjing tea. Legend suggests that Master Bianchai, an eminent monk of the North Song Dynasty, lived in seclusion in the Shousheng Temple, where he and Su Dongpuo (AD 1037–1101), an outstanding writer of the dynasty, often drank tea and sang poems in praise of the tea. Su also designed three characters meaning 'old Longjing' to show his love for this fine tea. The inscription is still visible on a cleft in the rock at the foot of Lion Peak Mountain. The Southern Song Dynasty saw further development in tea production as Hangzhou was established as the capital of the country (Konnal Long Jing Production and Trade Company *et al.*, n.d.).

By the middle of the Qing Dynasty (AD 1644–1911) special tea shops, tea stores and tea companies were appearing all over the city. And by the mid 18th century, tea was a well-established industry in the city. Hangzhou's Wenglongsheng Tea Firm, a company of great reputation selling the finest West Lake Longjing Tea plucked just before each of the three wnar festivals, Guyu, Qingming and Chunfen (China National Tea Museum, 2003).

Tea Tourism

The Zhejiang provincial government is well aware of the importance of tea tourism. As part of their continuing attempt to improve and market the most important agricultural product in the province the government suggests:

> The development of tea, culture and improvement of the specialty of teashops, and tea-related tourist industry is important. Hangzhou is a city full of tea products and depth of tea culture. Many legends, mythologies, poems, articles, songs and dances related to Longjing tea are passed on from one generation to another. They represent the tea culture, and also the essence of human practices. Based on Hangzhou's social, cultural, and economic conditions, and following the reform and opening stream, international exchanges should be carried out by use of tea as a bridge to make friends and help tea lovers spread tea culture at home and abroad. We should absorb both the essence of the traditional Chinese culture and the best elements of foreign high culture and combine them to create new ideas to make Hangzhou the international exchange centre for tea culture.

> The development of tea culture should be included in the larger Hangzhou tea industry, and occupy a position in the comprehensive program. We will search out and develop tea culture as a tourist source, and develop special teashops with culture significance. For example, a Tea Tourist Route could be designed centred on 'China National Tea Museum', and connecting to all the local tea attractions including Luyujing in Shuangxi Yuhang, 'the source of the tea ceremony', 'Longjing Tea at Dragon Well', 'Eighteen Empire Tea Trees', and 'Hupao'. During the trip, tourists can enjoy a series of tea dishes. When they are in Daqing Valley, they can experience the 'one day tea

planter' [helping with the planting and harvesting]. When they are at West Lake, they can enjoy the various tea products in the teashops. (Foreign Trade and Economic Cooperation Bureau of Zhijian Provincial, 2003)

These ideas, and the importance of tea to Hangzhou tourism, are supported by the *Strategy for Hangzhou Tourism Development* written in 2001. This document, produced at the request of City Council by the China Academy of Urban Planning and Design, pointed out that the potential of green tea as a tourism attraction was not being fully appreciated and had considerable potential. The plan states:

> The Tea Culture can be expanded and marketed. Longjing tea is one of the most famous and desired green teas in China and around the world, and it is the one thing that makes Hangzhou unique in China. As well as the importance of the tea itself, the culture that has developed because of its early cultivation in the area of Hangzhou is also unique. This combination of product and culture should be a major focus of tourism marketing. However, none of the Western visitors interviewed understood the importance of tea culture in the area and it is noted that the tea museum has relatively few visitors. These factors suggest a significant marketing and educational effort is needed. (Dewar & Li, 2001)

As a result of the provincial government's proposals and the city's strategic planning, tea was showcased for the first time in March 2002 when the first West Lake Longjing Tea Festival took place. The event included a series of tea ceremonies, performances and rituals in accordance with folk customs and traditions of the city. The China Tea Association was established at the same time as the first organization with a specific mandate to promote the product. This first event was a great success with more than 2000 visitors coming from overseas and around China on the opening day. Japanese and Korean tea lovers were the dominant international visitors to the festival. The success of the first festival encouraged officials to expand, adding Tea Beverage and Snacks expositions to the festival in 2003. The festival is now part of the permanent schedule of events for the city (Jiang, 21 November 2003, personal communication).

Since the publication of the Strategic Plan other attractions based on tea activities have also come on the market or have been developed. Besides more attention being paid to the China National Tea Museum and traditional tea houses around West Lake, other sites outside the town, such as Meijiawu Village in the western outskirts, have added to the popularity of tea as a tourism attraction. Besides Meijiawu Village there are three other tea villages in the area around Hangzhou, including Shi Feng (Lion Peak), Yun Qi and Hupao. The Longjing tea produced at Meijiawu Village is seen as being of the highest quality tea produced by the villages and volume of production is also larger, accounting for approximately 37% of total production (Li, 2002). Meijiawu has been transformed into a tourist attraction of the first order. Its many assets include beautiful rural scenery, fresh air, and food from the villager's vegetable gardens – as well as, of course, the famous tea. It has become a place for holidaymakers and urbanites to take weekend and short-break holidays. Approximately 170 tourists visited the village daily in 2002 and the number is increasing rapidly (Li, 2002). The tourism promoters of Hangzhou describe the village this way:

> The rustic food and tea in Meijiawu Village enjoys a very high reputation in Hangzhou. Every holiday, this village is full of the visitors having a cup of tea. Currently, a project called Meijiawu Tea Cultural Village is under construction. In the future, the whole area will become a tourism attraction featuring tea culture. Furthermore, the visitor can watch the tea performance and participate in the whole procedure of the tea production. Visitors also can purchase what they tasted later. The project is planning to cover an area of 207 acres including Mezhu Fishing Village. The layout of this tourism area includes several sight zones and a sight (sic) road. Sight zones include: A Village Tea Culture Tourism Center, New Farmer Leisure Tourism Zone, Xiaoyawu Natural Tea Garden Sights Area, Tiazhu Huzhong Tianti Leisure Tourism Zone. (Hangzhou Tourism Commission, 2004)

This site is one that will see a great influx of tourists over the next decade. How this will effect what is presented is unclear. Past history of similar sites in China would suggest that unless careful and sustainable planning is done soon it may turn into an over-commercialized sterile site of hawkers, beggars and pedlars and its reputation will be ruined.

The attractions of Hangzhou have been listed in a diversity of tourism sources including brochures, websites and tour maps. The tea-related attractions that appear most commonly in the literature are:

- China National Tea Museum
- Hupao Spring (Tiger Running)
- Meijiawu Village
- Longjing Village and
- Longjing Wen Cha 龍井問茶 (Discovery of Longjing Tea).

The China National Tea Museum, built in 1987 and opened to public in 1991 was the first tea museum in China and is increasingly the focal point for the interpretation of tea heritage both in the city and in China. It is situated in Longjing (Dragon Well) Tea plantation near West Lake. Its comprehensive collection of tea utensils and related artefacts is a national treasure and with some support should grow considerably over the next decades. The museum is made up of five themed buildings. The exhibition hall forms the main body of the museum. Branching off the main exhibit hall are areas dedicated to the history of Chinese tea, tea-drinking customs, tea utensils used in past dynasties, and the knowledge surrounding tea culture, including the complicated process of picking and roasting tea leaves (Warrior Tours, n.d.). According to the staff of the Museum, in 2002 international visitors were mostly from Japan and South Korea; European or American visitors only represented a small proportion of visits (Jun, 2003). Most visitors arrive as part of tour groups, with the average size being 20 to 30 people. The museum also attracts tea researchers and is a growing centre of excellence for the study and understanding of the natural and cultural history of tea. Its marketing efforts are still in their infancy and hampered by lack of funding. To develop and market this unique heritage more resources will be needed.

Longjing Wen Cha 龍井問茶 is another of the traditional tea-related scenic spots in Hangzhou relating to tea tourism. It is here you can find the famous Dragon Well which lies on the south west of West Lake, between the Northern High Hill and Sky House Hill. According to Chinese legend, the water in the Well never disappeared, even in the worst drought. People in the past believed that this water was linked to the ocean; because dragons are the emperors of the oceans and hence the name. Now Dragon Well is surrounded by a temple with the same name (Wu, 2000).

Longjing Village located on the peak of Lion Mountain is a site focusing on the history of the Qing Dynasty and was made famous by the visits of Qianlong (1736–95), one of China's most remarkable emperors. He paid four visits to the growing area of Longjing tea during his reign; and also left the world a number of poems and gave eighteen tea trees (the 'Royal Tea Trees') to the village. These trees allegedly still stand in front of the Hugong Temple. His poems and interest in tea are considered the catalyst for making green tea the national drink of China. Until recently the village was only a residential area for the local tea farmers, however the development of tourism has brought to the area many travellers seeking to purchase authentic Longjing tea and to visit this important part of Chinese heritage. In the past few years individually owned tea houses were established to cater to the growing tourist trade. With this shift to mass tourism travellers can now not only taste the great home-grown tea, but also purchase a variety of other tea-related products. Each individual tea house sets up its own tea-producing display to illustrate tea processing, as well to attract tourists (Zou, 2003). Bus tours are the major way that international visitors see the Hangzhou area. Flying Cloud Tea: China Tour is typical and offers this description in their itinerary:

> **Day 8:** We fly through Shanghai where we connect by train to reach the paradise of Hangzhou. The leisurely ride takes us through some of China's wealthiest agricultural areas, where we still see peasants at work in the fields. In Hangzhou, we will visit China's National Tea Museum and have a talk about the history of tea and its relationship to China's three major belief systems: Taoism, Buddhism, and Confucianism. (Great Strides Travel, n.d.)

China Merchants Travel Company, one of the largest local tour operators in Hangzhou, takes approximately 20,000 international visitors or 900 groups to Meijiawu Tea Village each year (Jiang, 2004). This is one of over 100 companies that regularly comes and visits the tea-related sites and the numbers of tours are growing rapidly. In most cases long-haul tourists do not specifically target Hangzhou and tea but visit as part of extensive two- or three-week tours of China. There are still very few companies that provide concentrated culinary tours of the area; Warrior Tours (http:// www.warriortours.com/intro/tea.htm) is an exception offering culinary-focused tours of China and Hangzhou with a two-and-a-half-day stop in the city.

Tea houses

Tea houses became progressively more important in the lives of the Chinese people as the Qing Dynasty (1644–1911) progressed. Tea culture and the magnificent buildings that were the centre of the traditions moved from the elite palaces into the lives of common people all over China. The tea house is now central to the local Hangzhou tea culture. Local people see these places as community meeting places much like the coffee houses of Europe, the pubs of England or the 'donut' shop of North America. Citizens like to spend time in the tea house exchanging information, meeting with friends and discussing business and hobbies, as well as playing *mah-jong* and feeding their caged birds. Into this calm relaxing environment tourists are now being added. New tea houses largely for tourism consumption are to be found throughout the tourists' districts particularly in the area of Xi Hu Park.

Plate 12.3 Tea house sign, West Lake, Hangzhou, China
Source: Wen Mei Li

Currently there are about 700 tea houses in Hangzhou (China Vista, 2002). Ms Jiang of the Hangzhou Tourism Commission suggested that this figure may be a conservative estimate. The tea houses tend to be grouped in areas such as Shuguang Road (called Teahouses Street) which is very popular with local people. This street is well known in Hangzhou not just for tea, but also for a diversity of cafés and pubs. It is a prime social area with a focus on multicultural cuisine and multicultural beverages. From Shuguang Road a visitor can connect to Longjing Road where some of the high-end tea houses are scattered. The China National Tea Museum and Longjing Village are also found there (Hangzhou Tourism Commission, 2003). As noted above, the surrounding tea-producing villages also have a good number of tea houses, especially Meijiawu Village and Longjing Village.

Tea houses vary in size and quality. Smaller one-room versions are dwarfed by the government-run three-storey Hupanju Tea House at the north end of West Lake (http://www.hzwestlake.com/english/hpje.htm).

Plate 12.4 Tea house exterior, West Lake Tea House, Hangzhou, China
Source: Wen Mei Li

Each level takes you to a better ambience, view, quality of service and, of course, a higher price bracket. Tea services are brought out and if you are a novice there are tea servers to help you through the ritual in several languages. Tea is the centrepiece, but there is a bewildering array of inexpensive snacks that can also be purchased. Following the custom of considering the *number* of dishes to be as important as their *content*, it is not unusual to see 20 or 30 snack dishes at a table, proudly overseen by the host. Tour groups can arrange private interpretation and instruction on the Chinese tea ceremony and how it is performed. The simple terracotta ceremonial teasets are available for purchase everywhere. Many tea houses also have shops selling tea and related paraphernalia, ranging from ceremonial tea services to ornate teapots, teacups and serving implements. Books, postcards, menus and other tea souvenirs are often available, if not inside the tea houses, then outside at hawkers' stalls. Several tea houses combine their operations with art galleries and upmarket souvenir shops.

Plate 12.5 Private tea house in the Gao House (*c.* 1700), West Lake, Hangzhou, China

Source: Wen Mei Li

Plate 12.6 Tea house pavilion, West Lake, Hangzhou, China
Source: Wen Mei Li

Tea Shops

If there are over 700 tea houses, then there are simply thousands of tea shops dotted all over the city. Most are small privately run businesses. Usually they do not serve tea as a major part of their business – although tea tasting is sometimes available. They sell tea, green tea, red tea (black tea) and *oolong* tea in vast quantities. It is an education to listen to the discussions of the merits of various types and blends of tea and the rhetoric of the expert behind the counter would put any wine taster to shame! Prices can range from a few Yuan to several hundred, even several thousand per 100 grams, depending on quality and fashion.

Other Culinary Traditions

Linked to sipping a fine cup of Longjing tea, Hangzhou offers further culinary delights related to and using local teas as a base or flavouring. The provincial government suggests a number of dishes that are available and can be promoted and enhanced as part of the industry:

> The tea dishes are gradually becoming better known. For example the tea-boiled eggs, the brown tea, green tea and Wulong tea beverages, tea wines, iced tea products, tea flavoured sweets, tea cakes, health care teas, medicinal tea, tea capsules and so on. The tea dishes have been developing quickly with the development of tea and food culture. The 'tea doctor' dish series includes: Longjing shrimps, Longjing roasted rabbits, honey perch, tin foiled steaks, Longjing fish stripes, fried Chabo, XO sauced vegetable, tea-flavoured duck, boiled bean duck, and Wulong beef steak. (Foreign Trade and Economic Cooperation Bureau of Zhijian Provincial, 2003)

One can now add the latest tea craze, Bubble Tea (Tapioca Pearl Tea or Boba Tea) to the growing list of culinary tea products. This tea, both black and green with flavoured milk, tapioca pearls and a very large straw is becoming a favourite among young people – much to the chagrin of their more conservative elders. Originally made with black (red) tea, the creations are now more elaborate and provide another outlet for producers to present tea to the public particularly tourists and the young (CNN, 2000). Tea-related products continue to grow as the tourism industry expands.

Marketing the Product

Tea as a significant tourism resource as suggested above has received considerable attention from the Hangzhou City Government as well as provincial officials. The City Government and the Tourism Commission are working to build on the growing interest in tea. They are developing tea programmes catering to the niche markets, particularly culinary and cultural tourists. Besides the tea festival, one of the strategies to promote tea tourism is by focusing on enhancing the local people's knowledge and appreciation of tea culture. City officials want to ensure tea tourism and tea culture will develop hand-in-hand with community involvement and understanding. Wisely the City Government has decided not to promote tea fully as an attraction until the community has 'bought into' the idea and has a basic understanding of the history of tea and its importance to Hangzhou. It is hoped that increased pride in their community will come with increased understanding. The ultimate goal is to make Hangzhou worthy of the name 'The City of Green Tea'. A number of community-based activities are proposed, including seminars on tea and health, tea consumption and the history of the city. Many folk activities such as tea poems, tea songs, tea

Plate 12.7 Early tea shop exhibit, China Tea Museum, Hangzhou, China
Source: Wen Mei Li

dances and tea catering and ceremony will be developed and promoted as well. A seminar on tea-house architecture and design is ongoing and the public is encouraged to participate. Tea tourism will develop in harmony with this local support campaign (Jiang, 21 November 2003, personal communication).

The China National Tea Museum is central to the City's campaign to educate the public. In the past, the museum has successfully held varied and interesting activities during the spring harvest time. The most popular of these activities emphasizes the new marketing campaign and includes the International West Lake Tea Party, Spring Tea Party, Wu-Wo Tea Ceremony, Public Contest Party of Tea, and Tea-skills Competition Party, as well as academic tea seminars. It is hoped these events bring tea lovers together from overseas and China to make new friends and exchange information on tea (China National Tea Museum, 2003). Another proposed programme is a competition that would involve the tea houses and local tea

Plate 12.8 Early tea shop exhibit, China Tea Museum, Hangzhou, China
Source: Wen Mei Li

producers. The top ten tea houses and outstanding tea farmers, tea pickers and tea blenders will be part of the promotional package taken to various tourism trade shows around the world. Related to the competition will be a tea auction for the top quality first pickings of Longjing tea also called First Spring tea. The finest Longjing tea is made from tea leaves picked just before the Qing Ming Festival (Pure Brightness Festival in the Chinese calendar, approximately 5 April each year). The highest auction price paid for the first spring tea picked at the time of the Qing Ming Festival, has been more than 10,000 Yuan (US$1250) per kilo (Jiang, personal communication, 21 November 2003). The normal price for the best quality tea picked before the Qing Ming Festival is around 5600 Yuan a kilo. However, the wholesale price from tea farmers is around 3200 Yuan a kilo. Apparently the sales make tea traders a substantial profit (Li X, 2002).

Besides the various festivals, competitions and programmes the Hangzhou Tourism Commission has selected four attractions to high-light as the main marketing focus for the tea destination campaign. They are Longjing Village, Longjing Theme Park, Meijiawu Village and, of course, the China National Tea Museum. Apart from the four lead-ing city tea attractions, Jingshan Temple, the first Buddhist temple in Jiangnan (Zhejiang and Jiangsu Province) is considered to be a niche market, particularly for Japan and Southeast Asia. Located at the north foot of Tianmu Mountain on the border of Yuhang and Linan Counties and within greater Hangzhou, Jingshan Temple (established by Monk Fa Qin in the Tang Dynasty) is well known all over the Buddhist world. Tradition says that the monk Fa Qin planted several fragrant tea plants there and plucked them for offerings. The monks and priests of the later ages always used the fragrant tea from the Temple to serve their guests. Over the course of time, a series of tea-serving ceremonies evolved from this simple courtesy and became known as the 'Tea Banquet'. It is these ceremonies that were the foundation of the modern tea ceremonies in both China and Japan. The Japanese not only imported the ceremonies but the tea itself. Yeisai, an eminent Japanese monk, came to China to study Buddhism twice during the Southern Song Dynasty. He took tea seeds and tea-tasting methods back to Japan and wrote a now famous book of technique, *Kitch Yojoki – The Book of Tea Sanitation* (China National Tea Museum, 2003).

Jingshan tea shares the honour of being one of the best teas in China. Today, around 1 April, Japanese believers come to Jingshan to pay their respects to their ancestors and to commemorate the restoration of the temple (Chinese Enterprise Net, n.d.). The combination of Buddhist tradition and tea is the motivation of a significant number of Buddhist pilgrims to the Hangzhou area from Japan as well as elsewhere and the spiritual bond between tea and religion is evident in much of the present-day culture and traditions. Tea is still seen as an important medicine as well a cultural and religious symbol. The intertwining of Buddhism, medicine and cultural factors is complex and beyond the scope of this chapter, but is a notable and growing element of tea tourism in Asia.

The tea tourism market in Hangzhou is still in its early stages and is already well patronized by Asia (Table 12.1) and domestic tourists. The City Government is planning an ambitious promotion of Hangzhou's tea tourism to European markets to coincide with their community efforts to educate the local people. The Tea Festival in 2004 is aimed at the European market to try to increase the market diversity beyond the traditional Japanese and Korean markets. There is great potential in this aspect of cultural tourism and it can bring great rewards to the city and its people. Care must be taken however to ensure that the area is managed in a sustainable way: there are growing signs of problems that need to be addressed.

Issues and Problems

The quickly growing Chinese domestic tourism market and the rapidly expanding international market will be both a boon and a threat to the Hangzhou tourism industry. Uncontrolled development and cut-throat competition, particularly between the small tea houses and tea plantations,

Table 12.1 Foreign tourists to Hangzhou by top ten countries 2003

Ranking	Country of origin	2003
1	Korea	142,379
2	Japan	94,459
3	Malaysia	47,548
4	USA	37,164
5	Singapore	22,050
6	Thailand	20,854
7	Indonesia	15,275
8	Germany	12,375
9	Canada	8,547
10	Australia	8,244

Source: Hangzhou Tourism Commission (2004)

could become an issue. Also, growing numbers of visitors may be an environmental threat to tourist attractions such as Xi Hu Park and other local destinations. Comments that are beginning to surface from Western visitors and domestic tourists alike indicate a small but growing dissatisfaction with the local tourism industry. Tourism demand and supply of and for tourism resources in Hangzhou should continue to be planned in a sustainable way to ensure a proper balance between use and protection. Short-term profits must not drive this planning. A realistic and long term strategic plan is essential (Dewar & Li, 2001).

FITs (fully independent travellers) – an ignored market

The China tourism industry is maturing particularly in popular tourist destinations, such as Hangzhou and Shanghai. The high-end hospitality industries including five-star and four-star hotels are on a par with similar cities in more developed markets. Tour groups organized by large tour companies travelling in China can expect to receive a high level of service. They are well looked after by their tour guide and tour company, and do not need to worry about how to get where they want to go and where to find genuine Longjing or Jingshan tea. They can enjoy drinking in a tea house without any real worries about being cheated on price. As long as the tour visitor has chosen a reputable company, the experience should be a good one. This is a result of the many companies that now have years of experience dealing with tour groups from all over the world. The market strategy has been to focus on these tour groups and the high level of service quality and infrastructure required.

The independent traveller, however, often does not have these advantages. In dealing with smaller businesses and having less information they are more vulnerable to problems. Disorderly and uncontrolled growth of the private sector is becoming an issue at many tourist attractions both in Hangzhou and elsewhere in China, and complaints and unhappy experiences are becoming more common. The problems include individuals being cheated, unfair prices being charged and false advertisements. An example of such an experience in Longjing Village by Zou (2003) shows how poor service leads to dissatisfaction and, if this dissatisfaction is expressed to friends and relatives at home, it can in the long run affect visitor levels, profits and the reputation of Hangzhou:

> The author's worst experience in Hangzhou occurred in Dragon Well Village, where there are a number of private teahouses on either side of the road. Employees from these teahouses were standing outside

seeking individual guests. The situation was disorderly and unpleasant. After the author had been invited to one of the teahouses, the owner showed up with a glass of some of 'the best Dragon Well tea' with hot water. The owner also had asked a very high price for the tea; the deal was completed at the price not even half of what the owner asked, (Zou, 2003: 20)

There is also the distinct possibility that many of the tea houses, particularly those in smaller communities both within Hangzhou proper and in the region surrounding it, will become tourist attractions and displace the local people from their favourite tea house. This can lead to resentment and hostility within the local community towards guests. Further, the arrival of large numbers of tour groups can be disruptive to the local community as a whole. Care will be required to manage the numbers of visitors and control access. The deterioration of good relationships between tourists and the host community is a well-understood phenomena in the tourism industry (Doxey, 1976).

Tourists' demands will diversify and intensify as the various market segments develop and there is some movement away from organized tours to independent travel. The organized tours will no doubt remain popular with first-time visitors, but as the market becomes more mature and sophisticated and the number of private vehicles increases, there will be a need to look more closely at what the individual and small group traveller wants (Dewar & Li, 2001). This idea is supported by Lew:

. . . China's international tourist products tend to be old-fashioned and highly structured. They have been largely designed for culture-oriented sightseeing tour groups . . . These kinds of products can no longer suit the demands of contemporary international tourists who are seeking more independence and greater flexibility and choice in developing their itineraries. (Lew *et al.*, 2003: 229)

Many Western FIT travelers are very sophisticated and have travelled widely, and their wants and needs can be very different. It is possible to generalize Western culture as aggressive, independent and goal-oriented, with the individual being more important than the group. In contrast, Eastern cultures have a greater emphasis on family and group affiliation, and the individual need is often suppressed. These differences must be taken into account when managing the ever-increasing numbers of tourists. Flexibility and a good degree of cross-cultural understanding will be needed by industry workers if all tourists are to have good quality experiences.

Armed with good market research, it is possible to design the facilities and infrastructure in such a way as to maximize potential visitation and provide optimum quality to those niche markets that choose to visit. Such elements as international or youth hostels, bed and breakfasts (highlighting Chinese culture and cuisine), car and bike rental businesses, visitor maps in English and other languages, more sophisticated web pages with travel details and local information, and high-quality guided tours (with properly certified guides) are just some of the areas that must continue to be improved if Hangzhou is to take advantage of the growing FIT market and its profit potential.

One of the important features for FITs is the Visitor Information/ Reception Centre (VRC). It is essential that easy-to-access, clear and unbiased information is available to the visitor. These VRCs are a world-wide tourism service organized by local or regional governments and are well understood by international visitors. The internationally recognized 'i' is an important part of any city's information system, and independent visitors seek this sign everywhere, at the airport, in city centres and at major attractions. The VRC is seen as a government source that can be trusted and information acquired from such locations can help ensure the visitor will have a pleasant stay.

FITs and small groups have an economic importance that can often be underestimated because it is hard to research and hard to quantify their spending. However, it is well known that individual travellers have a tendency to spend locally, buying from small merchants and local crafts people and eating in small restaurants and traditional food streets. There is also less economic leakage from the community back to the large corporations that typically manage the hotels, the major tour bus companies and suppliers of foreign goods. Despite FITs spending less than tour groups per day, they normally stay longer and contribute more to the local community both economically and in employment. FITs search for authentic experiences and are more likely to take an interest in the local customs and engage local people, simply because they are not restricted by the tight schedules of tour operators, nor are they herded into over-priced souvenir mills and 'Disney-fied' cultural attractions. FITs can counterbalance the large tour groups and may offer the local communities and neighbourhoods more by way of positive economic and social benefits, although they can also be more critical of poor quality. Hangzhou has not yet recognized the importance of the FIT segment of the market. However with growing demand and greater numbers of domestic and international visitors coming from outside of the traditional tour group the city will have to respond.

Trademarks and branding

The demand and prices for Longjing Tea are also beginning to cause problems. Counterfeit tea, particularly of high quality, is beginning to appear. Visitors are frequently warned about this problem by local tea merchants and guides (even cab drivers will warn of the problem), however at present there is no credible system of certifying tea which can be easily understood by visitors – even though branding and trademarks were developed and put in place in 1999 (Foreign Trade and Economic Cooperation Bureau of Zhijian Provincial, 2003). In 2004, at the beginning of the spring tea harvest, the villagers of Meijiawu dumped thousands of kilograms of tea into a nearby river. It was a protest aimed at attracting attention to the problems related to counterfeiting and the imports of cheap fakes, as even before the local people had started the spring harvest, tea shops all over Hangzhou were advertising new Longjing tea (Beijing Scene, 2004). The lack of control of the brand image and lack of enforcement of the existing system is damaging the local industry and degrading the credibility of the area as a tea producer.

The issue of copyright, trademarks and brand images are a major concern in China (Cunningham, 2004) and foreign companies are bringing ever-increasing pressure on the central government to help protect brands and brand images. The local market for unique products is also being damaged. There is no credible estimate of the loss of revenue to Hangzhou and the Longjing tea producers but it will run into the many millions of Yuan if enforceable certification programmes are not put in place. Fortunately there are models to be followed, the most important being with another beverage – Champagne. The province of Champagne took back its name in the late 1970s and has worked hard ever since to use international law and quality control to ensure those who work hard to produce this fine product get their reward and the public gets product they are paying for (Sharpe A. & Smith J., 1991). Chinese brands also have this kind of high potential in the international market if marketed properly. This view is expressed clearly in relation to manufactured goods but the same rules and ideas can be applied to Longjing and other top teas (Gao, 2003). Although Gao speaks specifically of the export market for goods, tourism can also be viewed as an export market and branding the destination and its unique key products is essential for maximum profits and employment.

Hangzhou, with its beautiful natural scenery, has long been known as the 'Paradise City of the Earth': there is a Chinese expression 'Up in the heaven, there is paradise; Down on the earth, there is Hangzhou and Suzhou, which is the best praise that can be given.' Its grand traditions and its tea are becoming important elements in the tourists' itinerary and with careful sustainable planning there are rich possibilities for the future.

References

Beijing Scene (2004) Hangzhou tea party. Online document: http://www. beijingscene.com/cissue/inshort.html (accessed 22 March 2004).

China National Tea Museum (2003) Hangzhou: China National Tea Museum.

China Vista (2002) Hangzhou launches famous tea houses. Online document: http://www.chinavista.com/entravel/show_news.php?id=488 (accessed 24 March 2004).

Chinese Enterprise Net (n.d.) Jingshan resort. (In Chinese) Online document: http://mengda.smeinchina.com/m32.htm (accessed 4 March 2004).

CNN (2000) Tapioca milk tea creating waves as fun coffee alternative. Online document: http://www.cnn.com/2000/FOOD/news/11/27/bubble.tea.ap/ (accessed 7 April 2004).

Cunningham, R. (2004) Brand owners confront counterfeiting threat. *Managing Intellectual Property*, China IP Focus 2004, 14–17.

Dewar, K. and Li, W. (2001) *Tourism in Hangzhou*. Beijing: China Academy of Urban and Regional Design.

Doxey, G.V. (1976) When enough's enough: The natives are restless in old Niagara. *Heritage Canada* 2 (2), 26–7.

Foreign Trade and Economic Cooperation Bureau of Zhijian Provincial (2003) The tea industry of Hangzhou:The current situation of the tea industry in Hangzhou and the adjustment direction after China's accession to the WTO – Online document: http://www.investzhejiang.com/en/modules/cyq/show (accessed 1 April 2004).

Gao, P. (2003) Can Chinese brands make it abroad? *McKinsey Quarterly*, Special Edition (4), 54–67.

Great Strides Travel (n.d.) Flying Cloud Tea China Tour – Online document: http://www.greatstridestravel.com/teatour.html (accessed 13 March 2004).

Hangzhou Tourism Bureau (2001) *2001 Tourism Survey*, public document. Hangzhou: Hangzhou Tourism Bureau.

Hangzhou Tourism Commission (2003) Go all over Hangzhou – douse in Hangzhou. Hangzhou: Zhijiang Photograph Press.

Hangzhou Tourism Commission (2004) Meijiawu Village leisure tour – tea culture village. Online document: http://www.gotohz.com/inter/en/showarticles (accessed 24 March 2004).

Hangzhou Xihu Longjing Tea Company Ltd (n.d.) The history of Dragon Well tea. Online document: http://www.chinalongjing.com/e-lsyb.html. (accessed 28 February 2004).

Jiang, M. (2004) Letter to Keith Dewar. Hangzhou, March.

Jun, J. (2003) Interview, Hangzhou Tourism Commission, 21 November 2003.

Konnal Long Jing Production and Trade Company *et al.* (n.d.) The history of Long Jing tea. Online document: http://www.chinatea-konnal.de/en/enkonnal-1. htm. (accessed 15 February 2004).

Lew, A.A., Yu, L., Ap, J. and Guangrui, Z. (2003) *Tourism in China*. New York: The Haworth Hospitality Press.

Li X. (2002) Life of a tea planter. Online document: http://www.chinatoday. com.cn/English/e20026/tea.htm (accessed 6 March 2004).

Long, Y. and Qin, C. (7 October 2003) Hangzhou hangs in. *China Daily*, October, p. 3.

People's Daily (2003) Different views on China's GDP growth in 2004. Online document; http://english.peopledaily.com.cn/200310/09/eng20031009_125603. shtml. (accessed 24 March 2004).

Sharpe, A. and Smith, J. (1991) Champagne's sparkling success. *International Marketing Review* 8 (4), 13–21.

Visit Britain *et al.* (n.d.) Overseas visitors to the UK – Top towns visited 2002. Online document: http://www.tourismtrade.org.uk/uktrade/Images/42_13657.pdf (accessed 6 March 2004).

Wang, L. (7 July 2003) Summit boost for Yangtze tourism. *China Daily – Hong Kong Edition*, July, p. 2.

Warrior Tours (n.d.) Tea culture. Online document: http://www.warriortours. com/intro/tea.htm (accessed 13 March 2004).

Wu, X.S. (2000) *The Scenery Beside West Lake*. (In Chinese) Hangzhou: Hangzhou Publishing Institution.

Xinhua News Agency (2001) Tourism profitable in East China Province. Online document: www.xinhuanet.com (accessed 12 June 2001).

Zou, P.B. (2003) Unpublished research report.

Chapter 13

Teapot Trails in the UK: Just a Handle or Something Worth Spouting about?

DEREK HALL AND STEVEN BOYNE

This chapter addresses the concept, nature and role of 'teapot trails' in the UK. Within the context of tea's imperial history, its national, social and gender influences, it examines relationships between the tea room, teapot trails and the potential for tea-related tourism in local and regional development processes. Challenges and opportunities are discussed, and the chapter concludes with recommendations that broaden tea-trail tourism into wider issues of sustainable development.

The UK Context

Although the Portuguese are credited as the first to bring tea to Europe, the commodity later became closely associated with the UK and Britain's imperial role, initially through the activities of the East India Company in the later 17th century. In the first decade of the 18th century, one Thomas Twining saw the need to give his London coffee house a competitive edge over the other 2500 such establishments then flourishing in the capital. No self-respecting lady would enter a coffee house, but, as a heavy tax had been imposed on tea two decades earlier, to diversify into this commodity would require establishing an ethos that would attract exactly those women, of a certain affluence, who hitherto did not frequent such public places. After ten years trading as a coffee house specializing in good quality tea, Twining bought three adjacent small buildings and converted them into one – probably the first – dry tea and coffee shop.

Being expensive, tea was kept, by those who could afford it in locked boxes, which became known as caddies. The lady of the house would keep the key to the caddy in her belt, offering the precious commodity only to the most important visitors. At such times she would typically use a small china teapot and (tea) bowls, imported from China.

She herself presided over the kettle, the measuring of the dry leaves with a caddy spoon, and the making and serving of the tea. That is how the British tea ceremony started. (Twining, 1989: 4)

From 1784, when the tax levy was reduced, tea drinking began to take on a popular appeal, and teapots became larger. Tea played an important role in the temperance movement's crusade against high levels of alcohol (particularly gin) consumption. Until 1839 all tea came from China. But in that year, the first Indian tea arrived in the UK, and subsequently became an important commodity in the British imperial relationship with the Indian subcontinent and later with East Africa. Tea from Ceylon began to be imported in 1879. The plantation economies that tea production and consumption generated, and the consequential environmental, social and cultural impacts that it imposed, were to define one of the more enduring mutual relationships of empire (Jolliffe, 2003; Pettigrew, 2001a; Twining, 1989).

Within the contemporary context of tea consumption, the role of tea as a tourism ingredient, and the promotion of tea-related tourism, is constrained by two key factors (Boyne *et al.*, 2003b: 133). First, there appears to be a lack of understanding of consumer behaviour in relation to food and drink within processes of tourism and recreation (e.g. Fields, 2002). Second, and closely related to this, there exist ambiguities surrounding the way in which food and drink production is conceived by consumers, and in particular the way in which regional food and drink products are perceived in the UK (e.g. Kuznesof *et al.*, 1997; Tregear *et al.*, 1998; MAFF/CA, 2000). The anthropological literature on drink, although slight (Douglas, 1987), suggests the importance of three themes in the role of liquid consumption: (1) as national or regional symbols; (2) as 'markers' of social relations; and (3) as 'markers' of gender roles (Delamont, 1995: 37). All three have strong relevance to tea consumption, in its historic and contemporary guises, and represent important dimensions for the analysis of tea-based tourism.

For the UK, tea consumption and the institutions surrounding it, such as tea rooms, tea shops and afternoon tea, have become national symbols. As markers of social relations and gender roles, tea and tea consumption developed a dual, almost schizophrenic identity in the 19th century; a legacy which, for good or ill, persists. On the one hand tea became the essential 'brew-up' and 'cuppa' of the working classes. Despite the efforts of industrialists, landowners and clerics up to 1820, the 'tea break' became enshrined as a national workplace institution, portrayed and interpreted in both positive and pejorative terms. On the other hand, by contrast, tea consolidated its early 18th-century role as the daintily feminine and refined accompaniment to cucumber sandwiches or jam and cream scones, liberating ladies in their ability to attend, unchaperoned, public places such as tea rooms.

Today, tea is said to represent some 42% of Britons' daily fluid intake (Trew, 2002). But while coffee brands have become 'cool' and fashionable, particularly among young adults, the tea industry appears to have been slow to appreciate the beverage's changing role as a social marker and has failed to innovate sufficiently in response to changing social and cultural circumstances, particularly in the promoting of the several apparent health and medicinal benefits of tea consumption (e.g. de Mejía, 2003: Kris-Etherton & Keen, 2002; Tea Muse, 2003).

Nevertheless, the social and cultural role of tea consumption in the UK is gradually being transformed. Well-known brand coffee houses such as Starbucks and Coffee Republic are now stocking tea. The Brooke Bond tea company has set up what are attempting to be fashionable 'tea bars' in Brighton and Bristol, employing the supposed 'cool' brand name of *Ch'a*. In the *Mumbo* tea bar in Manchester, tea has been repackaged as a fashion item, while *Plaisir du Chocolat* in Edinburgh sells 180 different teas (Trew, 2002). More than 3000 tea varieties are now available in the UK. Yet these often uncoordinated attempts to (re-)establish tea as a fashionable beverage represent relatively isolated actions in the face of the ever-burgeoning, heavily-branded multiple-choice flavour-style coffee houses. Further, and perhaps crucially for tea tourism development, there is a lack of specialist re-blending as well as a lack of association of tea with a sense of place and local or regional identity.

The Tea Room Tradition: A National Symbol

The tea room grew out of the tradition of the earlier coffee houses, which tended to be the exclusive domain of men. It was women, however, who were to be crucial in the growth of tea's popularity and through whom afternoon tea became an important part of life during Victorian times.

Although the taking of tea is often viewed as representing quintessential Englishness, the role of Scotland in tea's development has been no less important. The drink was introduced to Edinburgh in 1681 by Mary of Modena when her husband, the future James VII, was Duke of York and Lord High Commissioner at the Court of Holyrood.

It quickly became fashionable but was frowned upon by both medical and clerical men as bad for the body and the soul. Many ministers of the kirk considered it a greater evil than whisky, and some people resolved the quandary by adding a dram of whisky to their cup of tea to counteract its bad effects. Cinnamon was also sometimes added to enhance the flavour. (Warren, 1979: 82–3)

By the middle of the 18th century tea had replaced ale or spirits as the morning beverage in Scotland, but the practice of tea drinking as a social pastime in the morning and afternoon was considered by the self-righteous to be a great time-waster. Good quality tea remained expensive because of the high customs duties imposed upon it. As a result, a great deal of cheaper tea was smuggled in from continental Europe, and simulated teas were produced from the leaves of such local trees as hawthorn, ash and sloe. These were coloured and mixed with China tea to produce a brew known as 'smouch'. As elsewhere, coffee houses had long been popular meeting places for men but in 1884 the enterprising Miss Cranston opened the first

Plate 13.1 The Charles Rennie Mackintosh designed Willow Tea Rooms, Buchanan Street, Glasgow, Scotland

Source: Derek Hall

of her famous tea rooms in Glasgow, and the practice of going to take tea in a public place became an enjoyable and socially acceptable one, so much so that she was able to open a number of similar establishments and the fashion soon spread throughout Britain (Warren, 1979: 83).

Tea rooms may be housed in buildings and structures with a range of functions, styles and site characteristics, from humble converted terraced houses and cottages to castles (e.g. Conisbrough Castle, 2003) and cathedral closes (e.g. Pilgrim's, 2004). A good tea room should be worthy of a visit in its own right, albeit complemented by interesting places and activities within the locality.

> Yet what exactly is a tea room? For some it conjures up the image of a coy little cottage with pretty tablecloths, bone china and a display of cakes to make the mouth water; for others a smart hotel where waiters and waitresses seem almost to glide across the floor bearing finger sandwiches and patisserie on tiered stands. (Thornby, 2001: 1–2)

Although by no means a prescriptive list for all tea rooms, favoured elements and attractions of the good tea room highlighted by authors include:

- the availability of loose-leaf tea (essential);
- a personal welcome;
- home-made food (e.g. Kitty's Tearoom, 2004; Tealby Tea Rooms, 2004);
- the availability of organic tea and food (e.g. Compton Tea Rooms, n.d.; St Martin's Tea Rooms, 2004);
- an unhurried, tranquil atmosphere;
- smoke-free atmosphere (e.g. Brief Encounter, 2002);
- a summer garden (e.g. Pilgrim's, 2004);
- the playing of background classical music (albeit annoying to some); and
- the availability of current newspapers to read.

Each tea room should have its own particular style. This may include any or all of: an extensive range of speciality teas, a wide range of mouth-watering home-made cakes, cream teas, special quality of service, and the provision of a much-valued resting place for locals and visitors alike (Thornby, 2001). However tea room and tea shop habituation rarely appear in the literature about leisure shopping behaviour (e.g. Falk & Campbell, 1997).

Such establishments may not be purely commercial ventures. In Cliftonville, Kent, southeast England, Ashley's Tea Rooms have been

Plate 13.2 Tea on the terrace at The Palm Court Café, Ventour Botanical
Gardens, Isle of Wight

Source: Derek Hall

established by Thanet Mencap Society (2003) to provide those with a
learning disability the opportunity to work with the public. Tea-related
charity events are often held, such as the Red Cross Big Red Teapot event,
which encouraged the holding of tea parties during February and March
2004 to raise funds for the charity by inviting small donations from those
attending (Anon, 2004; British Red Cross, 2004).

Tea rooms may take on the character of their region – for example, cream
teas in the south of England (Jolliffe, 2003), including local clotted cream in
Devon and Cornwall. And the fare accompanying tea may also have explicit
local or regional affiliations, such as Bath buns, Chelsea buns and Banbury
cakes. Yet the actual tea itself, despite the development of signature blends
such as Twinings' *English Breakfast*, is rarely employed, through blending
or repackaging, as a means of articulating and promoting local or regional
identity. It is not unrealistic, however, to suggest that a number of particular
local blends could be developed; incorporating local or regionally related
tastes, names and imagery (e.g. see Bartlett, 2003).

The closest – indeed possibly the only – UK place-specific branded blend is Brodies' *Famous Edinburgh*, which is set alongside their *Scottish Breakfast* and *Scottish Teatime* blends (Brodie Melrose Drysdale, 2004). Brooke Bond's *Scottish Blend* claimed to be the first Scotland brand when launched in 1990; it was intended to 'match the softness of Scotland's water' (Unilever, 2004). *Welsh Brew Tea* is claimed by its blenders to be 'One of Wales' better kept secrets' (Murroughs, 2004), while *Yorkshire Tea* is one of the few blends branded for an English region, and in this case intended to complement hard water (Bettys & Taylors, 2004).

Afternoon tea, its traditions and myths (Smith, 1986), are central to the tea room experience. Related events, such as at home teas, tennis teas, nursery teas and tea dances have become institutionalized in their various ways, although, as exemplified by tea dances, they tend to be associated with participants of a certain (now unfashionable) age group.

> Afternoon tea, which is having a great revival today, can be served any time from 3.00pm to 5.30pm. It is still correct for the hostess to make and pour the tea. If two different teas are being offered, the most important of the lady guests is asked to pour the second pot. One will most likely be Earl Grey (named after the Prime Minister of 1835) and the other probably a Darjeeling tea from the foothills of the Indian Himalayas. Milk must always be offered, but never cream, and if milk is taken, it should always be put in the cup first. Sliced lemon should be available and white sugar should be on the table for those who must have it. (Twining, 1989: 7)

The fare offered with afternoon tea varies with the seasons: thin sandwiches with cucumber, lettuce and tomato in the summer, and with jam or meat paste in the winter. Invented by the eponymous earl in the 18th century, the tea-time sandwich is claimed to be at its best with one-day-old bread, such that it can be sliced very thinly, with crusts removed once the sandwich is filled (Mashiter, 1989: 11).

Themed Trails

Themed trails have been a familiar tourism construct since at least the early 1980s (Macleod, 2004), although the academic literature is still relatively sparse (e.g. Bartis, 1998; Leask & Barriere, 2000). At its most basic, a trail is a means of organizing and managing the visitor experience by creating a:

> route for walking, cycling, riding, driving or other forms of transport that draws on the natural or cultural heritage of an area to provide an

educational experience that will enhance visitor enjoyment. It is marked on the ground or on maps, and interpretative material is normally available to guide the visitor. (Silbergh, 1994: 123)

The notion of travelling along a predetermined route is a fundamental symbol of progress and the idea of the journey is often used as a metaphor for life and self-discovery (Macleod, 2004): 'journeying along a trail has long been a natural inclination as well as simple common sense' (Moulin & Boniface, 2001: 241). The sense of a historic journey accompanied by attractive landscapes and built heritage provides a satisfying sense of achievement for the traveller. And in their role of directing visitors to specific locations and sites and providing a meaningful visitor experience, trails have been employed increasingly in visitor management strategies.

There is an important contribution to sustainable tourism management here, and the value of trails in directing visitors away from densely congested sites and areas in order to explore under-visited areas has been recognized by those managing popular destinations, particularly historic town centres (Hall & McArthur, 1998). Indeed, the 'staggering in time and space of tourist and visitor flows' (WTO, 2001: 4), to which trails in less-visited locations can contribute, is a key objective of the World Tourism Organization's *Global Code of Ethics for Tourism*.

More recently, the development of trails has been predominantly marketing-led (e.g. Boyne *et al.*, 2003b), and new trails have been created as an attempt to give a clear visual identity to places not already on tourists' itineraries (Macleod, 2004).

Thus, trails are becoming an important element of local and regional cultural tourism and a means of knitting together sparse rural regions, linearly distributed attractions, and cross-border complementarities. The European Union (EU) has been supporting a number of these, one example of which is the *King's Road* (Anon, 2000; Finnish Tourist Board, 2000), an ancient highway of great cultural significance that follows an important medieval mail coach route, linking the Nordic capitals of Oslo and Stockholm with Turku and Helsinki in Finland and eastwards to St Petersburg in Russia. This 'trail' represents a good example of the marketing of cultural routes across Europe, to assist, through transit tourism, the regeneration of rural and peripheral regions through which it passes (Roberts & Hall, 2001: 79).

Theme trails are usually based on partnerships within and/or between public and private sectors. They are more than just a route along which visitors are encouraged to travel, but are intended to raise the level of activities and attendances at attractions, to promote the branding of an area and to enhance its image and identity among target markets. They provide an underlying linkage through which communication can be made with a region's own inhabitants as well as with its visitors (e.g. Meyer-Cech, 2003, 2004). Often, however, as in the case of Austria's 50 theme trails, many do not progress beyond the stages of product development and mutual sales promotion, such as creating a brochure (Meyer-Cech, 2003: 154–7). In Austria, the insufficient marketing of trails and missed opportunities for deriving added value, are echoed in UK tea-related trails. Meyer-Cech (2003, 2004) contends that the success of such trails depends crucially on effective management and the development and implementation of strategies that can embrace a wide range of stakeholders.

Critics argue that the employment of heritage themes, which tea tourism encompasses, creates a 'museumization' of public spaces (Relph, 1976: 101), where the museum idiom breaks away from the confines of the institution and penetrates wider cultural life. Yet many would argue that this is an inclusive, perhaps even liberating characteristic of the embracing of heritage and culture by the democratizing processes of tourism development.

Within the cultural heritage idiom, tea rooms and tea shops, while serving the functional purpose of providing a place of refreshment and rest, are also employed to reinforce a staged authenticity of heritage urban and rural recreations, where nostalgia for a slower pace of life and the presentation of Victorian and Edwardian attractions and values may be central under-pinnings. Nostalgia is a powerful force in the creation of such assemblages, and consequently aesthetically attractive aspects of the past are likely to be favoured at the expense of the less-pleasing or contentious, such as the rigid class system, gender inequalities, colonial exploitation and endemic poverty which underpinned such privileged environments (Hewison, 1987).

The commodification of tea has in part resulted from tourism pressures, both domestic and international. Books and other publications on tea have long existed, in many forms. Thus one genre contains recipes associated with tea-taking, for example as an accompaniment to afternoon tea (e.g. Mashiter, 1989; Pettigrew, 2001b). Another is the compilation of pertinent ephemera that may be loosely tea related, one of the better examples of which is a collection of tea-related quotations, poems and paintings (Exley, 1999). Small-scale pottery manufacturers specializing in the production of tea ware have also set themselves up as visitor attractions with their own, often imaginative, promotional material. Examples include the Teapottery, which has two production units (at Keswick in the Lake District and Leyburn in North Yorkshire) (Teapottery, n.d.), and the Teapot Pottery at Debenham in Suffolk (Carter, 2004). Collections of tea ware also appear, either singly or in combination with other museum exhibits, such as

Norwich Castle Museum's 3000-strong Twining teapot collection, with exhibits dating from 1720 onwards (Jolliffe, 2003).

Teapot Trails

Originally sponsored by Brooke Bond (now part of Unilever), the UK teapot trails are a collection of 33 regionally-based publications that devote a page each to a selected number (usually around 25) of tea-serving establishments within the catchment area of the volume. The entries are not graded, and the only explicit criteria for inclusion (although no reference is made to exclusion) are a series of characteristics in the introduction to each volume, approximating to those already noted above, such as 'they all have one thing in common – you will be sure of a friendly welcome, fresh wholesome home-made food, inviting cakes and pastries and, most important, a really good pot of tea!' (Coulthard, nd: 1). Each introduction (by the editor) suggests that every entry has been personally 'examined': 'For this book, I've sought out those places where you can enjoy both the tea-shops and the historic surroundings' (Alderson, 1992: inside front cover).

The teapot trail series of publications also provide a brief sketch of the town, village, hamlet or farm in which each establishment is located as well as important detail about the tea room itself. This emphasis on geographical context and the employment of a central regional map, indicating by number the location of each entry, highlight three basic elements of the trail's construction:

(1) Only occasionally does the trail exhibit a linear characteristic, and then usually fortuitously rather than by design: thus rarely is there an explicit geographical route that takes the traveller from point A onwards to a final destination point B while being able to appreciate intermediate attractions along the way. What is actually being represented is a regional clustering of complementary activities which the visitor can dip into, in virtually any order, but which may exhibit no coherent linking geographical route.

(2) There appears to be no means by which consolidation and further regional promotion of these trails can be accomplished. No evidence is offered of collaboration, partnerships or networking between the establishments listed. A wide range of both public and private sector organizations publish directories of tea rooms, often with a specific intent (Table 13.1), but rarely do they appear to be related to or integrated with tea trails.

Table 13.1 Sample sources of tea room directories

Area/ownership/ event	Title	Total listed	Reference source
Devon & Cornwall/ National Trust	Tea rooms and restaurants	16	National Trust, 2004
East Hertfordshire Council,	Smoke Free Eating Guide – Tea/Coffee Rooms/Cafes	11	East Herts 2003
Exmoor Food Festival	Cream teas	28	Exmoor Food Festival, 2003
Harrogate, Borough Yorkshire	Coffee Houses & Tea Rooms	18	Harrogate Council, 2004
Herne Bay, Kent Internet,	Internet Cafe & Tearooms	8	Herne Bay 2004
West Surrey	Tea rooms and cafes	36	West Surrey CTCDA, 2003

(3) There is only ever one entry for each location. Many establishments may therefore be omitted for no obvious reason. No claim is made that the establishment listed is the best one in the particular town, village or hamlet within which it is located. Thus the regional clusters presented are both arbitrary and partial. By contrast, for example, Margaret Thornby's (2001) *Guide to Tea Rooms of Britain*, which details over 250 tea rooms (but not their geographical context), often has multiple tea room entries for particular places.

By 2001 the Teapot Trail series had featured over 800 establishments, and in that year *Tea Rooms of Distinction* (Anon, 2001) was published, detailing 130 'of some of the finest tea rooms in the country'. Indeed, a regional scatter approach rather than selecting the very highest quality establishments was the intention of this publication. Because many tea rooms could not be included due to lack of space, 'a few were chosen from each region as examples of the kind of quality the British tea room now offers' (KRD Books, 2001: 1).

Other UK tea trails include booklet series carrying such titles as *Tea Shop Walks* and *Best Tea Shop Walks*, which are usually based on a geographical county such as Worcestershire (e.g. Boston, 1999), or a major topographic feature, such as the Chiltern hills (e.g. Patefield, 1994). These suggest the use of tea shops as the starting, finishing or stopping-off points for locally based walks, either linear or circular in nature. Just as with the teapot trails, there is no formal recognition, association or demarcation of a particular walking route in relation to tea as an object of visitor attraction. Published as a means of promoting the individual tea shops highlighted, *Tea Shop Walks* again provides no explicit evidence of collaboration, partnership or networking between the establishments themselves, nor with other private or public sector agencies.

There is limited evidence of organized walking experiences based on tea-related trails, although the Christian Guild Holidays (2004) programme includes week-long 'Teapot Trails & Coffee Shop Stops' walking holidays in the hills and villages of North Yorkshire in spring and autumn. These are designated by the Guild as a 'fun and fellowship' type of break.

At present, therefore, within the UK, tea-related trails – whether geographical routes or functional clusters – appear insufficiently promoted and integrated as coherent tourist attractions. They appear to have generated only limited collaborative partnerships, not having progressed beyond the promotion of individual establishments, and back-linkages with the local economy and tea industry appear minimal. Yet the potential for the tourism industry and food and drink sectors to work together to achieve mutual benefit at local and regional levels has been endorsed in a number of strategy documents (Boyne & Hall, 2003: 286; Boyne *et al.*, 2003a: 78). The general theme of such policy recommendations (DCMS, 1999; DETR, 2000; ETC, 2001; Scottish Executive, 2001, 2002) is to establish stronger links between tourism and sectors such as food, drink, transport and retailing that have a major influence on the tourism 'experience' and which also benefit from tourism.

Results from an independent study commissioned by the Tea Council in the early 1990s indicated that 'very few' of the thousands of tea-serving outlets across the UK were serving tea to the high standards that the Tea Council believed was desirable. The body therefore decided that recognition should be given to those establishments that meet high standards in both preparing and serving tea. This is undertaken by invitation to membership of a 'unique and prestigious' organization – The Tea Guild – which was founded in 1995 (Tea Council, 2002). All establishments must fulfil what are claimed to be 'exacting criteria' and pass inspection at least once a year by professional tea tasters. A list of Tea Guild members can also be found online (Tea Council, 2004): just 72 in the UK and 16 overseas. Further, the Tea Council (2003) publishes a *Guide to the Best Tea Places in Britain*, to which reference is made in promotion and marketing material by those establishments included (e.g. Forte Tea Rooms, 2004).

Conclusions and Recommendations

Although possessing a rationale rooted in English heritage, at present within the UK tea-related trails are insufficiently promoted and integrated, and appear to have generated only limited collaborative partnerships. Teapot trails in particular remain little more than an internally fragmented paper exercise serving as an umbrella vehicle for the promotion of a collection of individual establishments which may otherwise have little or no collaborative relationship nor derive any consequent external economies. Yet, having identified a series of apparent tourism micro-clusters, such trails can act as the basis for the further development and promotion of specialized regional products to help create economic and social opportunities in small rural and peripheral communities (e.g. Michael, 2003; see also Marsden & Arce, 1995).

The most obvious challenge to the incorporation and embedding of tea in regional initiatives and local economies is, of course, that, certain herbal fusions aside, tea is not a part of UK local quality produce, and as such cannot be incorporated into product circles and related collaborative ventures (e.g. see Ilbery & Kneafsey, 1998, 2000; Ilbery *et al.*, 2001). As a result, few public sector bodies have shown willingness to support and encourage tea-led or tea-related tourism initiatives. It has been found, for example (Boyne & Hall, 2003: 288–9; Boyne *et al.*, 2003b), that, owing to limited promotional space and the requirement to promote quality goods and services to visitors, area and regional tourist boards usually confer priority to those initiatives which may enjoy national or international recognition or can demonstrate high or exceptional levels of quality assurance.

Yet it is not unrealistic to suggest that local place-specific blends can be developed, incorporating local or regionally related taste and nomenclature (e.g. see Bartlett, 2003), particularly given that one or two place-related and several regionally branded blends and 'speciality' teas already exist in the UK. Certainly, added value, imagery and identity could be generated and projected through appropriate blend designation and repackaging.

But a further challenge here is posed by the structure of the tea-purveying industry in the UK. The large food corporations, of which tea production may be a small part, may not be prepared to be troubled by relatively small-scale, quality-related developments. Such initiative would therefore fall to the smaller, specialist producers who would anyway be better positioned to contribute to sustainable tourism initiatives. Locally branded blends could be developed as their property and responsibility. These should then be supported, where appropriate, by and in collaboration with, economic development agencies and other local and regional public and private sector stimulators of tourism and quality produce development and promotion.

Further challenges include the reality that, compared to coffee, tea largely remains a relatively unfashionable beverage, particularly for the young. Despite various industry efforts to reinvigorate its image and identity, tea's unfashionability and dated aura largely remains. Further, the taking of tea has rarely been encompassed by mainstream gastronomy studies, as reflected in the literature in that field (e.g. Bode, 1994). Indeed, tea drinking is often taken for granted as a basic, unpretentious 'cuppa', and as such faces strong resistance in any efforts to integrate its consumption in more up-market or fashionable contexts, other than 'afternoon tea'.

All of these challenges therefore raise serious questions concerning the wider roles that tea-related tourism initiatives, such as teapot trails, can pursue in aspects of local and regional economic development. Nonetheless, from a sustainable development perspective, a number of opportunities offer themselves. As part of promotional and branding exercises, certain tea rooms and tea shops should embrace 'fair trade' principles and more prominently emphasize the availability of organic tea and accompanying organic food as a means of demonstrating their and their customers' commitment to:

- sustainable development and moves towards global equity and better employment conditions for the 'others' who work in the tea production industry in less developed countries;
- environmentally sensitive tea production, processing, distribution and waste recycling; and
- healthy eating and drinking set within a health-conscious environment – such as encouraging a more rigorous pursuit of the *Heartbeat Award* – a nationally recognized scheme supported by the Health Education Council and the Chartered Institute of Environmental Health to reduce coronary heart disease and encourage caterers to promote good health (e.g. Kent Education Authority, 2004).

Agencies such as *Tourism Concern* could have an important role to play here in both promoting tea tourism as a sustainable development option, and in integrating the local and global within and between the tourism and tea sectors led by an ethically rigorous 'fair trade' ethos.

References

Alderson, C.J. (1992) *The Teapot Trail. A Taste of Northumbria* (2nd edn). Darlington: CP Printing and Publishing.

Anon (2000) *Guide to Baltic Capitals and King's Road*. Tallinn: EU PHARE/TACIS and INTERREG IIA.

Anon (2001) *Tea Rooms of Distinction. The Connoisseur's Guide to the Finest Tea Rooms of Great Britain*. Darlington: KRD Books.

Anon (2004) 'Mack' time for a cuppa. *Ayrshire Post*, 13 February.

Bartis, H. (1998) A national black heritage trail in the Eastern Cape Province, South Africa: is it an option? In: D. Hall and L. O'Hanlon (eds) *Rural Tourism Management: Sustainable Options* (pp. 17–28). Auchincruive: Scottish Agricultural College.

Bartlett, B. (2003) Tourists could pour into city for tea. *Telegraph-Journal* (Saint John, Canada), 7 October. Online document: http://canadaeast.com/apps/pbcs.dll/article.

Bettys & Taylors (2004) *Yorkshire Tea*. Harrogate: Bettys & Taylors. Online document: http://www.yorkshiretea.co.uk/home.asp.

Bode, W.K.H. (1994) *European Gastronomy: The Story of Man's Food and Eating Customs*. London: Hodder & Stoughton.

Boston, I. (1999) *Best Tea Shop Walks in Worcestershire*. Wilmslow: Sigma Leisure.

Boyne, S. and Hall, D. (2003) Managing food and tourism developments: Issues for planning and opportunities to add value. In C.M. Hall, L. Sharples, R. Mitchell, N. Macionis and B. Cambourne (eds) *Food Tourism Around the World: Development, Management and Markets* (pp. 285–95). Oxford: Butterworth-Heinemann.

Boyne, S., Hall, D. and Williams, F. (2003a) Integrating sectors and efforts: Communities, agencies, food and tourism in rural development. In: J. Collen and G. Richards (eds) *Gastronomy and Tourism* (pp. 75–91). Gravenwezel/Schilde, Belgium: Academie voor de Streekgebonden Gastronomie.

Boyne, S., Hall, D. and Williams, F. (2003b) Policy, support and promotion for food-related tourism initiatives: a marketing approach to regional development. *Journal of Travel and Tourism Marketing* 14 (3/4) 131–54.

Brief Encounter (2002) *Brief Encounter Tea Rooms*. Keighley: Brief Encounter. Online document: http://www.brief-encounter.org.uk.

British Red Cross (2004) *Regional Fundraising Events*. London: British Red Cross. Online document: http://www.redcross.org.uk/event.asp?id=19512.

Brodie Melrose Drysdale (2004) *Products*. Edinburgh: Brodie Melrose Drysdale & Co. Ltd. Online document: http://www.brodies1867.co.uk/products.htm.

Carter, T. (2004) *Teapot Pottery*. Debenham: Teapot Pottery. Online document: http://www.cartersteapots.com.

Christian Guild Holidays (2004) *Special Breaks*. Matlock: Christian Guild Holidays. Online document: http://cgh.edenhosting.co.uk/holidays/.

Compton Tea Rooms (n.d.) *Compton Tea Rooms*. Eastbourne: Compton Tea Rooms. Online document: http://www.meadsvillage.com/tearooms/compton_right.html.

Conisbrough Castle (2003) *Conisbrough Castle: South Yorkshire's Best Kept Secret*. Doncaster: Conisbrough Castle. Online document: http://www.conisbrough castle.org.uk/tea_rooms.htm.

Coulthard, J. (n.d.) *The Teapot Trail. A Taste of Strathclyde & the West Coast*. Leyburn: Trail Publishing.

DCMS (Department of Culture, Media and Sport) (1999) *Tomorrow's Tourism*. London: DCMS.

Delamont, S. (1995) *Appetites and Identities*. London: Routledge.

DETR (Department of the Environment, Transport and the Regions) (2000) *Our Countryside: the Future. A Fair Deal for Rural England*. London: DETR.

Douglas, M. (ed.) (1987) *Constructive Drinking*. Cambridge: Cambridge University Press.

East Hertfordshire Council (2003) *Smoke Free Eating Guide – Tea/Coffee Rooms/ Cafes*. Bishops Stortford: East Herts Council. Online document: http://www.eastherts. gov.uk/healthpr/tea_rooms.htm.

ETC (English Tourism Council) (2001) Working for the countryside. A strategy for rural tourism in England, 2001–2005. London: ETC.

Exley, H. (1999) *Time for Tea*. Watford and New York: Exley Publications.

Exmoor Food Festival (2003) *Cream Teas*. Exmoor: Exmoor Food Festival. Online document: http://www.exmoorfoodfestival.co.uk/cream_tea/cream_ tea.htm.

Falk, P. and Campbell, C. (eds) (1997) *The Shopping Experience*. London: Sage.

Fields, K. (2002) Demand for the gastronomy tourism product: motivational factors. In: G. Richards and A.-M. Hjalager (eds) *Tourism and Gastronomy* (pp. 36–50). London: Routledge.

Finnish Tourist Board (2000) *The King's Road*. Helsinki: Finnish Tourist Board. Online document: http://www.thekingsroad.com.

Forte Tea Rooms (2004) *The Forte Tea Rooms and Restaurant*. Winchester: The Forte Tea Rooms. Online document: http://www.thefortetearooms.co.uk.

Hall, C.M. and McArthur, S. (1998) *Integrated Heritage Management: Principles and Practice*. London: The Stationery Office.

Harrogate Borough Council (2004) *Harrogate: Coffee Houses & Tea Rooms*. Harrogate: Harrogate Borough Council. Online document: http://www.harrogate.gov.uk/ tourism/restnts/tearooms.htm.

Herne Bay Internet (2004) *Herne Bay Internet: Cafe & Tearooms*. Herne Bay: Herne Bay Internet. Online document: http://www.hernebaymarket.co.uk/café.htm .

Hewison, R. (1987) *The Heritage Industry: Britain in a Climate of Decline*. London: Methuen.

Ilbery, B. and Kneafsey, M. (1998) Product and place: promoting quality products and services in the lagging regions of the European Union. *European Urban and Regional Studies* 5, 329–41.

Ilbery, B. and Kneafsey, M. (2000) Producer constructions of quality in regional speciality food production: A case study from south west England. *Journal of Rural Studies* 16, 217–30.

Ilbery, B., Kneafsey, M., Söderland, A. and Dimara, E. (2001) Quality, imagery and marketing: producer perspectives on quality product services in the lagging rural regions of the European Union. *Geografiska Annaler: Series B, Human Geography* 83 (1), 27–40.

Jolliffe, L. (2003) The lure of tea: history, traditions and attractions. In: C.M. Hall, L. Sharples, R. Mitchell, N. Macionis and B. Cambourne (eds) *Food Tourism Around the World: Development, Management and Markets* (pp. 121–36). Oxford: Butterworth-Heinemann.

Kent Education Authority (2004) *Heartbeat Award*. Canterbury: Kent Education Authority. Online document: http://www.kenthealthyschools.org/heheartbeat. html .

Kitty's Tearoom (2004) *Kitty's Tearoom and Bed & Breakfast, New Galloway*. New Galloway: Kitty's Tearoom. Online document: http://www.swscotland.clara. net/kittys/tearoom.html.

KRD Books (2001) *Tea Rooms of Distinction*. Darlington: KRD Books. Online document: http://www.teapottrail.co.uk/troomsdistinc.htm.

Kris-Etherton, P.M. and Keen, C.L. (2002) Evidence that the antioxidant flavonoids in tea and cocoa are beneficial for cardiovascular health. *Current Opinion in Lipidology* 13 (1), 41–9.

Kuznesof, S., Tregear, A. and Moxey, A. (1997) Regional foods: A consumer perspective. *British Food Journal* 99 (6), 199–206.

Leask, A. and Barriere, O. (2000) The development of heritage trails in Scotland. *Insights*, January, A117–A123.

Macleod, N.E. (2004) Seeing places: A critique of the heritage trail as a visual interpretation of place. *LSA Newsletter* 67, 35–42.

MAFF/CA (Ministry of Agriculture, Fisheries and Food/Countryside Agency) (2000) *Tourists' Attitudes Towards Regional and Local Foods*. London: MAFF. Online document: http://www.defra.gov.uk/foodrin/helpmark/report.pdf.

Marsden, T. and Arce, A. (1995) Constructing quality: emerging food networks in the rural transition. *Environment and Planning A* 27, 1261–79.

Mashiter, R. (1989) *A Little Book of Afternoon Teas*. Belfast: Appletree Press.

de Mejía, E.G. (2003) El efecto quimioprotector del té y sus compuestos. *Archivos Latinoamericanos de Nutrición* 53 (2), 111–18.

Meyer-Cech, K. (2003) Food trails in Austria. In C.M. Hall, L. Sharples, R. Mitchell, N. Macionis and B. Cambourne (eds) *Food Tourism Around the World: Development, Management and Markets* (pp. 149–57). Oxford: Butterworth-Heinemann.

Meyer-Cech, K. (2004) Regional co-operation in rural theme trails. In D. Hall, I. Kirkpatrick and M. Mitchell (eds) *Rural Tourism and Sustainable Business*. Clevedon: Channel View Press.

Michael, E.J. (2003) Tourism micro-clusters. *Tourism Economics* 9 (2), 133–45.

Moulin, C. and Boniface, P. (2001) Routeing heritage for tourism: Making heritage and cultural tourism networks for socio-cultural development. *International Journal of Heritage Studies* 7 (3), 237–48.

Murroughs (2004) *Welsh Brew Tea*. Swansea: Murroughs. Online document: http://www.welshbrewtea.com.

National Trust (2004) *Tearooms & Restaurants in Devon & Cornwall*. London: The National Trust. Online document: http://www.nationaltrust.org.uk/main/ shopping/trooms_devon_cornwall.

Patefield, J. (1994) *Tea Shop Walks in the Chilterns*. Wilmslow: Sigma Leisure.

Pettigrew, J. (2001a) *A Social History of Tea*. London: The National Trust.

Pettigrew, J. (2001b) *Tea-time Recipes*. London: The National Trust.

Pilgrim's (2004) *Pilgrim's*. Brecon: Pilgrim's. Online document: http://www. computer.brecon.co.uk/pilgrims/indnov3.htm.

Relph, E. (1976) *Place and Placelessness*. London: Pion.

Roberts, L. and Hall, D. (2001) *Rural Tourism and Recreation: Principles to Practice*. Wallingford: CABI Publishing.

St Martin's Tea Rooms (2004) *St Martin's (All Organic) Tea Rooms*. Chichester: St Martin's Tea Rooms. Online document: http://www.organictearooms.co.uk.

Scottish Executive (2001) *A Forward Strategy for Scottish Agriculture*. Edinburgh: Scottish Executive.

Scottish Executive (2002) *Tourism Framework for Action: 2002–2005*. Edinburgh: Scottish Executive.

Silbergh, D. (1994) A strategy for theme trails. In J.M. Fladmark (ed.) *Cultural Tourism* (pp. 123–46). London: Donhead.

Smith, M. (1986) *Michael Smith's Afternoon Tea*. Basingstoke: Macmillan.

Tea Council (2002) *An Introduction to the Tea Guild*. London: The Tea Council. Online document: http://www.teacouncil.co.uk/newtc/cate/index.htm.

Tea Council (2003) *Guide to the Best Tea Places in Britain*. London: The Tea Council.

Tea Council (2004) *Tea Guild Home*. London: The Tea Council. Online document: http://www.tea.co.uk/tBreakN/guild/index.htm.

Tea Muse (2003) The benefits of tea. *Tea Muse*, May. Online document: http://www.teamuse.com/artcile_030501.html.

Tealby Tea Rooms (2004) *Tealby Tea Rooms*. Tealby: Tealby Tea Rooms. Online document: http://TealbyTeaRooms.com.

Teapottery (n.d.) *Teatime Will Never Be the Same Again*. Leyburn and Keswick: The Teapottery.

Thanet Mencap Society (2003) *Ashley's Tea Rooms*. Cliftonville: Thanet Mencap Society. Online document: http://www.thanet-mencap.co.uk/tea/ .

Thornby, M.V. (2001) *Guide to Tea Rooms of Britain*. Leicester: Whitehill Publishing.

Twining, S. (1989) Introduction. In R. Mashiter, *A Little Book of Afternoon Teas* (pp. 3–8). Belfast: Appletree Press.

Tregear, A., Kuznesof, S. and Moxey, A. (1998) Policy initiatives for regional foods: Some insights from consumer research. *Food Policy* 23 (5), 383–94.

Trew, J. (2002) Tea turns over a new leaf. *Scotland on Sunday*, 9 June.

Unilever (2004) *Scottish Blend*. London: Unilever Bestfoods UK. Online document: http://www.brookebond.co.uk/product/beverages_scottish.asp.

Warren, J. (1979) *A Feast of Scotland*. London: Hodder & Stoughton.

West Surrey CTCDA (District Association of the Cyclists Touring Club) (2003) *Tea Rooms and Cafes*. Guildford: West Surrey CTCDA. Online document: http://www.westsurreyctcda.org.uk/coffee.htm.

WTO (World Tourism Organization) (2001) *Global Code of Ethics for Tourism*. Madrid: World Tourism Organization.

Chapter 14

Tea Tourists and Tea Destinations in Canada: A New Blend?

LEE JOLLIFFE

The tea traditions of Canada reflect the diverse origins of those who inhabit the country. The indigenous population has its own traditions such as those reflected by the Inuit herbal teas of the north. Tea cultures imported into Canada include those from Britain, reflected in the English-style tea rooms of Victoria, BC and from France as seen in the tea salon tradition in Montreal, Quebec. New immigrants to Canada are also bringing their own tea cultures with them. This is indicated by the recent establishment of a number of Asian-style 'bubble tea' shops in the Toronto, Ontario area and of shops reflecting Asian tea cultures in Charlottetown, Prince Edward Island. For the tourist dedicated to searching out these tea experiences there is much to discover. For the tourism industry there is the potential for using tea in destination development.

However, tea products and experiences must indeed be searched for and this chapter examines the context for the further development and enhancement of tea-related tourism in Canada. This includes a review of the role of the contemporary tea trade and a discussion of the characteristics of the tea-tourism consumer and the domestic tea tourist in Canada. A number of localities with tea history and tea-service facilities in Canada are examined in terms of their emergence and development as tea destinations.

Tourism in Canada

As a tourism destination Canada has much to offer in terms of nature, attractions and culture. The country ranks seventh (after France, Spain, United States, United Kingdom, China and Mexico) in terms of international tourism arrivals with 20.1 million visitors, excluding same-day trips (WTO, 2002). In the same year travel by Canadians in Canada consisted of 187.9

million trips (CTC, 2004). In the following year 2003 there was a decrease in Canadian travel within Canada, due to a number of adverse factors that included the war in Iraq, SARS, a major power failure in Ontario, and forest fires in British Columbia (CTC, 2004). However, despite this temporary decline in tourism demand it is evident that there is still a considerable market for both international and domestic tourism in the country.

The Canadian Tourism Commission (CTC) has encouraged the development of the culinary tourism aspect of Canada's tourism product with national roundtables (discussion groups) on the topic, a conference, and funding for product development through a product club (CTC, 2001a, 2001b). These developments reflect a growing global interest in culinary tourism that consists of travelling to experience culture through food and drink. For communities Wolf (2003: 11) identifies culinary tourism as 'a very lucrative niche that holds strong benefits for community economic development'. The author furthermore identifies some of the activities of culinary tourism, including, for example: eating and drinking at a hard-to-find 'locals only' restaurant or bar; attending cooking classes; driving a 'culinary route'; meeting the chef/owner of a noted restaurant; searching for hard-to-find food ingredients (farm and farmers' markets, 'u-picks', local shops). Briedenhann and Wickens (2004) argue that the establishment of such routes as culinary routes holds potential for stimulating partnership and cooperation between local areas and stimulating the start-up of tourism in less-developed regions. Previous work has identified the potential of tea as a tourism-development tool for destinations (Jolliffe, 2003a). Based on the experience of other countries such as the UK (as discussed by Hall and Boyne in Chapter 13) where teapot trails have been developed, it is not difficult to imagine that similar developments might occur in Canada.

As illustrated by Table 14.1, domestic travel within Canada includes visiting friends and relatives, pleasure trips and business and convention visits; all market segments that could be attracted to the 'tea tourism' experiences profiled later in this chapter. Expenditure statistics also show that these visitors spend a considerable amount on food and beverage, which will include the consumption of tea and tea-related meal services. Tea can be viewed as a sign of hospitality in both the commercial and non-commercial hospitality sectors. Tea consumption, enjoyment and experiences, although undocumented, are likely to affect a large percentage of the Canadians travelling within Canada. Since 66% of Canadians consume tea at home it is likely that these consumers will also be inclined to consume tea while away from home (Tea Council of Canada, 2004).

Tea experiences are also available to travellers making same-day trips, identified as 85.9 million in 2003, as a stop for a cup of tea, or a visit to a tea

Table 14.1 Canadian travel within Canada

	2002	*2003*
Total trips (millions)	**187.9**	**172.2**
Intraprovincial trips	164.6	151.2
Interprovincial trips	23.3	21.0
Same day trips	92.7	85.9
Overnight trips	95.2	86.3
Visiting friends or relatives	65.3	61.4
Pleasure	74.5	67.4
Personal	24.5	23.8
Business and convention	23.6	19.6
Total nights (millions)	**308.0**	**278.5**
Non-commercial nights	186.6	170.1
Commercial nights	121.4	108.4
Total expenditures ($millions 1997)	**27,968**	**25,444**
Transportation	10,655	9,591
Accommodation	4,692	4,402
Food and beverage	6,582	5,983
Recreation and entertainment	1,910	1,711
Other	4,129	3,757

Source: Canadian Tourism Commission, 2004

room, tea café or tea bar (where available) would be easy to fit into a same-day itinerary. Canada's Tim Hortons chain of 'donut' and coffee shops has recently introduced 'steeped' tea and has mounted a massive national advertising campaign to let Canadians know that the chain now uses 'loose' tea leaves and 'steep' their tea, referring to it as a time-honoured tradition. The chain consists of 'more than 2350 stores across Canada and a steadily growing base of 228 locations in key markets within the United States' (Tim Hortons, 2005). Moves such as this by the food and beverage industry, as well as the continued media coverage of the health benefits of tea, are sure to promote the idea of tea among Canadian consumers, and this is a platform upon which the tourism industry can build in terms of developing tea-related tourism products, experiences and destinations.

Plate 14.1 Steeped tea campaign, Tim Hortons, Saint John, New Brunswick, Canada

Source: Keith Dewar

The Tea Trade in Canada

In Canada, as in other countries, the tea industry is recognized as consisting of a layering of producers, dealers or brokers, distributors and retailers. As no tea is grown in Canada it must all be imported, the major sources being India, Sri Lanka and Kenya. The companies purchasing tea are sent samples both directly from tea gardens, and from the weekly tea auctions such as those in Mombasa (Kenya), Colombo (Sri Lanka) and various locations in India, including Jakarta. The teas are purchased or bid on for purchase through a broker who represents the producers, and the companies subsequently blend a number of teas into signature tea blends. This allows for a consistent product to be offered year after year. As Smith (1986: 32) observes: 'The taster's blend must match up with previous blends in order to achieve a continuity of flavour, almost in the same way as a blended wine must have no recognizable differences from its predecessor.' Much of the tea retailed in Canada consists of quick-brew tea bags blended from black tea but there is an emerging trend towards the offering of speciality teas.

The contemporary tea trade in Canada is represented by the Tea Council of Canada, a 'not-for-profit association of leading companies and producing countries, including Sri Lanka, India, and Kenya dedicated to the promotion of quality tea to Canadians' (www.tea.ca). Members embrace tea-producing countries, tea blenders and distributors, tea retailers, bulk tea suppliers, and equipment and service providers. The council's objectives include increasing the awareness of quality tea and its health benefits. It does this in a number of ways: through its web site, Canada's Tea Zone (www.tea.ca), through media coverage of trends in tea consumption and of the benefits of tea, through a quality service programme in which establishments serving tea can become certified (four star tea-grading programme) and through an annual industry conference. Positive media coverage also promotes the consumption of tea and the council periodically issues press releases reflecting current research on tea consumption and trends.

A number of large companies and their brands dominate the retail tea trade in Canada (for example Tetley and Lipton), and most tea is sold in grocery stores, so it is natural that the trade will concentrate its marketing and development efforts on the domestic tea consumer. Tea sales are increasing alongside the growing interest of the public in the health benefits of tea. Experts recognize that this recent vogue for tea may be attributable to public awareness of research findings. Furthermore, to encourage the proper use of tea in a food service setting the Tea Council of Canada, in cooperation with George Brown College in Toronto, Ontario, is currently planning for the introduction of a tea sommelier course (Roberge, 2004, personal correspondence). This will build on the council's efforts to encourage quality standards in the serving of tea. The Fairmont Royal York Hotel in Toronto is the first hotel in Canada to have a tea *sommelier* on its staff (www.fairmont.com).

There is great potential for the tea trade to use tea tourism to promote its own blends and brands, as the use of particular brands of tea in tourism promotions and products could enhance brand recognition. Examples of this type of endeavour already exist: for example, Red Rose has produced a Heritage Inns calendar, encouraging visits to the inns where their tea is sold; and the Barbours Company in Sussex, New Brunswick has contributed to the opening of a local King Cole Tea Room (Jolliffe, 2003a) and periodically sponsors a 'King Cole Tea Tent' (for example in June 2004 on the occasion of the centenary of the establishment of the town of Sussex). These efforts reflect not only the potential for marketing of tea but also the natural role that tea plays in the provision of hospitality, in this latter case in a special event context.

Tea Consumers and Tea Tourists in Canada

Tea is consumed both at home and as part of leisure, recreation and touristic pursuits. In a previous work the tea tourist was defined as a tourist whose decisions, purchases and habits are motivated by an interest in the various aspects of tea (Jolliffe, 2003a). Information on the tea tourist in Canada can thus be derived by examining the domestic consumption of tea as well as investigating the possible motivations of these consumers as tourists.

Data on tea consumption available from the Tea Council of Canada shows that 66% of Canadians consume tea at home. Differences in tea consumption and perceptions of the benefits of drinking tea are evident between men and women. For all types of tea, more women than men drink tea. This affects the profile of tea tourists, as it could generally be expected that women are more likely to be tea tourists than men. In addition, differences in tea consumption are demonstrated between different age groups. In response the question 'What type of tea do you drink?', Tea Council research indicated: 'regular black tea is favoured by the 55 years plus group while younger Canadians are more interested in ice tea. More people are drinking teas in all age segments.' This demographic information has implications for tea-related tourism as it is clear that the older age group will appreciate traditional tea offerings whereas the younger group will be attracted by other offerings, for example iced tea. Canadians consider green tea to be healthy – in a 2001 survey, 73% indicated they thought green tea was healthy versus 50% who thought black tea was healthy (Tea Council of Canada, 2004). Theories about tourist motivations can also be applied to examining the potential characteristics of the tea tourist. It is generally agreed that the primary motive for pleasure tourism is a need to get away from the routine situation of the home, workplace and normal physical environment (Williams, 1998).

Both data on tea consumption and a discussion of tourist motivations thus reveals some inherent characteristics of the tea tourist in Canada. The Canadian tea tourist is likely to consume tea as a beverage at home. At present these tea tourists are also likely to be from an older age group and to prefer traditional offerings of black tea as well as some of the associated meal services, such as afternoon tea. Younger Canadians who prefer speciality tea and iced tea may not be as interested in the existing tea offerings, and new products and services may have to be developed for these consumers. The awareness of health benefits has implications for the use of green tea in developing new services for these potential tea tourists, perhaps corresponding with the current interest in health and wellness tourism.

The typology of tea tourists (Table 14.2) is informed by the demographics of tea drinkers and by participant observation by the author, not only as proprietor of Mrs Proffitt's Tea Shop in Prince Edward Island and a

Table 14.2 Typology and characteristics of tea tourists

Type	*Characteristics*
Accidental	• Enjoys a tea experience when they come across it • Will not actively seek out tea experiences • Does not make vacation decisions based on the availability of such experiences
Dedicated	• Actively seeks out tea experiences • Introduces their family and friends to tea experiences • Vacation decisions are influenced by access to tea services and experiences
Extreme	• Will go anywhere for tea experiences • Searches out tea-related collectables • Purchases tea souvenirs • Makes vacation decisions based on availability of tea facilities and potential tea experiences

Source: Jolliffe (2003a)

researcher at the 1810 Carter House Tea Room in New Brunswick but also as a tea tourist visiting and experiencing other tea rooms. It has been observed most visitors are dedicated tea consumers, many are interested in the tea experience and some purchase tea-related collectables (tea accessories, teapots, books about tea, etc.). In both situations local residents regularly brought their visiting friends and relatives for tea.

Culinary tourism in Canada

This section reviews the current context for the development of tea-related tourism in the form of the trend towards culinary tourism. It also provides a snapshot of the products currently available for tea-related tourism. These products provide examples from which lessons can be extracted for the further development of tea-related tourism.

Culinary tourism consists of travelling to experience culture through food and drink (Boniface, 2003). In recent years an interest in culinary tourism in Canada has been evidenced by a number of initiatives. The Canadian Tourism Commission has sponsored the National Tourism and Cuisine Forum (held in 2000), recognized cuisine as a cultural tourism product line (2001), and produced a handbook for developing cultural tourism products (2003). An increase in the number of Canadians seeking heritage activities is projected as 3.7 million in 2026 (CTC, 2003), a market segment that would also have an interest in culinary tourism. Furthermore, the International Culinary Tourism Association identifies this type of tourism as 'a very lucrative niche that holds strong benefits for community economic development' (Wolf, 2003: 11), identifying activities that could also include tea such as culinary routes, cooking classes and experiencing local restaurants. Tea, as the most commonly consumed beverage in the world after water, has a natural role to play in the development of culinary tourism products in a country like Canada.

For potential tea tourists, as well as for tourists wanting a cultural experience related to tea, there are products, services and experiences widely available in Canada. Previous research has profiled the global existence of dedicated tea tours, tea rooms, tea trails, tea events, afternoon tea services and tea exhibitions (Jolliffe, 2003a). A dominant activity in tea-related tourism is the tea tour, a tour of tea attractions that includes experiencing local, traditional tea services (Cong & Jolliffe, 2002). Different types of tours include those that are focused on tea and those that utilize tea to enhance traditional tours.

The product base for tea-related tourism in Canada is different from that previously identified on a global basis, as it includes tea attractions, tea establishments – food service establishments where tea is served – and tea souvenirs. However, evidence of the dedicated tea tour found in other countries was not found in the case of Canada. Resources for building up tea tourism are particularly evident in the services provided by the Tea Council of Canada, which include certification for quality tea services as well as the resources provided on its web site. A variety of individual products available for tourism activities related to tea are reviewed here in the categories of: tea attractions, tea services and tea souvenirs.

Tea Attractions in Canada

Tourist attractions related to tea take many forms. They may include:

- dedicated tea museums;
- exhibitions on tea within other museums;
- interpretive programmes related to tea;
- special events with a tea theme; and
- historic sites with a relevance to the history of tea.

While Canada does not have any dedicated tea museums, as found in other countries (for instance, China, Japan, Taiwan and England), there are a number of museums as well as special programmes and exhibitions that deal with tea. For example, the Gardiner Museum of Ceramic Art in Toronto deals with some of the material culture related to tea. The museum also hosted the special exhibition The Artful Teapot (2003). Other museums also occasionally host special exhibitions and programmes dealing with tea. For instance, during the summer of 2003, the Montreal Botanical Gardens hosted an interpretive programme, Japanese Green Tea Tasting. Another illustration is the World Tea Party an exhibition held at the Art Gallery of Victoria, Victoria, BC, 2004. The exhibition is referred to as:

> a comprehensive celebration to the modest, fragrant leaf, that according to exhibition co-curator Dr. Judith Patt, has had wide-reaching effect on the visual arts, the decorative arts, architecture, social ritual and contemporary cultural production. (*National Post*, 2004)

This is the third such exhibition, the first having been held during the summer at Presentation Gallery in 1993. The World Tea Party is not just an exhibition. Its organizers portray it as a sharing of and celebration of tea traditions, reflecting how tea is a catalyst for human connection and communication (Dion *et al.*, 1995).

These programmes and exhibitions provide opportunities for tourists to experience tea histories and cultures. In combination with tea services provided either on site or nearby such events contribute to building the resource base that is necessary for the development of tea-related tourism at a destination.

Tea Services in Canada

The serving of tea many be exactly that – just a cup of tea – or there may be additional elements to the service that contribute to form a 'tea experience'. This may be accomplished in part through special meal services that incorporate tea. The serving of tea on a commercial hospitality basis takes many forms. A number of levels of service exist, including:

- afternoon tea;
- cream teas;
- high teas;
- special teas;
- daily tea services;
- lodging packages that include tea services; and
- activity packages that include tea services.

The setting for serving tea is as important as the hospitality provided. This may range from small cosy tea rooms and cafés to the elegant tea lobbies of some hotels. For the food service industry tea also means the opportunity for added revenue through tea services such as afternoon tea. In Canada, this is demonstrated by the number of hotels that offer afternoon tea as a service. For example, within the Fairmont chain, a number of hotels offer an afternoon tea service, including the Fairmont Algonquin in Saint Andrews by the Sea, New Brunswick, which offers The Algonquin Afternoon Tea. The Fairmont chain developed its own line of tea, serving to further brand the afternoon tea experience at its properties. The Fairmont Empress in Victoria, British Columbia has its own specially selected 'Tea at the Empress' tea blend. Tea services also have the potential to increase guest satisfaction, as the tea meal service is likely to be relaxed and, for the tea consumer, to make a lasting impression that reflects their stay. In situations where concentrated tea history and appeal is limited, tea services are often added to other types of tourism products for added charm and profile.

With roots in 19th-century England and Scotland (Pettigrew, 2001) the tea room has developed as a very popular form of food service establishment that offers tea and related meal services. This may include traditional cream teas and afternoon tea services. Boniface (2003: 116) describes the tea room genre: 'the tearoom can be a more wide and diffuse entity than that serving afternoon tea – frequently it is open all day and offers snacks and light lunches and coffee and other drinks – but its whole culture and aura derive from that seen as pertaining to afternoon tea.' In Canada examples of different forms of tea rooms include: The Red Tea Box in Toronto, Ontario; Rita's Tea Room, Big Pond, NS; and the McFarland House Tea Garden, Niagara on the Lake, Ontario. These establishments all provide a different ambience and service in the context of tea. The Red Tea Box provides a 'tea and food' experience, pairing tea with food, and also retails fine loose-leaf tea and the related accessories needed for its preparation. Rita's Tea Room is owned and operated by Cape Breton singer Rita MacNeil. As such, it serves traditional maritime fare, and a hearty blend of black tea is available, attracting locals, tourists and fans of the popular singer. The McFarland House Tea Garden, located in the historic house of the same name operated by The Niagara Parks Commission near Queenstown, Ontario serves tea, home-baking and Niagara wines in a historic garden setting. This is one of a number of historic house museums in Canada using tea as a complement to the interpretation of their properties and as an added service.

Tea Souvenirs from Canada

There are over 3,000 varieties of tea in the world (Pettigrew, 1999). With this variety and the trend towards blending there is great potential for the custom blending of tea and for individual tea establishments to develop their own signature blends, which can also be retailed as souvenirs. The availability of such tea packaged as souvenirs could be important in providing visitors with memento. One Canadian company, the Metropolitan Tea Company, has built up a wholesale tea business, which is based in part on the development of souvenir tea blends attractively packaged for different geographical and interest markets in Canada. For example, the company has developed both a Lighthouse Tea Blend and a Maple Tea Blend. This company and others also assists retailers to develop their own signature lines of souvenir teas. The 1810 Carter House Tea Room in Kingston New Brunswick has thus introduced (2004) two signature blends, a Heritage Blend and a Maple Blend. Kingston Heritage and the manager of the site,report that there has been considerable interest in this new offering by both locals and tourists (Baxter, 2003).

The above review of sample products for tea tourism provides examples of a range of products available in Canada for the potential tea tourist. These existing products serve as models for the development of other tea-related products. It is evident that, in the cases of the tea establishments reviewed, all have a theme and purpose and provide a number of tea-related services. A clustering of products is necessary for the development of this specialized form of tourism, both within individual establishments and within destinations: tea tourists, particularly those who might be identified as dedicated or extreme, will want to have a variety of different experiences while visiting individual establishments and destinations at different locations.

Tea Destinations in Canada

A few destinations in Canada are known for their historical and contemporary connections with tea. This includes the port cities of Saint John, New Brunswick on the east coast and Victoria, British Columbia on the west coast. Other cities are becoming known for developing a contemporary tea scene through the establishment of tea shops, tea houses and tea-related businesses. An example is the city of Charlottetown, Prince Edward Island in eastern Canada. These three destinations are profiled here.

Saint John, New Brunswick

The port city of Saint John, New Brunswick is known as the 'birthplace' of several of Canada's well-known tea blends. In addition, the city is home to the New Brunswick Tea Company, which operates out of the Saint John City Market, and two nearby communities have established tea rooms: the 1810 Carter House Tea Room is operated by Kingston Heritage (in Kingston) and the King Cole Tea Room is operated by an artist's cooperative (in Sussex). Exhibits at the New Brunswick Museum in Saint John tell, in part, the story of the emergence of the Red Rose Tea Blend and a number of historic buildings in the city have ties to this history, including the Red Rose Factory (now an office building) and the Red Rose Mansion (now a bed and breakfast).

Canada's well-known tea brands, Red Rose and King Cole were both developed in Saint John, New Brunswick (Cong & Jolliffe, 2002). The King Cole Blend was created by the G.E. Barbour Company, founded in Saint John in 1867, and the Red Rose blend was created by the T.H. Eastbrooks Company, established in Saint John in 1894. The special blend of Indian and Sinhalese teas was launched under the name Red Rose in 1899. It is reported that this company was one of the first to commercialize the sale of tea in small packets wrapped in foil; and it started putting tea in bags in the 1930s. In 1931, T.H. Eastbrooks was sold to the large English firm of Brooke Bond, which was itself bought in 1985 by the multinational Unilever. Unilever merged it with Lipton's, who then took over marketing and development of the popular Red Rose blend.

The rich history of tea in Saint John includes other tea companies, as well as companies importing china associated with tea (such as Hayward & Warwick) and tea rooms operating in local department stores in the 1950s (Cong & Jolliffe, 2002). Today, tea is no longer blended in the city (although King Cole is blended in the nearby town of Sussex), however there remain remnants of this history that can be utilized for tea tourism. For example, an exhibit at the New Brunswick Museum interprets the tea history of the city; and the Hayward & Warwick China Museum presents special exhibitions such as Tea for Two – The Story of the Tea Cup' shown in 2003. An analysis of the strengths, weaknesses, opportunities and threats for developing tea tourism in the city and surrounding area follows (see Table 14.3). In 2004 a new contemporary tea shop called Infusions opened in the City Market building, adding to the tea venues and attractions in the city.

This analysis shows that the Saint John region offers much for the tourist interested in tea and its related traditions, from tea rooms to cafés serving tea, and from museum exhibits to heritage buildings related to tea

Table 14.3 Tea and tourism SWOT analysis: Saint John, New Brunswick

Strengths	*Weaknesses*	*Opportunities*	*Threats*
• Strong tea traditions and history • Number of attractions related to tea • Tea rooms in area for day trips • Tea service at some inns and cafes • Archival resources • Day trip and visit destination • Tea and tea souvenirs available at City Market	• No regular afternoon tea services • No dedicated tea rooms in city • Limited range of 'tea souvenirs' • Little interpretation of tea history in the city • Existing tours include but do not focus on tea	• Development of a tea room, and afternoon tea as a meal service in existing establishments • Potential to interpret the rich tea history of the city • Packaging of products into a tea tour	• There may not be sufficient interest to sustain such businesses on a year round basis

Source: Jolliffe (2003b)

production. What the city lacks is a method of unifying this tea history. While it is locally known that both the Red Rose Tea and the King Cole Tea brands originated in the city, few visitors are aware of this fact. This history is reflected in the Red Rose Mansion (bed and breakfast), the Red Rose building and a New Brunswick Museum exhibit. Cruise ship visitors experience tours that include afternoon tea (at area inns such as the Inn on the Cove and also at The Fairmont Algonquin in Saint Andrews), but casual visitors to the city do not have access to these services. The New Brunswick Tea Company, now located inside the City Market, has an opportunity to pass on the city's tea lore through its retailing of tea blends and fine china. Visitors to the city can be served tea at the Loyalist House by the Mayor, but only if they happen to visit on a Wednesday afternoon during July and August. While there has been some limited tea tourism growth one might conclude that Saint John has ignored its tea history and focused on other themes (e.g. Loyalist history and Bay of Fundy tides) to market itself to visitors, and to date has ignored potential for development using tea (Bartlett, 2003).

Victoria, British Columbia

It is reported that, by the latter half of the 19th century, afternoon tea had become a popular form of entertainment in well-established households in Canada (Abrahamson, 1980). Today, reflecting its British heritage, the tradition of afternoon tea has become a predominant tea activity and indeed a tourism attraction in the port city of Victoria, British Columbia. The publication *Afternoon Tea in Victoria* (n.d.) lists some of the establishments serving afternoon tea including: The Empress Hotel, Adrienne's Tea Garden, Oak Bay Beach Hotel, The Blethering Place, James Bay Tearoom, Point Ellice House, Windsor House Tearoom and Willow's Beach Tearoom. These establishments provide a number of different services that include afternoon tea, traditional high teas, tea room fare and gift shops retailing tea impedimenta.

The Empress Hotel, part of the Fairmont hotel chain, is reported to serve more afternoon teas than most hotels in London, England with 800–1000 people a day coming to enjoy the tradition. Tourism Victoria notes that 'The Fairmont Empress serves its world-famous tea more than 100,000 times a year' and that 'afternoon, or high tea, is served at more than a dozen places throughout Victoria' (Tourism Victoria, 2003).

Air Canada's in-flight magazine *Enroute* (2003) in the Gostello Report on 'hotels and what to do worldwide' rates the Fairmont Empress as third in 'The List: 10 Best Afternoon Teas: 'Over 115,000 afternoon teas are served a year.' Food service establishments serving tea in Victoria range from hotels to tea rooms to tea gardens, providing a variety of services, menus and settings. This concentration of tea services and facilities in Victoria offers definite opportunity for the development of tea tourism. Services not listed in above include specialty tea shops such as Murchie's Tea and Coffee Ltd and Special Teas Inc. Tea is also served at Butchart Gardens, where Tourism Victoria indicates it has been served since 1904.

The destination management organization Tourism Victoria is contributing to the development of tea-focused tourism in Victoria, as evidenced by web site listings on afternoon tea and tea gardens in Victoria (http://www.tourismvictoria.com), but has not to date made a concerted effort to develop tea tourism. However, through private enterprise, additional tea services and activities are being added to the city's roster of tea activities. For example, at the Silk Road, tea is used as part of spa treatments: there is a tea bar, an events calendar that includes cooking with tea and in-store Japanese tea ceremonies. The Globe and Mail (Rosen, 2004) indicates: 'tourists and locals alike come to browse and buy from this chic retail experience.' Because of this clustering of tea products, services and related marketing Victoria could understandably be classified as a tea destination. As such, it should be able to use tea to extend the length of stay of dedicated tea tourists and to market to both the dedicated and the extreme tea tourists who will visit because of the quality and the variety of tea experiences offered (Jolliffe, 2003b).

Charlottetown, Prince Edward Island

The city of Charlottetown, Prince Edward Island, is known as the birthplace of the Confederation of Canada. As a port city, tea would have been imported and distributed from here. However, none of Charlotte-town's original tea businesses have survived. For example, Milton's Tea Room located at 151 Kent Street was advertised in *Mrs Flynn's Cookbook*, originally published in 1930 (PEI Heritage Foundation, 1980). The book also carried an advertisement for the locally blended Brahmin Tea, sold by Higgs and Company Limited. Today, all that remains of the latter enterprise is a business sign which is on exhibit at Charlottetown City Hall.

Prince Edward Island was the home province of author Lucy Maud Montgomery, author of *Anne of Green Gables*. This fame offers an opportunity for the development of tea-related tourism. One example of such an enterprise was Anne's Tea Party, which recently operated for several years. At this shop, located adjacent to the Anne Store, one could take afternoon tea with the servers costumed as characters from *Anne of*

Green Gables who also presented a mock concert to 'raise funds for the African mission' during the serving of tea. The menu of set teas also reflected the *Anne* theme, with a Green Gables Tea, Marilla's Cream Tea and Diana's Dessert Tea. Away from Charlottetown, other tea-related *Anne* products have also been created. For example, at the Anne of Green Gables Museum at Park Corner it is possible to participate in Anne's Perfectly Scrumptious Wild Rose Tea Party, a package that includes a museum tour, afternoon tea, and making a floral decked hat, accompanied by author and interpreter Carol Collins (http://www.gov.pe.ca/visitorsguide). Both of these tea party events provide a good example of how tea menus and services can be customized to a locality, transforming tea into a tourism experience.

However, in recent years a number of other tea establishments have emerged in the city. Recent additions to the Charlottetown tea scene include the Formosa Tea House, serving teas and authentic snacks from Taiwan. Several other Asian-style tea houses have also emerged in the city. A number of tea shops are also available for visitors wishing to take day trips away from the capital city. This includes The Spot of Tea Restaurant formerly operated in Stanley Bridge and the Blue Moon Tea Room in New London.

Comparing Tea Destinations

In the preceding section three destinations in Canada that are at different stages in their development as tea destinations have been profiled. This section now compares these destinations and considers the stages in the development of a location with tea history and traditions into a 'tea destination'. The three locations, Saint John (New Brunswick), Victoria (British Columbia) and Charlottetown (Prince Edward Island), all have resources and attractions that contribute to their development as destinations with a tea focus (Table 14.4). This includes traditional tea histories and now contemporary tea offerings.

Saint John, New Brunswick, a city with a rich tea heritage, shows potential for attracting the dedicated tea tourists previously identified in the typology of tea tourists. However, to date, these tea resources have not been extensively developed for the purpose of tourism, and potential developments will perhaps be part of the city's transition from an industrial to a service economy (Bartlett, 2003). Tourism planners in the city could take advantage of the growing market of cruise ship visitors to develop tea services and products of interest to this market segment.

Table 14.4 Comparison of tea destinations profiled

Destination	Tea resources	Tea attractions
Charlottetown, Prince Edward Island	Tea history Tea shops Tea services in hotels and bed and breakfasts	Tea shops in city Tea activities in area, e.g. Workshops at the Shining Waters Tea Room
Saint John, New Bunswick	Tea History Red Rose Mansion Red Rose Building Tea Service in inns and bed and breakfasts Tea rooms in region	Tea exhibit at New Brunswick Museum Red Rose Mansion (Bed and breakfast) Red Rose Building
Victoria, British Columbia	Tea history Tea service in hotels, tea rooms and other locations Retail tea shops Tea rooms Tea gardens	Afternoon tea at the Empress Hotel Tea at Buchart Gardens Tea at Point Ellice House Occasional tea exhibitions (e.g. The World Tea Party)

Victoria, British Columbia, a city with a rich tea history, could be considered a more mature tea destination. The city has the infrastructure for a variety of tea services and experiences offered to the visitor, and a tea trail certainly could be developed, as could special events which had a tea focus. A number of guides to tea rooms do exist – for example, Afternoon Tea in Victoria – and this guide and others may provide the closest example that we have of tea-trail activity, similar to the Teapot Trail Series produced in the UK, as tourists use the guides on their journey from one tea room to another. These guides cater to those who Boniface (2003) refers to as 'tea room enthusiasts'.

In Charlottetown, Prince Edward Island the city's traditional colonial tea history is being supplemented by the establishment of tea shops reflecting other tea cultures and traditions (Taiwan, Japan). There is however, considerable potential for developing tea experiences related to the well-known author Lucy Maud Montgomery's fictional character Anne (from *Anne of Green Gables*), whose fame attracts tourists to the island. The tea scene in Charlottetown is now evolving to reflect new traditions and interests from other tea cultures as evidenced by the establishment of new tea shops introducing tea culture and experience to both visitors and tourists alike. However, without a dedicated concentration of tea products, services and attractions the city could be identified as one in a very early stage of development as a tea destination.

Tourism destinations are recognized to have cycles of development, a cycle of evolution similar to the life cycle of a product (Butler, 1980). In the case of tea destinations, for a particular location to develop there should be tea resources in terms of both tea histories and traditions and there must also be a resultant clustering of tea services and activities. There is also some potential for destinations without a history and tradition of tea to use 'tea' as an instrument for tourism development. Another critical element is for destination management organizations and tourism planners to be aware that tea can be used as an instrument for tourism development. When viewed on a continuum of development, the destinations reviewed here could be seen as being in the involvement (Charlottetown), development (Saint John) and consolidation (Victoria, BC) stages of development. Ongoing development will depend not only on the tourism development agencies in these areas but also on private entrepreneurs who may – in response to market trends and interests in tea – develop the products and services sought out by the savvy tea tourist.

The State of Tea Tourism in Canada

With a strong tradition of tea consumption there is clearly potential for the development of tea-associated tourism in Canada. The population of tea drinkers provides a ready market for the development of tea tourism products that may include the consumption of speciality tea services as well as the purchase of tea as souvenirs and the experiencing of tea through attendance at tea-themed exhibits and events. With a growing interest in culinary tourism international tourists will also be interested in experiencing Canada's historical and contemporary tea traditions.

However, the tea trade in Canada seems to be fairly conservative in terms of its activities and to date its efforts regarding the promotion of tea do not include tea tourism per se but rather focus on promoting the consumption of tea in both the domestic and food service situations. The Tea Council of Canada has a potential role to play in changing this outlook and in promoting the development of tea tourism that will also fulfil the goals of the organization. The current involvement of the council in the development of a tea *sommelier* programme provides an assurance of quality in the area of tea service.

It is also evident that destination management organizations and tourism developers have not grasped the opportunity to use tea as a tool for tourism development, rather than just viewing tea as a food service element or as an activity available to tourists. One might conclude that there is a new role for the 'cup of tea' in the context of Canada's emerging cultural tourism industry and economy as an instrument for the development of tourism. Tea and tourism may become the 'new blend', affording opportunities for the development of both industries.

References

Abrahamson, H. (1980) *Victorians at Table*. Toronto: Ministry of Culture and Recreation.

Afternoon Tea in Victoria (n.d.) Victoria: Kiwanas Clubs of Greater Victoria.

Bartlett, B. (2003) Tourists could pour into city for tea. *Telegraph-Journal* (Saint John, Canada), 7 October.

Baxter, J. (2003) Personal correspondence.

Boniface, P. (2003) *Tasting Tourism: Travelling for Food and Drink*. Hampshire: Ashgate.

Briedenhann, J. and Wickens, E. (2004) Tourism routes as a tool for the economic development of rural areas – vibrant hope or impossible dream? *Tourism Management* 25, 71–9.

Butler, R.W. (1980) The concept of a tourism area cycle of evolution: Implications for management of resources. *Canadian Geographer* 24 (1), 5–12.

CTC (Canadian Tourism Commission) (2001a) *National Tourism & Cuisine Forum*, Proceedings and Final Report, Halifax, 11–13 June 2001.

CTC (2001b) *The Heritage Product Club Newsletter*, No. 18. Ottawa: Canadian Tourism Commission.

CTC (2003) *Canada's Heritage Tourism Enthusiasts – A Special Analysis of the Travel Activities and Motivations Survey*, Research Report 2002–8, Ottawa.

CTC (2004) Canadian Travel Survey (CTS) Fact Sheet Q4 and year 2003. Online document: http://www.canadatourism.com (accessed 18 September 2004).

Cong, Y. and Jolliffe, L. (2002) *Tea History, Traditions and Tourism*. Unpublished paper.

Dion, D., Mulvihill, B. and Patch, M. Suschnee (1995) *World Tea Party*. North Vancouver: Presentation House Gallery.

Enroute (2003) Gostello Report, The list: 10 best afternoon teas. Montreal: Enroute, June.

Government of Prince Edward Island (2004) *Visitors Guide*. Online document: http://www.gov.pe.ca/visitorsguide (accessed 28 July 2004).

Jolliffe, Lee (2003a) The lure of tea: history, traditions and attractions. In M. Hall, L. Sharples, R. Mitchell, N. Macionis and B. Cambourne *Food Tourism Around the World: Development, Management and Markets* (pp. 121–36). London: Butterworth-Heineman.

Jolliffe, L. (2003b) Something's brewing: Tea and tourism in Canada. Presented at Travel and Tourism Research Association, Canada Chapter, Saint John, New Brunswick, October 2003.

PEI Heritage Foundation (1980) *Mrs Flynn's Cookbook* (Reprint of 1930 edition). Charlottetown: Prince Edward Island Heritage Foundation.

Pettigrew, J. (1999) *Tea and Infusions*. London: Carlton.

Pettigrew, J. (2001) *A Social History of Tea*. London: National Trust.
Prince Edward Island Visitors Guide (2004) Charlottetown: Government of Prince Edward Island.
Rosen, Amy (2004) *World of Wellbeing Silk Road, Victoria*. Toronto: The Globe and Mail.
Smith, M. (1986) *Afternoon Tea*. London: Macmillan.
Tea Council of Canada (2004) Online document: http://www.tea.ca (accessed 26 July 2004).
Tim Hortons (2005) Online document: http://www.timhortons.com/ (accessed 26 November 2004).
Tourism Victoria (2003) *Afternoon Tea in Victoria*. Online document: http://www.tourismvictoria.com (accessed 30 July 2003).
Williams, S. (1998) *Tourism Geography*. London: Routledge.
Wolf, E. (2003) *Culinary Tourism: A Tasty Economic Proposition*. Oregon: International Culinary Tourism Association.
WTO (World Tourism Organization) (2002). Online document: http://www.world-tourism.org.

Part 5: Conclusion

Chapter 15

Towards a Research Agenda for Tea Tourism

LEE JOLLIFFE

So, what have we learned about tea and tourism? This volume has built an interim account of the state of tea tourism in different countries and at differing destination locations. Case studies and narrative investigations of tea-related tourism development came from major tea-producing countries such as China, India, Sri Lanka and Kenya, and from significant tea-consuming countries such as the United Kingdom, Canada and China. Tea, as an agricultural commodity, is produced and processed in 57 countries and, of necessity, only a sample of producing countries has been profiled. This reality is one of the limitations of this volume. In addition, with tea as a beverage being consumed worldwide, only a small number of tea-consuming countries can be examined. The volume can therefore be seen as an entry into the potentially rich area of tourism research.

The State of Tea Tourism Research

The work therefore reflects current research and thinking on the existence, development and trends in the area of tourism related to tea, with views on tea tourism being presented from the diverse yet interrelated perspectives of a number of tourism researchers. The background and viewpoints of these researchers has been discussed in Chapter 1. This work has made use of existing theories in tourism including: theories of tourism motivation (Iso-Ahola, 1982); material cultural studies (Pearce, 1992); the study of souvenirs as the material culture of tourism (Graburn, 2000); destination development theories and theories related to assessing heritage assets (McKercher & du Cros, 2002).

The chapters of this book reveal areas for future study that draw their strength from the contributions of different disciplines that include history, anthropology, political ecology, museology, cultural heritage management, marketing and regional development. In addition the body of tourism studies knowledge has been drawn upon. Research threads emerging include: tea and tourism contexts (including tea tourism and social change); tea culture and tourism; tea travel and tea souvenirs; tea tourism products; tea tourist behaviour and characteristics; tea tourist experiences; tea destinations; tea tourism development and development projects; tea interpretation; tea tourism ecommerce; and tea and associated hospitality perspectives.

From the editor's perspective five interrelated tea tourism research threads emerge that have particular relevance for both academics and practitioners in the hospitality and tourism industries. These are:

- tea, tourism and social change;
- tea tourist behaviour, characteristics and experiences;
- the emergence, development and marketing of tea destinations;
- tea tourism development projects; and
- tea and hospitality.

Research findings and proposals for future research in these areas are briefly discussed below.

Tea, Tourism and Social Change

The story of tea is one of social change, and the concept of travel has been intertwined with these changes. Tea has played a role in trade and travel, as well as in conquests and colonization. Tea has become a global commodity and its consumption has been adopted and adapted to both local and regional customs and traditions. Tea cultures and traditions offer a rich tapestry of potential experiences for today's mass tourists. For the more specialized and dedicated tea tourists, seeking out either commoditized or authentic tea experiences, there is much to discover. Tea tourism is inherently linked with social change, as inherited tea traditions are as much related to social change as the commoditized tea exchanges that are the direct result of changes in society. There is a rich research potential in this area. For example, researchers could investigate the tea traditions and cultures of individual destinations and then examine how tea experiences are being presented to tourists and experienced by them. Sites for research investigation can include tea houses, tea rooms, tea festivals and events, tea exhibitions, and tea shops.

Tea Tourist Behaviour, Characteristics and Experiences

An understanding of the behaviour and characteristics of the tea tourist will contribute to the building of a theoretical framework for planning and evaluating experiences for tea tourism. There is a need to survey tea tourists at the places where these experiences take place, for example in hotels serving afternoon tea, at tea rooms, and at tea exhibitions held by museums and commercial galleries. Tea is a major world commodity, and there is research being carried out on tea consumers and markets; this body of knowledge should be useful to tea tourism researchers, giving them a starting point and a research advantage, as demonstrated by Leung Kin Han (Chapters 2 and 4) who utilized the figures on importation and consumption available from the International Tea Committee. Studies contributing to the market positioning of tea can also be accessed.

Emergence, Development and Marketing of Tea Destinations

A number of destinations around the world have the ability to be developed and branded as 'tea destinations'. Tea has the potential to be utilized in the branding of these destinations, as shown by the example of Hangzhou, China discussed by Dewar and Li in Chapter 12. For other locations with a tradition of tea consumption, tea can be utilized in developing new tourism products and experiences, and there is a need for applied research to guide and inform such development.

Tea Tourism Development Projects

In both tea-producing and developing countries tea has the ability to be the theme of tourism development projects. In tea-producing countries there is the potential for tours of tea gardens and tea factories and for experiencing unique tea traditions. More work is needed on the potential of tea when used for tourism to adjust the gender employment and remuneration imbalances in tea gardens. Furthermore, in tea-consuming countries, tea rooms, tea trails and tea exhibitions can be employed as instruments for regional development of the products for tea tourism.

Tea and Hospitality

Tea is closely related to hospitality in many cultures and societies: it is offered as a sign of hospitality; and it forms an important part of hospitality management, both in terms of a beverage offering in the hospitality context and as a meal service. The investigation of the tea hospitality connection could focus on the historical development of the serving of tea, a theme touched on briefly by some authors (Walton, 2001; Visser, 1991; Boniface, 2003). Research in the tea and hospitality context could also investigate the contemporary context for tea's role in hospitality services. The training of staff, in terms of tea history, cultures and traditions relevant to the particular hospitality context is also to be desired and the current state of this training should be investigated. Business case studies of hospitality enterprises that have used tea to brand their establishments, to create additional revenue streams and to increase guest satisfaction could be utilized. The popular afternoon tea services offered by many hotels could be benchmarked against published listings of the best afternoon teas, contributing to providing quantitative and not qualitative listings such as those that have been published in the past. An example is the Gostello Report (listing of 10 best afternoon teas among world hotels) as seen in Air Canada's in-flight magazine *Enroute* (2003). Research into any of these aspects of tea service and provision will address an apparent gap (Jolliffe, 2004) within the hospitality management literature in the study of tea and hospitality.

Research Agenda

A research agenda in tea tourism will be relevant to the tea and tourism industries and their consumers in tea-producing and tea-consuming jurisdictions. Overall objectives for such research could:

- contribute to understanding of tea cultures, traditions in relation to tourism and social change;
- detail, study and assess the current state of tea tourism products;
- reveal the demographics of the tea tourist and contribute to understanding the motives and experiences of this type of tourist;
- develop an understanding of the nature of tea destinations, extracting lessons for other destinations and identifying issues for continued development;
- create awareness of the need to preserve and manage tea's material culture;
- contribute to sustainable tea tourism projects in tea-producing countries as a form of 'pro-poor' tourism;
- assist with the development of local and regional tea tourism projects in tea-consuming countries, as part of local economic development initiatives.

Conclusion

In summary, the book has positioned tea tourism within a number of areas of the existing body of literature on tourism. It has made a beginning towards the study of tea tourism as part of the study of cultural heritage and the transformations that can occur through tourism as an aspect of one culture's heritage is adopted, adapted and interpreted by other cultures. It has also profiled tea tourism as a niche area of tourism is closely related to both cultural tourism and culinary tourism. The potential of tea tourism has been noted as an instrument of tourism development, in both tea-producing and tea-consuming countries with considerable potential for use in 'pro-poor' tourism development. In addition the relationship of tea and hospitality has been discussed as a potential area of study within hospitality management.

The significance and contribution of this work can be seen as introducing a discussion on establishing tea tourism as a niche area of tourism worthy of independent study. It has accomplished this by identifying the existence, nature and development of tea tourism worldwide. It has also provided concrete examples of how tea is changed through tourism, providing products, experiences and destinations for tourists interested in the rich history, culture and traditions related to tea. An agenda has been proposed for future research in this area and a cadre of tourism researchers (the contributors to this volume) has been created to ensure that further enquiry takes place into the meanings and significance behind the consumption and promotion of the culture associated with the ubiquitous cup of tea when it is consumed and experienced around the globe in a hospitality and tourism context.

References

Boniface, P. (2003) *Tasting Tourism: Travelling for Food and Drink.* Aldershot: Ashgate.

Enroute (2003) Gostello Report, The list: 10 best afternoon teas. Montreal: Enroute, June.

Graburn, N.H.H. (2000) Preface. In Michael Hitchcock and K. Teague (eds) *The Material Culture of Tourism* (pp. xii–xvii). Aldershot: Ashgate.

Iso-Ahola, S.E. (1982) Towards a psychological theory of tourism motivation. *Annals of Tourism Research* (9) 2, 256–62.

Jolliffe, L. (2004) 'Not just a cuppa: Tea and commercial hospitality'. Proceedings of Bangkok International Conference on Applied Business Research. Bangkok, Thailand: Faculty of Business Administration, Kasetsart University.

McKercher, B. and du Cros H. (2002) *Cultural Tourism: The Partnership between Tourism and Cultural Heritage Management.* Binghamton, NY: The Haworth Press.

Visser, M. (1991) *The Rituals of Dinner: The Origins, Evolution, Eccentricities and Meaning of Table Manner*. Toronto: Harper Collins Publishers.

Walton, J.K. (2001) The hospitality trades: A social history. In C. Lashley and A. Morrison (eds) *In Search of Hospitality* (pp. 56–74). Oxford: Butterworth Heinemann.

Index

1810 Carter House Tea Room, Canada, 231, 234

Abrahamson, 237
action-based research, 14
Adler, 125
Administration Committee of Taimu Mountain, 136
Administration Committee of Wuyi Scenic Areas and Resorts Districts, 125
Administrative Bureau of Taimushan Scenery District, 135
Adrienne's Tea Garden, Canada, 237
Africa, 26, 33, 84
African Highland, 150
afternoon tea, 5, 6, 13, 212, 233, 237
Afternoon Tea in Victoria, 237
Agfa Film Company, 172
agri-tourism, 115, 119
Air Canada, 237, 250
Air Lanka, 89
Aitken Spence & Co. Ltd, 92
Alefran Tours and Safaris Ltd., 157
Amani, Tanganyika, 33
An'xi County Government, 128
An'xi County, China, 116, 122, 127
Andersen, 57
Anhui, 24
Anne of Green Gables, 238
Anne of Green Gables Museum, 239
Anne's Tea Party, Canada, 238
Ansi, China, 135
anthropology, 248
Arab, 101
Arce, 218
Art Gallery of Victoria, Canada, 49, 232
Artful Teapot Exhibition, 41
Arunchal Pradesh, India, 72, 74, 81
Ashley's Tea Rooms, UK, 210
Asia, 84
Asia Society and Museum, 41
Assam, India, 13, 16, 17
Assam Accord, 76
Assam Movement, 76

Assam State Tourism Development Corporation, 81
Assam Tea, 81
Association of Tea Growers, Kenya, 151
Australia, 86, 100
Austria, 214
Autumn Moon Festival, China, 170
Avieli, 123

Babbie, 116
Bai, 99
Bailey, 71
Bandaranayake International Airport, Sri Lanka, 90
Bandarawela, Sri Lanka, 17
Bangladesh, 72, 73
Barbour Company, Canada, 229, 235
Barriere, 212
Barringer, 39
Bartis, 212
Bartlett, 211, 218, 237, 239
Baruah, 72, 73, 74, 75, 77
Battuta, 85
BBC, 75, 76, 77
Beijing Scene, 203
Beijing, China, 3, 63, 122, 124
Bengal, India, 72
Bengali, 75
Best Tea Shop Walks, 216
Bettys & Taylors, 212
Bhattacharya, 77, 81
Bhutan, 72
Big Pond, Canada, 234
Bihar, India, 73
Blaikie, 71
Blofeld, 116
Blue Moon Tea Room, Canada, 239
Bode, 219
Bodhinayake, Nihal, 93
Bodo, language, 75
Bodoland, India, 75
Bodum, 42
Bogoria, Kenya, 149
Bonavia, 174

Boniface, 6, 39, 42, 45, 213, 231, 233, 250
border tea, 167
Boston, 216
Botswana, 148
Boyd, 86
Boyne, 18, 207, 213, 217, 225
Bramah, 45, 149
Bramah Tea and Coffee Museum, 41, 45, 46
brand images, 203
Briedenhann, 225
Brief Encounter, 210
Brighton, UK, 208
Bristol, UK, 208
British Columbia, Canada, 225, 235, 237
British Red Cross, 211
British tea ceremony, 207
British Tea Council, 42
Brooke Bond, 150, 154, 208, 215, 235
Brookfield, 71
Bryant, 71
bubble tea, 60, 195
Buck, 85
Buddhism, 24, 30, 36, 56, 116, 190, 198
Burcaw, 40
Burma, 62, 77
Burnet, 152
Butchart Gardens, Victoria, Canada, 238
Butler, 241

Cachar, India, 32
caffeine, 167
Calcutta Botanical Gardens, 33
Camellia sinensis, 3, 40
Campbell, 210
Canada, 3, 19, 32, 247
Canada's Tea Zone, 228
Canadian Dictionary of the English
    Language, 45
Canadian International Development
    Agency, 135
Canadian Tourism Commission, 225, 231
Carter, 214
Central Highlands, Kenya, 149
Central Province, Kenya, 152
Cerhan, 101
Ceylon, 5, 33, 85, 207, *see also* Sri Lanka
Ceylon Hoteliers Association, 89
Ceylon Tourist Board, 89, 90
Champagne, 203
Changsha, China, 98, 99, 104, 106, 108, 111
Charles II, 32
Charles Rennie Mackintosh, 209
Charlotte, North Carolina, 49
Charlottetown, Canada, 224, 235, 238

Charters & Ali-Knight, 54
Chatterjee, 73, 74, 81
Chengde, China, 177
Chiltern Hills, UK, 216
China, 3, 4, 5, 7, 9, 13, 36, 207, 224, 247
China Academy of Urban Planning and
    Design, 187
China Agriculture Association, 127
China International Tea Culture Research
    Association, 125
China International Tea Culture Society, 172
China Merchants Travel Company, 190
China National Tea Museum, 63, 186, 189,
    191, 198
China National Tourism Administration,
    56, 102, 119, 178
China National Tourism Agency, 117
China Tea and Culture Tour, 43
China Tea Association, 125
China Tea Museum, 46, 183
China Travel Service, Fujian, 126
China Vista, 191
Chinese Enterprise Net, 198
Chinmen Islands, Taiwan, 59
Chongqing Province, China, 62
Chow Dynasty, 56
Christian, 75
Christian Guild Holidays, 217
Civitello, 24
Clark, 41, 47
cliff tea, 124
Cliff Tea Festival, 125
Cliftonville, Kent, UK, 210
CNTA, 115
Coffee Republic, 208
Cohen, 123
Collins, Carol, 239
Colombo, Sri Lanka, 90, 228
Committee of Tea Culture, 33
Confucianism, 190
Conisbrough Castle, 210
copyright, 203
Cornwall, UK, 211
Coulthard, 215
Cranston, 209
cream teas, 233
culinary tourism, 231
cultural heritage management, 248
cultural landscape, 170
Cultural Revolution, China, 102
Cunningham, 203
Cutty Sark, 41

Daily Nation, 155

Dali, China, 172, 175, 176, 178
Da-Ping, China, 127
Darjeeling International Tea Festival, 81
Darjeeling, India, 11, 32, 35, 36, 57
Das, 76
Dayan Ancient Town, China, 169, 172, 177
de Alwis, 91
de Mejía, 100, 208
Debenham, UK, 214
Dehua County, China, 121
Deng, 99
Deng Xiao-ping, 103
Denham, 33
Deqing, China, 172
Devon, UK, 211
Dewar, 18, 43, 249
Dieke, 146
dim sum, 56
Dion, 232
Dodd & Bigotte, 54
Dong, 99
Dongting Lake, China, 98
Dorchester Hotel, 11
Douglas, 207
Doxey, 201
Dragon Well Longjing tea, 18
Dragon Well Village, Hangzhou, China, 200
du Cros, 12, 18, 174, 247
Duangmee, 39
Duke of York, 208
Duncan, 86
Durban Botanical Gardens, 33
Dutch East India Company, 31

E'shan, China, 172
East Africa, 207
East Africa Tea Trade Association, 152
East India Company, 38, 73, 74
Eastern Produce, 150
Eastern Province, Kenya, 152
eco-tourism, 94
Eden, 33
Edinburgh, UK, 208
Edward Adventure Tours, 175
Eichu, 30
England, 3, 4, 6, 13
Enroute magazine, 237, 250
Entebbe, Uganda, 33
ephemera, tea-related, 214
Eryuan, China, 172
Euromonitor, 6, 61
Europe, 100, 213
Evans, 149
Exley, 214

Fa Qin, Chinese Monk, 198
fair trade, 219
Fairmont Algonquin Hotel, Canada, 233
Fairmont Empress Hotel, Canada, 5, 11
Fairmont Hotels, 237
Fairmont Royal York Hotel, Canada, 229
Falk, 210
Feiner, 173
Fernando, 86, 87, 92, 95
Fields, 207
Finland, 213
Finnish Tourist Board, 213
Flagstaff House Museum of Tea Ware, 47
Flowerdew, 92
Flying Cloud Tea: China Tour, 190
FML Tea Trading Co., 102
Foreign Trade and Economic Cooperation
    Bureau of Zhijian Province, China, 187
Formosa Tea House, Canada, 239
Forte Tea Rooms, UK, 217
France, 32, 224
Frochot, 54
Fuding Foreign Trade Corporation, 135
Fuding Ocean and Fishery Bureau, 136
Fuding Ocean Tourist Agent, 136
Fuding Statistic Bureau, 136
Fuding Taimu Dianoxin Hotel, China, 135
Fuding Taimu Famous Tea Company, 139
Fuding Yuda, 139
Fuding, China, 18, 129
Fujian Agriculture and Forestry University,
    135, 142
Fujian Province, China, 18
Fujian Tea Association, 125
Fujian Tourism Administration, 116, 128
Fujian Tourist Authority, 135, 137
Fujian, China, 30, 43
Fuzhou, China, 13, 39, 117

Gandhi, Rajiv, 75, 89
Gao, 203
Gardella, 13
Gardiner Museum, 49
Gardiner Museum of Ceramic Art, Canada,
    232
George Brown College, 228
George Williamson, 150
Germany, 33
Getty Conservation Institute, 174
Gilmore, 105
Global Code of Ethics for Tourism, WTO,
    213
Globe and Mail, 65
Gondwanan rainforest, Sri Lanka, 94

Goodwin, 7, 38, 39, 45, 134
Gostello Report, 11, 237
Gou, 23
Goushiu tea, 24
Graburn, 46, 247
Graham, 25, 30
Great Exhibition of 1851, 39
Great Rift Valley, Kenya, 148
Great Strides Travel, 190
Great Wall, China, 173
Greenfield tea plantation, Sri Lanka, 94
Grove, 73
Guangdong Province, China, 32, 57, 100, 117
Guangxi Province, China, 62
Guangzhou, China, 100, 104, 122
Guan-Qiao, China, 127
Guha, 73
Guide to Tea Rooms of Britain, 216
Guide to the Best Tea Places in Britain, 217
Guizhou Province, China, 62
Gunasekara, 17, 41
Gunn, 9
Guwahati, India, 79, 80

Haitian Hotel, 104, 106
Hakim, 100
Hall, 17, 18, 43, 213, 217, 225
Hall *et al.*, 54
Hamel, 38, 39
Hangzhou Tourism Bureau, 181, 182, 183
Hangzhou Tourism Commission, 183, 188, 191, 198
Hangzhou, China, 3, 13, 18, 63, 116, 249
Hannam, 17, 78
Haputale, Sri Lanka, 94
Harler, 13, 145
Hayward & Warwick Company, Canada, 236
He, 172
Health Education Council and the Chartered Institute of Environmental Health, UK, 219
Helsinki, Finland, 213
Henan, 24
Heng Mountains, China, 99
Hethersett Estate, 92
Higgs and Company Limited, Canada, 238
Hilton, 149
Hindi, language, 75
Hindu, 75
Hitchcock, 38, 39, 46
Hjalager, 8
HNTA, 103

Ho, 175
Hong Kong, China, 3, 47, 57, 62, 122, 124, 175, 181
Horne, 40
Hoshiyama, 101
hospitality, 4, 249
hotels, 4
Hotels Corporation, Sri Lanka, 89
Howard, 6, 39
Huang, 17, 43, 103
Hubei, 24
Hudson, 47
Hui, 99
Hunan, 24
Hunan Province, China, 17
Hunan Tea General Corporation of China, 107
Hunanese cuisine, 107
Hupao Village, China, 188
Hussain, 11

Il'yasova, 101
Ilbery, 218
Imperial Tea Court, 43
India, 4, 5, 7, 9, 26, 27, 33, 53, 152, 207, 228, 247
indigenous health care, 94
Indonesia, 27, 152
Infusions Tea Shop, Canada, 236
Institute of Tourism and Travel Management, 79
International Culinary Tourism Association, 231
International Fairtrade Tea Register, 94
International Tea Committee, 53, 56, 249
International Travel Service, China, 54
International West Lake Tea Party, Hangzhou, China, 196
Inuit, 5
Iran, 33
Iraq, 33
Iraq war, 181
Ireland, 32
Islam, 27, 36
Iso-Ahola, 10, 247
IUCN, 78

Jakarta, India, 228
James Bay Tearoom, Canada, 237
Japan, 3, 6, 25, 30, 38, 175, 187, 198
Japanese Green Tea Tasting, 232
Japanese tea ceremony, 44
Jian, 101
Jianchuan, China, 172

Jiang, 187, 190
Jiangsu Province, China, 24, 198
Jiangxi Province, China, 117, 134
Jianzhong, 183
Jin Dynasty, 24
Jinghong, China, 172, 177
Jingshan Temple, China, 198
Jolliffe, 5, 7, 9, 10, 14, 16, 18, 19, 54, 96, 102, 129, 145, 207, 211, 215

Kamm collection, 41
Kandapola, Sri Lanka, 92
Kandy, Sri Lanka, 90
Kaziranga, India, 78
Keen, 100, 208
Kent Education Authority, UK, 219
Kenya, 3, 5, 13, 18, 33, 228, 247
Kenya Association of Tour Operators, 156
Kenya Tea and Forests Conservation Zone, 159
Kenya Tea Development Agency, 12, 150, 151
Kenya Tea Research Foundation, 152
Kenya Tourist Board, 146, 155
Kenyan Highlands, 155
Kericho Tea Hotel, Kenya, 154, 155, 157
Kericho, Kenya, 149, 155, 156
Keswick, UK, 214
Kiambethu Tea Estate, 156
Kiambethu Tea Farm, 155, 157
King Cole Tea Room, Canada, 229, 235
King Cole Tea Tent, 229
King's Road, Europe, 213
Kingston, Canada, 234
Kirby, 14
Kirschemblett-Gimblett, 47
Kitch Yojoki – The Book of Tea Sanitation, 198
Kitty's Tearoom, UK, 210
Kneafsey, 218
Kongque Ping, China, 172
Konnal Long Jing Production and Trade Company, China, 186
Korea, 12, 25, 175, 187
Kotler, 145, 147
KRD Books, 216
Kreps, 38, 40
Kris-Etherton, 100, 208
Kuang, 172
kung-fu, 122
kung-fu tea, 116
Kunming, China, 63, 172, 177
Kuo, 59
Kuznesof, 207
Kyoto, Japa n, 30, 35

Lake Nakuru, Kenya, 149
Lamb, 152
Lanka Monthly Digest, 91
Laos, 62
Lavery, 146
Leask, 212
Leung, 16, 17, 249
Lew, 201
Leyburn, UK, 214
Li, 18, 43, 249
Liberian Tigers of Tamil Ealem, 89
Lijiang, China, 172, 175, 177, 178
Lim, 32
Limuru, Kenya, 33, 156
Lin, 140
Linswchoten, 38
Lion Peak Mountain, Hangzhou, China, 185
Lipton, 32, 228, 235
Liu, 103, 109
London Tea Auctions, 41
London Tea House, Taiwan, 61
London, England, 3, 11, 14, 39, 183, 237
Lonely Planet, 149, 150, 154, 155
Long Beach, California, 49
Longjing (Dragon Well) tea, 180
Longjing Village, China, 189, 191
Longjing Wen Cha, Hangzhou, China, 189
Longyan, China, 117
Lord Bentinck, 73
Lord Byron, 124
Lu Yu, 13, 24, 29, 42, 185
Lu Yu Tea Art Centre, 60

Macao, 181
MacCannell, 125
Macleod, 212, 213
MacNeil, Rita, 234
Mae Salong, Thailand, 12, 14
Malawi, Africa,3, 33, 152
Malaysia, 36
Maldives, 91
Malik, 101
Manchester, UK, 208
Manil, 4, 32, 33
Manipur, India, 72, 81
Mao Zedong, 99
marketing, 248
Marsden, 85, 218
Mary of Modena, 208
Mashiter, 212, 214
Matsu Islands, Taiwan, 59
McArthur, 213
McDonnell, 157
McFarland House Tea Garden, Canada, 234

McIntosh, 41
McKenna, 14
McKercher, 12, 174, 175, 247
Meghalaya, India, 72, 74, 81
Meijiawu Tea Cultural Village, 188
Meijiawu Tea Village, 186, 190
Meijiawu Village, China, 187
Mennell, 115
Metropolitan Tea Company, Canada, 234
Mexico, 224
Meyer-Cech, 214
Mezhu Fishing Village, 188
Miao, 99
Michael, 218
Miller, 49
Millie, 86
Milton's Tea Room, Canada, 238
Ming Dynasty, 124
Ministry for Tourism, Kenya, 146
Ministry of Agriculture, China, 127
Ministry of Tourism and Culture, India, 80
Ministry of Tourism, India, 72, 78, 80
Mitchell, 157
Miththapala, 93
Mizoram, India, 72, 74, 80, 81
Mohei, China, 172
Mojiang, China, 172
Mombasa, Kenya, 154, 228
Momsen, 17, 41
Montgomery, Alabama, 49
Montgomery, Lucy Maud, 238
Montreal Botanical Gardens, Canada, 232
Montreal, Canada, 224
Morris, 47
Morrison, 33
Moulin, 213
Mount Kenya, Kenya, 148, 149
Moxham, 5, 7
Mrs Flynn's Cookbook, 238
Mrs Proffitt's Tea Shop, Canada, 230
Mt Mengding, China, 167
Mueller, 152
Muhati, 18
Mumbo Tea Bar, 208
Murchie's Tea and Coffee Ltd., Canada, 238
Murroughs, 212
museology, 248
Museum of Modern Art, 42
Museum of Worcester Porcelain, 46
Muslim, 56, 75
Mutai, 155
Myanmar (Burma), 72

Nagaland, India, 72, 74, 80, 81

Nagano, 101
Nairobi, Kenya, 155, 156
Namibia, 148
Nanping, China, 117
Napa, California, 49
Narobi, Kenya, 157
Natal, Africa, 33
National Day, China, 183
National Post, 232
National Tourism and Cuisine Forum,
    Canada, 231
Naughton, 7
New Brunswick Museum, Canada, 235
New Brunswick Tea Company, Canada,
    235
New Brunswick, Canada, 231, 235
New Delhi, India, 72
New Tea Appreciation Festival, 4
New York, 41, 90
New Zealand, 32
Ngong Hills, Kenya, 155
Niagara on the Lake, Canada, 234
Nianyong, 109
Ningde, China, 117
Norfolk Museums Service, 49
North Bengal, India, 11
North Yorkshire, UK, 217
Northern Song, 185
Norwich Castle Museum, UK, 48, 51, 215
Norwich Museum, 46
Numitea, 169
Nuwara Eliya estates, 87
Nuwara Eliya, Sri Lanka, 86, 92
Nyago Tea Zone, 159
Nyanza Province, Kenya, 152
Nyayo Tea Zone Development
    Corporation, 152

Oak Bay Beach Hotel, Canada, 237
Oh, 129
Okakuro, 45
Ondaatjie, 91
Ontario, 225
Operation Bajrang, 77
Operation Rhino, 77
Opium War, 27, 32
Oregon, USA, 42
Organic Growers Organizations, 94
origins of tea, 23
Orissa, India, 73
Oslo, Norway, 213
Oxford English Reference Dictionary, 9, 44

P'enghu Islands, Taiwan, 59

Patt, 49, 232
Pearce, 40, 247
Peet, 71
Peluso, 71
People's Daily, China, 133, 134
Perennial Tea Room, 49
Perry, 7
Peters, 100
Pettigrew, 6, 23, 31, 32, 41, 133, 207, 214,
   233, 234
Phukan, 74
Pidurutalagala Peak, Sri Lanka, 84
Pilgrim's Cathedral Close, 210
Pine, 105, 129
Ping Lin Tea Museum, 46
Ping Lin, Taiwan, 3, 12
Pinpinxiang Tea Factory, 139
Plaisir du Chocolat, 208
Plog, 10
Point Ellice House, Canada, 237
political ecology, 71, 248
Porter's Five Forces Analysis, 145
Potteries Museum and Art Gallery, UK, 46
Pratt, 6, 31, 33, 43, 44, 46, 145, 149
Premadasa, Ranasinghe, 90
Prentice, 57
Presentation Gallery, Canada, 232
Prince Edward Island, Canada, 230, 235,
   238
Pristine Pottery, UK, 42
pro-poor tourism, 251
Public Contest Party of Tea, Hangzhou,
   China, 196
Puer, China, 172
Purchas, 38
Putian, China, 117

Qianlong, 189
Qin, 23
Qing Dynasty, 29, 186, 189, 190
Qing Ming Festival, China, 198
Qu, 103
Quanzhou Municipal Administrative
   Region, China, 121
Quanzhou Municipal Government, 128
Quanzhou Municipality, China, 127
Quanzhou, China, 117
Queenstown, Canada, 234

Ramayana, 85
Ratnapala, 89, 91
Red Cross Big Red Teapot Event, 211
Red Rose Factory, Canada, 235
Red Rose Mansion, Canada, 235

Red Rose Tea, 41, 229
regional development, 248
Regional Plantation Companies, 92
Relph, 214
restaurants, 4
Rettie, Clare, 88, 89
Richards, 8, 57
Rift Valley, Kenya, 149, 152
Rita's Tea Room, Canada, 234
Ritz-Carlton Hotel, UK, 11
Riungu, 159
Roberge, 229
Roberts, 213
Rose House, Taiwan, 61
Rosen, 238
Royal Institute of Chartered Surveyors, 93
Ruan, 23, 27
Russia, 3, 31

Sadler, 13, 42, 44
Saga, 30
Saint Andrews by the Sea, Canada, 233
Saint John City Market, Canada, 235
Saint John, Canada, 235
SARS, 181, 225
Sartippour, 101
Saudi Arabia, 100
Scotland, UK, 13, 208
Scottish Executive, 217
Seattle, 49
Sesso, 100
Shalleck, 38, 42, 44
Shanghai, China, 63, 104, 122, 124, 183
Shaoshan, China, 99
Shapira, 6, 7
Sharpe, 203
Shaxi Valley, China, 172, 173, 177
Shen Nung, 23, 56
Shi Feng Village, China, 188
Shigu Town, China, 172
Shiliguri, India, 72
Shimen Village, Taipei, 12
Sichuan Province, China, 23, 24, 30, 62, 167
Sideng Market, China, 173
Sideng, China, 177
signature tea blends, 211
Sikkim, India, 81
Silbergh, 213
Silk Road, 18, 24, 39, 172, 174, 177
Silk Road Spa, Victoria, Canada, 238
Simao County, China, 169
Simao Tourism Office, 172
Simao, China, 172, 176, 177
Sindiga, 146, 154, 160

Sinharaja World Heritage Site, 94
Smith, 7, 10, 38, 40, 44, 45, 46, 203, 212, 228
South, 148
South Kensington Museum, 39
Southern Song Dynasty, 185, 198
Souzhou, China, 183
Spain, 224
Special Teas Inc., Canada, 238
Spencer, 43
Spring Tea Party, Hangzhou, China, 196
Sri Lanka, 3, 5, 12, 13, 17, 26, 27, 32, 53, 134, 152, 228, 247
Sri Lanka Association of Inbound Tour Operators, 95
Sri Lanka Tourism Cluster, 94
Sri Lanka Tourist Board, 89, 95
Sri Lankan Airlines, 95
St Martin's Tea Rooms, 210
St. Petersburg, Russia, 213
Starbucks, 208
Stash Tea Company, 42
State Council of China, 135
State Tourism Administration, China, 54
State Tourism Bureau, 183
Stebbing, 74
Stockholm, Sweden, 213
Stoke-on-Trent, England, 42, 46
Strizzi, 137
Su, 101
Su Dongpuo, 185
Suez Canal, 86
Sung Dynasty, 27, 29, 35
Sussex, Canada, 229, 235
Sylhet, India, 32

T.H. Eastbrooks Company, Canada, 235
Taiji, 122
Taimu Mountain State Key Scenic Spot, 135
Taimu Mountains, China, 135
Taimushan Tourism Economic Development Zone, 135
Taipei, Taiwan, 3, 62, 63
Taiwan, 4, 6, 17, 36, 181
Taiwan Tourism Bureau, 59
Tamil, 88
Tamil Tigers, 89
Tan, 99
Tang Dynasty, 24, 35, 198
Tanzania, 148
Taoism, 36, 56, 190
Taoist, 116, 122
Taylor, James, 32, 86
tribute tea, 24
Tea and Horse Trade Route, 26, 39

Tea and Tourism Festival, Assam, 81
tea and travel, 14
tea arts, 122
tea auctions, 13
Tea Banquet Ceremony, China, 198
Tea Board of Kenya, 152
tea break, 207
Tea Capital An'xi, China, 128
tea ceremonies, 10
tea classifications, 25
Tea Council of Canada, 225, 228, 229, 232, 241
Tea Council, UK, 217
tea councils, 5
tea cuisine, 12
tea cultivation, Sri Lanka, 87
tea culture, 115, 175
Tea Culture and Art Festival, 125
Tea Culture Tourism Festival, 128
Tea Districts Labour Association, 74
tea exhibitions, 49
tea factories, 11
Tea Factory Hotel, Sri Lanka, 12, 17, 41, 92
tea festivals, 13
Tea for Two – The Story of the Tea Cup Exhibition, 236
Tea Gardens Project, China, 135
tea gardens, Assam, 78
tea hotels, 13
tea houses, 13, 36
tea landscape, 107
Tea Master's Contest, 122
Tea Muse, 208
Tea Museum in Shizaku Prefecture, 46
tea museums, 13
tea plantations, 53
Tea Research Institute, China, 167
tea room, 6, 208
Tea Rooms of Distinction, 216
Tea Shop Walks, 216
tea sommelier, 241
tea souvenirs, 39
tea tourism research threads, 248
tea tourism, definition, 57
Tea Tourist Route, Hangzhou, China, 186
tea tournaments, 7
tea trails, 8
tea types, 100
tea walks, 8
TeaCup, 49, 51
Teague, 38, 39, 46
Teahouses Street, Hangzhou, China, 191
Tealby Tea Rooms, UK, 210
Teapot Pottery, 214

Teapot Trail Series, 240
teapot trails, 206, See tea
Teapot Trails & Coffee Shop Stops, 217
Teapotmania, 49
teapots, 207
Teapottery, 214
Tea-skills Competition Party, Hangzhou,
　China, 196
Temple of the Tooth, Sri Lanka, 90
Terry, 101
Tetley, 228
Thailand, 4
Thanet Mencap Society, 211
The Artful Teapot Exhibition, 232
The Blethering Place, Canada, 237
The Empress Hotel, Canada, 237
The Four Seasons Hotel, 11
The Globe and Mail, 238
The Niagara Parks Commission, 234
The Palm Court Café, UK, 212
The Red Tea Box, Canada, 234
The Spot of Tea Restaurant, Canada, 239
The Tea Guild, UK, 217
The Tianhu Fairy Tea Interpretive Centre
　and Tea House, 142
The World Tea Party, 49
Thomas Garraway, 31
Thornby, 210, 216
Thorp, 46
Tian, 99
Tianfu Tea Museum, China, 119
Tianhu Tea Company, 136, 139
Tianmu Mountain, China, 198
Tibet, 25, 36, 39, 62, 72, 167
Tiger Leaping Gorge, 172
Tim Hortons (coffee shops), Canada, 226
Tongchen Hotel, 104, 106
Toronto, Canada, 49, 65, 224, 228, 232, 234
Totally Teapots, 49
Tourism Concern, 12, 134, 219
Tourism Marketing Bureau, Sri Lanka, 89
Tourism Trade Administrative Committee
　of Fuding, 135
Tourism Victoria, Canada, 11, 237, 238
tourism, China, 56
Tourist Hotels Association of Sri Lanka, 95
trademarks, 203
trails, 213
tea-related, 214
Travel Agents Association of Sri Lanka, 95
Travel and Tourism Fair, Ahamadebad,
　India, 93
Tregear, 207
Trew, 208

tribute tea, 167
Tripura, India, 72, 80, 81
Tsar Alexis, 31
Tsing Dynasty, 23
tsunami, 90
Tu, 172
Tujia, 99
Turkey, 36
Turku, Finland, 213
Twining, 41, 102, 206, 207, 212, 215
Twining & Company, 49
Twinings, 48, 50, 211
Twinings Company, 41

UK Teapot Trails, 215
UNEP, 78
UNESCO, 78, 99, 124
UNESCO Regional Advisor for Culture in
　Asia and the Pacific, 93
Unilever, 212, 215, 235
United Kingdom, 100, 152, 224, 247
United Liberation Front of Assam, 72, 76
United States, 224, 226

Vancouver, Canada, 13
Ventour Botanical Gardens, Isle of Wight,
　UK, 212
Victoria and Albert Museum, 39
Victoria, British Columbia, 13
Victoria, Canada, 5, 11, 224, 232, 235, 237
Vietnam, 62
Visitor Information Reception Centre, 202
Visser, 250

Wade Pottery, 41
Walker, 4, 41
Walton, 250
Wang, 99, 183
war in Iraq, 225
Warren, 209, 210
Warrior Tours, 189
Washington, 90
Watts, 71
way of tea, 31
Weihai, 24
Weiner, 75
Weishan, China, 172, 178
Wenglongsheng Tea Firm, China, 186
West Bengal, India, 73
West Han Dynasty, 24, 56
West Lake Longjing Tea Festival, 187
West Lake, Hangzhou, China, 116, 191
Western Province, Kenya, 152
Whitcomb, 38

Wicentowski, 60
Wickens, 225
Wickremasinghe, 92
Wild Grass Resort, 78
Williams, 10, 230
Willow Tea Rooms, Glasgow, UK, 41, 209
Willow's Beach Tearoom, Canada, 237
Windsor House Tearoom, Canada, 237
wine tourism, 8, 54
Wolf, 8, 225, 231
Wolk, 101
Women's Centres in China, 142
Women's Voice of Yunnan Magazine, 172
Woodlands Network, Bandarawela, 17, 94
Woolcott, 101
Worcester, England, 46
Worcestershire, UK, 216
World Bank, 172
World Commission on Environment and
    Development, 134
World Community Development Education
    Society, 13
World Heritage Convention, 172
World Heritage Site, 78, 99
World Monument Fund, 173
World Tea Party Exhibition, 232
World Tourism Organization, 54, 175, 182,
    213
Wu, 99, 101
Wu Town, China, 183
Wuhan, China, 63
Wuliang Mt., China, 172
Wulingyuan Scenic and Historic Interest
    Area World Heritage Site, 99
Wu-Wo Tea Ceremony, Hangzhou, China,
    196
Wuxi, China, 183
Wuyan County, China, 134
Wuyi Cliff Tea Festival, 122
Wuyi Travel, 125
Wuyi World Heritage Site, 123
Wuyi, China, 135
Wuyishan City Government, 122, 125
Wuyishan City, China, 124
Wuyishan, China, 116

Xi Hu Park, Hangzhou, China, 184, 190, 200
Xian, China, 39
Xiang, 99
Xiao, 18, 105

Xinhua News Agency, 180
Xi-Ping, China, 127
Xishuangbanna, China, 167, 172, 175
Xi-xing, China, 43
Xizhou, China, 172

Yang, 100, 101
Yangtze River, China, 98, 180, 183
Yeisai, Japanese Monk, 198
Yellow Pages Kenya, 155
Yi Qin Yuan Tea Room, 108
Ying-Xian-Pu, China, 127
Yixing teapots, 49
York, 65
Yso, 99
Yuan Dynasty, 124
Yuanjiang, China, 172
Yuen Dynasty, 26
yum chea, 56
Yun Qi Village, China, 188
Yunnan Province, China, 23, 39, 167
Yunnan Provincial Ministry of Culture, 173
Yunnan Provincial Tourism Association, 178
Yunnan Tourism, 175
Yunnan, attractions, 63
Yunnan, China, 17, 24, 30, 35
Yuxi Cigarette Factory, 172

Zbinden, 4, 32, 33
Zen, 30
Zen Buddhism, 6
Zen Buddist, 44
Zhang, 103
Zhangjiajie National Forest Park, China, 99
Zhangzhou Municipal Administrative
    Region, China, 119
Zhangzhou, China, 117
Zhejiang Province, China, 63, 117, 135, 186,
    198
Zhong, 99
Zhongdian, China, 172, 177
Zhou Dynasty, 23, 26
Zhou Village, China, 183
Zhoucheng, China, 172
Zhu, 109
Zhuang, 18, 99, 129
Zhuge, 109
Zimbabwe, 148
Zoe, 136
Zou, 190, 201